ADVANCE PRAISE FOR *DAMAGED HERITAGE*

"J. Chester Johnson is of that generation of southern-born white people who came of age in the 1960s, deep in the heart of American apartheid, in hometowns they were taught to see as perfections of the American dream. Then they were tortured first by personal discovery of the white supremacist evil that suffused their idyllic worlds, then tortured by the failure of peers to make the same discovery, and finally tortured by revelations of the complicity of people they loved and admired most. In *Damaged Heritage*, Johnson poignantly reveals the demons he discovered in his own life and family, ties to one of the worst racial horrors in American history, his personal anguish, and his efforts to make amends and fill a desperate empty place in our hearts. Only a poet can see this clearly, be this honest, and still hope this much."

—Douglas A. Blackmon, author of *Slavery by Another Name: The Re-Enslavement of Black Americans from the Civil War to World War II*, Winner of the Pulitzer Prize

"Johnson poignantly tells of a personal family history that stretches from the darkest days of 1919 to a moment of grace nearly a century later, when he met with Sheila Walker. A moving and inspiring read."

—Robert Whitaker, author of *On the Laps of Gods*

"'It is not permissible,' wrote James Baldwin, 'that the authors of devastation should also be innocent . . . it is the innocence which constitutes the crime.' In J. Chester Johnson's *Damaged Heritage*, a native son has given up that threadbare old claim to white innocence, as he grapples with a beloved grandfather's role in the Elaine Race Massacre of 1919, in which more than a hundred African American sharecroppers were killed. This is a heartfelt and deeply personal contribution to the literature of white remembrance, and a serious reckoning with the past."

—Patrick Phillips, author of *Blood at the Root: A Racial Cleansing in America*

"If you think as a culture we have reached an immovable impasse, read this book. If you hold the belief that where we've been doesn't bleed into the way we live now, read this book. If you are beginning to suspect we are a people who have lost the desire to heal, read this book. J. Chester Johnson has done more than tell us a story that must be told—he has laid the healing tools in our hands, and left instructions. This is how it starts."
—Cornelius Eady, Co-founder, Cave Canem Foundation;
Finalist for the Pulitzer Prize

"Johnson is making a profound contribution to that sacred healing work with his truth telling of this long overdue story."
—Catherine Meeks, PhD, Executive Director of the Absalom Jones Center for Racial Healing, co-author of *Passionate for Justice: Ida B. Wells, As Prophet For Our Time*

"*Damaged Heritage* reverberates. This is not just an Arkansas story, not just a Southern saga, but a national one. If we can achieve reconciliation and genuine relationships that span the racial gulf, then this book is a beacon of hope shining a light on that possibility."
—David Billings, author of *Deep Denial: The Persistence of White Supremacy in United States History and Life*

"I read *Damaged Heritage* in one sitting. It's wonderfully written, a proverbial page-turner, and the right book for the present. I sincerely hope this volume becomes a bestseller. It certainly deserves to be, not least because of its timeliness and accessibility."
—Larry Rasmussen, author and Reinhold Niebuhr Professor of Social Ethics Emeritus, Union Theological Seminary, New York City

PRAISE FOR J. CHESTER JOHNSON

St. Paul's Chapel & Selected Shorter Poems (2010):
"Undoubtedly, this is a work headed for literary permanence."
—Major Jackson, poet and author of *Leaving Saturn;*
Hoops; Holding Company; Roll Deep: Poems

"Johnson's 'St. Paul's Chapel' is one of the most widely distributed, lauded, and translated poems of the current century."
—*American Book Review* (Fall, 2017)

Now And Then: Selected Longer Poems (2017):
"The scope of *Now And Then* is epic. It provides its readers with the same amplitude of intelligence, passion and formal achievement as our great American epics—Melville's *Moby Dick*, Whitman's *Leaves of Grass*, and Ginsberg's *Fall of America*. It is a book of fierce spiritual and moral witness, energy and power."
—Lawrence Joseph, poet and author of
Into It: Poems; So Where Are We?: Poems; and
The Game Changed: Essays and Other Prose

"J. Chester Johnson is one of our country's literary gems. From his work on the *Book of Common Prayer* with Auden to his chronicling and advocating for civil rights in the American South . . . Johnson offers rare glimpses into what William Carlos Williams called 'news that stays news.' Elegant, truthful, heartfelt, spiritual, beautiful. This is a book to savor and admire. Highly recommend this impressive book."
—Elizabeth A. I. Powell, Editor-in-Chief,
Green Mountains Review; poet and author of
Willy Loman's Reckless Daughter and *The Republic of Self*

Auden, the Psalms, and Me (2017):

"J. Chester Johnson's account of his long service on the drafting committee for the Episcopal Church's project . . . to retranslate the Psalter is a wonderfully cautious, sensitive and even-handed book . . . Johnson is a fine poet himself. He is to be praised for his verbal attentiveness throughout the book, and not least for his orderly and sculpted expository style. A delightful book."

—John Fuller, Fellow Emeritus, Magdalen College, Oxford University; one of England's best-known and favored poets writing today; author of *W. H. Auden: A Commentary*

"J. Chester Johnson tells a remarkable and illuminating triple story: the story of the English psalms in the past and present, the story of W. H. Auden's profound engagement with the language of the psalter, and the story of Chester Johnson's engagement with Auden, the psalms, and the church. I hope this well-told story will be widely read."

—Edward Mendelson, Lionel Trilling Professor of Comparative Literature at Columbia University; literary executor and principal biographer for W. H. Auden; author of *Early Auden; Later Auden*; and *The Things That Matter*

DAMAGED HERITAGE

DAMAGED HERITAGE

THE ELAINE RACE MASSACRE
AND A STORY OF RECONCILIATION

J. CHESTER JOHNSON

FOREWORD BY SHEILA L. WALKER

PEGASUS BOOKS

NEW YORK LONDON

DAMAGED HERITAGE

Pegasus Books Ltd.
148 W. 37th Street, 13th Floor
New York, NY 10018

First Pegasus Books cloth edition May 2020

Interior design by Maria Fernandez

Library of Congress Cataloging-in-Publication Data is available.

ISBN: 978-1-64313-466-6

10 9 8 7 6 5 4 3 2 1

Printed in the United States of America
Distributed by Simon & Schuster
www.pegasusbooks.us

To *Freda*, as always;

to *Sheila L. Walker*, whose forgiveness
and friendship altered history;

and to the memory of *Scipio Africanus Jones*,
who'll someday be remembered
for the American hero he is.

CONTENTS

Major Sites
For Damaged Heritage

Legend

Elaine

Helena:
County seat/site of
Elaine Massacre Memorial.

Hoop Spur:
Site of significant killing fields for
Elaine Race Massacre.

McGehee:
Lonnie's Hometown/MoPac hub
for Southeast Arkansas.

Monticello:
Author's Hometown.

Tillar:
Location of Birch (Lonnie) Farm.

Winchester:
Headquarters for Progressive Farmers
and Household Union.

Created by: JonCarlo Curiale

INTRODUCTION

Would I have written this book in the absence of the recent resurgence of white nationalism and unapologetic white racism that have now reached through every state to every hamlet and crevice in our nation? Possibly not, for there are elements in this book harkening back to an earlier time, even to the pre-civil rights period of the American South, which we may have previously and erroneously thought were gone forever. And yet, that is precisely where so many whites in this country have taken us at the beginning of the third decade of the 21st century. Subtle and not-so-subtle public slogans and public pronouncements encourage whites to be pitted against persons of color, while American governments seek to suppress votes of black and brown Americans and our tawdry and egregious immigration policies punish black and brown immigrants and would-be immigrants. These are infamous, but evidentiary examples of a revived, distended white racism that is present today in our United States. The presidency of Donald J. Trump has ripped off the ameliorative, national band-aid to expose the open wound that constitutes our more public and noxious racism now exercised by so many white Americans against persons of color, particularly African-Americans.

So, we should examine how we got here, how a "damaged heritage" has summoned forth white Americans to that certain vision of race relations prevailing for centuries, notably in the American South, and how that vision inspires many white Americans still, even beyond the South, for the dehumanization of others to satisfy the formidable urge for whites to dominate persons of color again and again. While its partner in crime, filiopietism, that excessive veneration of ancestors and tradition, operates alongside, damaged heritage has come to us too simply, but that is not surprising, for heritage itself is one human feature that cannot be easily separated from who we are. One philosopher characterizes our tightly bound linkage to the past this way:

> What I am, therefore, is in key part what I inherit, a specific past that is present to some degree in my present. I find myself part of a history and that is generally to say, whether I like it or not, whether I recognize it or not, one of the bearers of a tradition.[1]

For most white Americans, I do not think there is a need to provide a definition for the phrase, "damaged heritage." I think the meaning is obvious on its face in terms of the influence that "damaged heritage" has had on the unending recurrence of racism and racial subjugation of African-Americans, century after century. Regarding this book, why do I use this phrase as a constant theme throughout the pages? In today's America, it is not enough for white folks to identify the damaged heritage of their ancestors. Rather, it is critical, at this time, for white Americans to establish and annunciate the marked and unalloyed differences in attitude and practice between that past and their own actions; that is what can be done affirmatively in setting a juxtaposition with that past, that damaged heritage. The relevance of the phrase lies in the immoral grounding that white Southerners and many other Americans have regularly inherited for generations, the immoral grounding that evolves from the explicit and implicit racism that has been perniciously present in most every part of those lives. Damaged heritage is not of our individual creation or making, but it is an important part of our past, our inheritance with which we have to deal. Of course, everyone is born with a degree of damage in her or his heritage, for theologians have repeatedly reasoned that we humans are born into sin. But the damaged heritage of which I speak is different, entirely different, for white children receiving this legacy that relies on racism for economic and social foundations are expected, actually compelled, to support a blatant, prime facie immorality as a primary, if not the primary function of existence. This damaged heritage goes beyond the normal human condition of being born into sin. Generations of white Americans, especially white Southerners, have been expected, without even deliberate or considered acceptance, if not outright glorification, to base their very lives on this institutionalized immorality, this "damaged heritage."

Roger Frie, a German-born writer of today, facing a similar challenge and circumstance dictated by his own damaged heritage, put it starkly: "I was transported to a past that was not of my making, but to which I nevertheless belonged."[2]

Throughout this book, I descend into the nature of American white racism, and to that end, I've described the seemingly immutable repetition of this disease emanating from meaningful parts of our American culture. Indeed, I have found that damaged heritage and filiopietism are inextricably bound together. In fact, filiopietism—that excessive veneration of the past and traditions—is necessary for white Americans, especially white Southerners, to sustain and tolerate the cruelty, intolerance, madness, and repulsion of damaged heritage. The highly reverential filiopietism excuses, camouflages, and sufficiently inoculates damaged heritage. Simply put, the influence of damaged heritage on white racism could not continuously exist without the psychological cover of filiopietism. I am a white American; more particularly, I grew up and matured during the turbulent 1950s and 1960s civil rights period within the confines of severe segregation on the cusp of the Mississippi River Delta in southeast Arkansas.

From these experiences, including, at the end of the 1960s, my return to southeast Arkansas to teach in an all African-American public school before integration of the local education system and by my own demonstrable rejection of a segregated way of life, I write freely about the forms and features of racism that have significantly impacted a large swath of my life's journey. By giving my own personal slant to these issues, relying on the constructive path to racial reconciliation, particularly with Sheila L. Walker, an African-American woman whose antecedents were victims of the largely undiscovered Elaine Race Massacre in which my own grandfather participated, I describe one white Southerner's pilgrimage to achieve racial reconciliation through a belief in the pursuit of the "genuinely human" in our black brothers and sisters. I also believe that part of the solution to our racial tyranny lies in a full acceptance by whites of forgiveness from African-Americans for the pervasive and malevolent "damaged heritage" that so many white Americans have, without critical thought or comprehension, ingested from birth for a lifetime of prejudice, if not villainous hatred, against our African-American sisters and brothers.

Of course, neither Sheila nor I was directly involved in the Elaine Race Massacre, and yet, in a larger sense, we are creatures of history, of near history, near history more so than far history. Because of the past's often cruel and menacing ways, we must accept conclusively that the Massacre helped to shape us. History does that. Even if no one had said a word about this murderous conflagration, it still brought with it a persuasive, peculiar, certain manner of seeing things, of acknowledging the world in which we were born and matured. The fact that the particulars of the Massacre were pertinent in this way but closed off from sensibility and discussion declares with an almost deafening roar the importance that the Elaine event holds for us, for people like Sheila and me.

When one thinks of damaged heritage in the context of racial prejudice and racial subjugation, there is a tendency for non-Southerners to think of the American South as the place where the term applies most suitably and directly. However, damaged heritage of white Americans employed against blacks penetrates into the very core of our nation. Just as examples, two American icons outside the South—the White House and Trinity Church Wall Street—utilized black slaves for the original construction of their structures. Furthermore, according to *The New York Times*:

> New York City in the late 18th century was an epicenter of the slave trade, holding more Africans in chains than any other city in the country, with the possible exception of Charleston,

S.C. New York City's addiction to the immediate fruits of slave labor—and to the profits that it reaped from servicing the business needs of the South—made for a slow and tortured path to emancipation there.[3]

Indeed, on the matter of black subjugation, there is more than enough damaged heritage that has been perpetrated outside the South to call it an American curse. The U.S. Constitution, another prime example of our national legacy of damaged heritage, calculated the value of black slaves at only 60 percent of a free white person. So, please do not assume this book is meant for the Southern reader alone. While the South may carry a more glaring history of damaged heritage and its effect on racial prejudice and racial subjugation, let us not be misled: damaged heritage is a *national* problem, and wherever its use by whites against African-Americans exists, then the message of this book is relevant.

During the time I wrote the "Litany of Offense and Apology" for the national Day of Repentance (October 4, 2008) when the Episcopal Church, the American branch of the Anglican Church, formally apologized for its role in transatlantic slavery and related evils, I discovered a treatise entitled *The Arkansas Race Riot*, written by the African-American historian and anti-lynching advocate, Ida B. Wells. Her piece described the hidden and more appropriately named Elaine Race Massacre, one of the worst racial onslaughts against African-Americans in our country's history with over a hundred and possibly hundreds of African-American sharecroppers and members of their families perishing in the fall of 1919 at the hands of white posses, white vigilantes, and white federal troops in rural Phillips County, Arkansas, along the Mississippi River. As a result of my grandfather's participation in this murderous event and its victimization of Sheila's family, she and I were drawn together to rely on our mutual association with the Massacre, though from opposite sides, to form this pursuit of racial reconciliation. We each had taken different paths of attention to the Massacre, but they converged into not only reconciliation but also a very valued friendship. For six years now, Sheila and I have secured reconciliation, notwithstanding the history that brought us together. Early on, she forgave my grandfather, Lonnie, for his role in the attacks, a special act of unsolicited forgiveness that established a firm foundation for our exceptional journey. With the Elaine Race Massacre as stage or habitat and our friendship as terra firma, I have seen my way clear then to harvest a series of germane and necessary junctures and experiences for this book, for this life lived in black and white.

FOREWORD

by Sheila L. Walker

I n 2013, I met Robert Whitaker, the author of *On the Laps of Gods*. As a descendant of Albert Giles, one of the historically important Arkansas Twelve of the Elaine Race Massacre legacy, I wanted to thank Whitaker for writing the very comprehensive account of the Massacre. During my first meeting with Whitaker, he asked if I would be interested in talking to a white man whose relative, his grandfather, had participated in the Massacre. Without giving it much thought, I agreed.

A little more than six months later, Robert Whitaker introduced me, by email, to J. Chester Johnson. In his first email, Chester sent as an attachment his article for the *Green Mountains Review*, "Evanescence: The Elaine Race Massacre." There were two distinct things in the essay title that stood out to me. First was calling what happened in Elaine a *massacre*. That word echoed my feeling of how to properly classify the events in Elaine, after I learned details of what happened. Second, the word *evanescence*. It encapsulated my fears that the Elaine Massacre would continue as a crucial historical event, fading and unknown. How could I honor my ancestors that were involved?

In 1973, my grandmother started to tell me about something she witnessed when she was fifteen. She started to cry and became hysterical without finishing her story. As the years passed, Grandmother would attempt to tell her story several times, resulting in her going into hysterics each time. She died in 1991. I was clueless about what caused her to appear to suffer from what is now known as post-traumatic stress syndrome. I was almost fifty when my mother told me Grandmother had been trying to tell her story of the *"Elaine Riots."* I had never heard of Elaine! I researched and read vintage newspaper accounts, but I mostly relied on two books, *Blood in Their Eyes: The Elaine Massacres of 1919* by Grif Stockley and *On the Laps of Gods* by Robert Whitaker. Both books named my granduncles, Albert and Milligan Giles, as surviving victims of the Massacre.

Chester had depended on these same books as primary references for his *Evanescence* essay. The message he conveyed stood out, not as a selfish release of "white guilt," but as an accountable acknowledgment of the truth. Chester's writing was able to allow me, a descendant on the "other side," to relate and empathize with his perspective.

Our first phone conversation lasted over two hours. I knew if there was any way possible, we had to meet face to face. After I mentioned to him that my husband and I would shortly be visiting our son and his family in Boston, Chester and I decided to meet at my son's home. I was happy, but apprehensive. Was the connection we made over the phone genuine? Both Chester and I reached out to Robert Whitaker, who asked to join us. My daughter-in-law and son, both experienced media producers, thought our meeting should be filmed, worthy for a possible future documentary.

When Chester and I met face to face, instead of a handshake, we embraced like old friends. Kindred spirits. Our conversation was honest and frank. Chester expressed his desire to memorialize what happened on September 30, 1919 and the days following as part of his reconciliation. For my part, I treasured the information I had learned about my family's involvement in the Massacre, and I wanted to ensure it didn't become obscured again for my family or any of my people. But how? I had sent books to my family hoping they would read about what happened and pass the information on to their children. But what I discovered is that my family found it very hard to read about Elaine, in spite of and because of our family's involvement. As it is to Chester, contributing to other means of memorializing the Massacre is of key importance to me. As I listened to Chester speak about his personal voyage toward reconciliation, I realized this was a hard task for either of us to take on as individuals. The act of us coming together seemed a divine intervention. God was making possible what we could not do alone.

The capacity to personally forgive Chester's grandfather became easy. I know that all humans are born with inherent goodness which can often be overshadowed by an oppressive society that teaches us hate and individual circumstances that are far from ideal. The result: we all make mistakes, and some of us do very bad things. If we are lucky and blessed, we get the opportunity to make an honest account of the hurt surrounding us and then mend fences with both those we have hurt and those who have hurt us. Truth, reconciliation. Chester and I strive to support each other and our people on the path of truth and reconciliation for everyone touched by the Elaine Massacre. This book is one of many steps that Chester has taken on that path, and I am pleased to now be a friend and witness to his journey.

1

A CHANGING OF AMERICA

cross the sweeping canvas of American history, two markers, inherited and ineluctable, from the Elaine Race Massacre of 1919 in Phillips County, Arkansas, invite a degree of attention yet to be fully received from the country's public consciousness. First, the sheer number of persons who died in the Massacre—more particularly, the countless African-Americans who perished—would certainly cause this massacre to be judged one of the deadliest racial conflicts, perhaps the deadliest racial conflagration, in the history of the nation. Second, the American Civil Rights Movement during the 1950s and 1960s drew constantly from the wellspring of the 1923 U.S. Supreme Court's decision in *Moore v. Dempsey* that emerged out of the legal proceedings in Phillips County against African-American defendants, charged with the murders of whites allegedly committed during the Massacre. The ruling in *Moore v. Dempsey* broke a long chain of Supreme Court decisions brutally adverse to the safety and rights of African-Americans.

Two heroes whose individual backgrounds could not have been more dissimilar share in this saga of a changing of America. Most apparent, Scipio Africanus Jones, African-American lawyer, who began work in Arkansas' fields to become a twentieth-century Moses, climbed, through brilliance and tenacity, to forensic heights to free the black sharecroppers, unjustly found guilty of crimes in the aftermath of the Massacre. At the same time, he developed the legal strategy that ultimately, through the intervention of the U.S. Supreme Court, gave life to the Fourteenth Amendment of the U.S. Constitution to guard the individual rights of and due process for American citizens. The other hero, Oliver Wendell Holmes, Boston patrician and distinguished jurist, who wrote the majority opinion for *Moore v. Dempsey*, not only opened the door to freedom for wrongfully convicted Arkansas sharecroppers, but also articulated a new judicial precedent and principle under which the federal government would more forcefully thereafter engage in the constitutional protection of all its citizens.

*Portrait of Scipio Africanus Jones. Courtesy of the Butler
Center for Arkansas Studies, Central Arkansas Library System*

Notwithstanding the historical and legal significance of the Elaine Race Massacre, outside a handful of advocates and a somewhat wider audience that those advocates engendered, the Massacre and its aftermath have been largely ignored. Whether this inattention can be explained by the Massacre's remote location, by the desire of many blacks and whites in Phillips County and throughout Arkansas to keep quiet about the conflagration, or by the rush of other affairs affecting the state and the nation, we just don't know. It is certainly time for more airing of those days at the end of September and early October, 1919, and subsequent, associated, and gravid moments, if, for no other reason, than to debunk the erstwhile success of silence and avoidance.

By the time of my birth in 1944, my maternal grandparents, Alonzo Birch, known as "Lonnie," and Hattie, had moved to Little Rock from McGehee when he was transferred by the Missouri Pacific Railroad (MoPac) from the company's southeastern Arkansas hub to its larger transportation center. Lonnie was thin, not tall, not short, white, and a native of the Arkansas Delta. Bespectacled with large pale frames, he had thick, often unmanageable gray hair. An inveterate smoker and a proud agnostic, Lonnie bore a tranquil demeanor, and for me, remained always available. At the time Lonnie became my principal caretaker, he was retired from MoPac, which had an indelible and indisputable part in the Elaine Race Massacre. For several years following my father's death in 1946, before I had reached the age of two, I lived with Lonnie and Hattie until my mother brought my older brother and me together under one roof in Monticello, one of the many small towns in southeast Arkansas. Upon our father's death, my brother spent much more of his time with the paternal side of the family. Soon after I left Lonnie for Monticello, he died of a cerebral hemorrhage, but even today, I reminisce over the love and sensibility we shared with each other. I can recall times I sat in his lap on the front porch of my grandparents' home in Little Rock, when Lonnie and I watched cars and people go by, and I played with a porch chair that could be overturned and magically—soon after the end of World War II—become a fighter pilot's cockpit. Lonnie and I celebrated birthdays and other holidays together. When I fell down, he picked me up and gently assuaged my scrapes and bruises.

Out of the blue—I must have been in junior high school—without provocation or for any apparent reason, except that the integration of Little Rock Central High School had just begun, Mother casually mentioned that before she became a teenager, Lonnie participated in a "well-known" race riot while in the employ of MoPac. Later on, she editorialized about it now and then: how he traveled on a MoPac train from McGehee to the battle between the races, how the place of bloody engagement with the blacks had been close to the railroad tracks and among cotton rows. Looking back at the time that followed the end of World War I, when the Elaine Race Massacre occurred, what other race massacre or so-called race riot had there been near McGehee, except for Elaine? There wasn't one. History did disclose lynchings or the burning alive of African-Americans around that time in Star City, Monticello, McGehee, and Lake Village within southeast Arkansas, but no massacre or riot, except for Elaine. Whenever she mentioned the race riot, Mother frequently referred to Lonnie, in a matter-of-fact tone, as a member of the Ku Klux Klan.

At the time of the Elaine Race Massacre in 1919, Lonnie worked as a railroad engineer for MoPac. The Birch family, pioneer residents of Desha County, immediately south of Phillips County, consisted of planters, but, unlike other male family members who chose to farm, Lonnie instead took a job with MoPac in McGehee, only a few miles from the Birch farms. Home for Hattie, Lonnie, and their several children and a relatively short train ride to and from Elaine, McGehee had become MoPac's regional center for southeast Arkansas. If anyone in that part of the country found it necessary to get to Phillips County by railroad, the easiest mode of non-local land travel in the early part of the twentieth century, the path generally led through McGehee. Arkansas Governor Charles Hillman Brough brought federal troops from Little Rock to Elaine via McGehee to "restore" order, and except for those coming through Memphis, outside contributors or witnesses to the Elaine Race Massacre, if they came by rail, were likely to pass through Lonnie's hometown.

Much later, I made the simple connection that the race riot to which Mother alluded and the Elaine Race Massacre were one and the same. It was not very difficult to conflate the related factors leading to Lonnie's participation in the Massacre: his employment with MoPac; the routine, quasi-police role MoPac undertook during that time in that region of the state; Lonnie's chthonic views about race, evidenced by his membership in the Ku Klux Klan; and the history, conveyed by Mother's verbal remembrances. I had learned that Lonnie, though employed by MoPac, kept in contact, for kinship and financial reasons, with his brothers who farmed the family lands, and would have therefore undoubtedly known of the rumored threats of unionization by African-American sharecroppers in the Arkansas Delta to negotiate for higher cotton prices with the white planters. After all, Robert Hill, the black organizer of black sharecroppers, and his Progressive Farmers and Household Union, both being indivisibly bound to the Massacre in Phillips County, resided in Winchester, a small hamlet only a handful of miles north of the family farm.

I can indeed link the convincing pieces that led to the conclusion Lonnie took part in the Elaine Race Massacre, but I cannot reconcile my love for Lonnie and his apparent views about and contributions to racism, as practiced in the Arkansas Delta by whites during the first part of the twentieth century. In my readings that dealt with the period, I recollect references to the Arkansas Delta as the heart of darkness for African-Americans, and it may have been—with my own grandfather's propensity adding, in goodly supply, no doubt, to the pool of darkness that spread murderously and perniciously over the land. Yet, he was always kind to me, much kinder than virtually anyone else. So, I will not try to reconcile the two—it would be false, serpentine, and artificial. But maybe he couldn't reconcile the two either. He was who he was, and now that he is dead, I can only ponder the questions with the answers secluded and forever distant. Still, I know unreservedly my own path to Elaine was, in part, to uncover a slice of him that eludes my memory and baffles my personal conscience.

In 2008, as I was writing the "Litany of Offense and Apology" in poetry and prose for the national Day of Repentance when the Episcopal Church formally apologized for its role in transatlantic slavery and associated evils, I dove headlong into research to refine my recollection of and familiarity with consequential African-American writers and leaders. As I re-read or read fresh various books, letters, essays, and sundry materials by such notables as W. E. B. Du Bois, James Weldon Johnson, Ida B. Wells, and numerous others, I occasionally came across references to and comments about the Elaine Race Massacre of 1919. Although reared—a white male—during the 1950s and early 1960s in southeast Arkansas, some sixty miles or so from Elaine (as the crow flies), except for episodic and somewhat abstruse and brief allusions about Lonnie's participation, as relayed by my mother, which I later employed to make connections to the Massacre, I could recount nothing I'd heard or read in those earlier years about the event.

I never learned about the Elaine Race Massacre during my school days in history classes, even in Arkansas history instruction; I never heard it discussed in family circles or in casual conversations at local restaurants or coffee shops or at church and social gatherings. A small number of whites died, but many more African-Americans lost their lives—several writers say hundreds, others say less—mostly in "the killing fields" north of Elaine. Ida B. Wells, the fervid lynching critic, traveled from Chicago to Arkansas in early 1920 to hear about the white attacks up close and to interview African-American prisoners at The Walls penitentiary outside of Little Rock, when she posed as a family member of one of the prisoners to gain access to the Elaine Twelve, who were repeatedly scheduled for execution, convicted of murdering whites during the Massacre. After her time at The Walls, Ida B. Wells wrote about the incident in a short volume of some seventy pages, *The Arkansas Race Riot*. But I had known nothing. I contacted several friends from Monticello High School with whom I've continued a rather close relationship; they likewise had no or little information to bear on the matter. A void, the silence, evanescence, if you will, of neglected history.

During the course of my research, which grew in intensity, I learned the Massacre had gradually crept into the public consciousness among some Arkansans, as, over time, information and transmitted recollections seeped into the open air. Indeed, I eventually discovered that a symposium had been held a few years previously in Phillips County, allowing African-Americans and whites to combine information that people gleaned over the years about the Massacre and its immediate aftermath. I also learned that three excellent books, which discussed the Massacre, had been published since 2000: Robert Whitaker's *On the Laps of Gods* and Grif Stockley's two books: *Blood in Their Eyes: The Elaine Race Massacres of 1919* and *Ruled by Race*. These books built on earlier information about and studies of the Massacre.

Notwithstanding these books, the silence of neglected history prevailed. I soon contacted, on several occasions, the Arkansas branch of a national African-American organization to ascertain whether it had plans, even preliminary ones, for a centennial observance of the Massacre. After all, if there were a significant set of programs, memorials, or general reflections to be scheduled for the centennial in 2019 for commemoration of the event, initial planning and fundraising should soon begin. No return calls, no letters written in response to my inquiries. In additional instances, outreach to others met with similar silence. On the other hand, I did find interest by some Arkansans for giving more attention to the Massacre through public forums or other public acknowledgments. I've nonetheless had to conclude there was an unwritten agreement, among many blacks and whites, for silence about or only modest recognition of the Massacre and associated, unsettling history. Indeed, in her book, *One With Others*, published in 2010, both a poetic and investigative account of the 1969 March Against Fear, a march for racial freedom and justice, from West Memphis, Arkansas to Little Rock, Arkansas, C. D. Wright altered or omitted true names nearly a half century after the actual march, presumably as a result of vicinal responses to various inquiries Wright pursued about the past epoch. I guess I'm forced to consider seriously the cynical words of one elder, white Arkansan, who told me a few years ago: "We should have learned that racism is a scab that never heals. If you poke at it enough, it'll start to bleed, and we've had more than enough blood spilling out of that wound."

A new, threatening world gripped the white planter class in the Arkansas Delta at the conclusion of World War I. African-American men, returning in consequential numbers from Europe, were different than those who left the shores of the United States to fight. Europe had shown respect for black Americans, and many were decorated heroes. After risking their lives for this country, these African-Americans expected to be treated with greater fairness and equity upon their return. As an immediate concern to the white planters, these African-American veterans knew how to take care of themselves and how to use firearms. Nevertheless, as soon as these blacks set their feet back on home soil, whites were determined to make it clear that nothing at all had changed; maybe, it had even gotten worse in early 1919 with lynchings, shootings, or the burning alive of African-American veterans and other blacks in places like Star City and El Dorado, Arkansas, and in the near-by states of Louisiana and Mississippi.[1]

At the same time, communism had recently swept Russia and promoted a world-wide conquest; in the United States, did this mean vigorous unionization of farm workers among African-Americans, who tilled the Arkansas Delta cotton fields? Fear of the radicalization of the African-American in the United States, assumed to be inspired by Bolshevist agitation, became rampant.[2]

Racial confrontations broke out everywhere in the country during the summer of 1919: Chicago, South Carolina, Washington, D.C., Texas, Georgia, Tennessee, Nebraska, and as far west as Arizona—prompting the black poet, James Weldon Johnson, to coin a double entendre for the nation's upheaval, "Red Summer of 1919." Numerous journalists, in and out of the United States, believed the internal American conflict, at that time, constituted a race war.

Throughout the months leading up to the fall of 1919, rumors and tense times pervaded the white citizens of Phillips County, Arkansas, home to many substantial cotton farms along the Mississippi River. Indeed, a committee, composed of County officials and plutocrats, most of whom lived in Helena, the county seat, had formed to monitor any potential problems that might surface among African-Americans. In fact, white planters heard from "spies" and other sources that a certain Robert Hill, a newly returned African-American veteran, residing outside of Phillips County in Winchester within nearby Drew County, Arkansas, planned to organize black sharecroppers in Phillips County into a union, the Hoop Spur Lodge of the Progressive Farmers and Household Union. The union would give black sharecroppers enhanced leverage to bargain over cotton prices and to eliminate the "take it or leave it" power among white planters that had kept prices at which sharecroppers could sell their cotton artificially low. There was a hot, disturbing rumor associated with the union's organizational efforts that a list existed of white planters in Phillips County targeted for murder and that a black uprising could be forthcoming.

Late into the evening on Tuesday, September 30, 1919, existing and prospective African-American members of the newly formed union and Robert
Hill were meeting in the Hoop Spur Church, right off Highway 44, on the
northern outskirts of Elaine, some twenty miles southwest of Helena. In
addition to the men present, women and infants attended—in all, about
100 persons, including Sheila Walker's antecedents: Sallie, Albert, and
Milligan Giles.[3] A little after 11:00 P.M., a Model T Ford, whose passengers consisted of Charles Pratt, the Phillips County deputy sheriff; W. A.
Adkins, a security agent from MoPac; and Kid Collins, a black "trustee"
(prisoner from the County jail) pulled up next to a bridge that crossed the
Govan Slough within eyesight of the guards posted outside the church in
case someone tried to interfere with the union proceedings. Within minutes, bullets streamed and whistled through the air and into the church;
people inside fell to the floor and over each other, and some crawled out
windows and began running into surrounding fields. Outside, next to the
car, the MoPac agent lay dead with a load of buckshot in his belly and
with another shot in his neck; the Model T Ford was riddled with bullets.
The deputy sheriff—with a bullet wound to his knee—crawled to safety
along the MoPac tracks, which paralleled Highway 44; he would later
climb aboard a passing train. The unharmed "trustee" walked to a nearby
community. The Hoop Spur Church burned to the ground the next day,
disguising bullet shots that had sprayed the interior.[4]

Within three hours, the County sheriff's office had been informed of
the deadly shootout; a few hours later, Helena posses of white men were
deputized and were on the hunt to crush a black insurrection, which
County fathers now feared had begun with the gunfire at Hoop Spur. Mid-
morning, the Helena posses, once past the Hoop Spur Church, continued
south a short distance and turned west on a dirt road where blacks were
living; then, the shooting of African-Americans commenced; in addition
to the Helena white posses, another one headed from south to north out
of Elaine.[5] Blacks hid in the woods, coppices, and in the slough that ran
roughly along Route 44. Several blacks emerged from the slough holding
up their hands, but they were shot and killed. Other African-Americans
simply ran, but they too were gunned down among lineated cotton rows at
the hands of the posses. Approximately at this point in the attack both Albert

and Milligan Giles were shot: Milligan, at fifteen, had been shot in the face by Henry Smiddy of MoPac, and Albert was struck with bullets several times, one traversing "through his skull" to depart close to his left ear.[6]

According to a note I received from Robert Whitaker, author of *On the Laps of Gods*, approximately fifteen to twenty African-Americans were killed that first morning. Two whites also died, either from blacks shooting at posse members or from friendly fire between bands of white shooters.

Groups of whites started to arrive from close Arkansas communities and the states of Mississippi and Tennessee, and it is reported that these white vigilantes were responsible for much indiscriminate killing of blacks, including those who were simply working cotton fields in Phillips County, well away from Hoop Spur and unaware of the incidents.

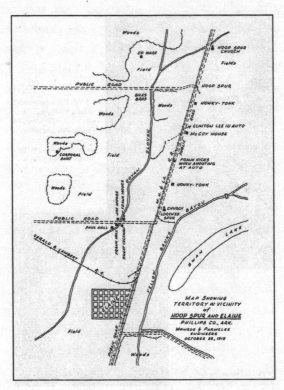

This map depicts certain important locations within the Elaine Race Massacre. Courtesy of the Butler Center for Arkansas Studies, Central Arkansas Library System.

Soon after noon on that day, October 1, with the total tally of whites killed by then at three though reported to be four (the fourth turned out to be only a minor wound), a call went out from Phillips County to Arkansas Governor Charles Hillman Brough for help; in turn, Brough sent a message to the nation's war secretary indicating that four whites had been killed and African-Americans were ready to mass an attack. Specifically, the Governor requested authorization to use federal troops from nearby Camp Pike,[7] located outside of Little Rock, thereby bypassing a required step for Governor Brough first to call out the Arkansas National Guard, but the war department quickly consented to the request, and the Governor and the federal troops were shortly on their way by train to Phillips County via McGehee. According to Whitaker in a following note, most of the African-Americans killed in the Massacre were slain by the federal troops, including immolation of one African-American. The largest number of killings by the military occurred on Thursday, October 2, soon after the troops arrived in Phillips County, but a scattering of killings of African-Americans by the military continued into the weekend.

With guns in hand, white men from neighboring communities and states
began to arrive to assist the posses the day following the shootings at
the Hoop Spur Church. Courtesy of the Arkansas State Archives.

How many died in the Massacre? There is plenty of documentation on the five whites killed: one security agent from MoPac, three locals, and a corporal with the federal soldiers. However, one meaningful aspect of the Massacre remains unknown and will undoubtedly remain unknown forever: how many African-Americans lost their lives in the Massacre? A reporter from the *Arkansas Gazette* at the time estimated that over 850 blacks died,[8] but this figure is uniformly discredited as being too high. Possible deaths, among African-Americans, now range from as few as fourteen,[9] a figure which is discredited as being too low, to hundreds. To attempt to bring order to this chaos, created, in large part, by the necessity of looking retrospectively over nearly 100 years, Robert Whitaker developed a map for his book entitled "The Killing Fields," demonstrating, according to his best estimates, the location, the number of deaths from the attacks at those locations, and those responsible for the deaths. As a consequence of my own interest in this unresolved (and likely unresolvable) factor—that is, quantifying the number of African-Americans killed during the Massacre—I reached out to Robert Whitaker to determine the extent to which he could even more specifically estimate or reaffirm the total deaths among African-Americans, based on "The Killing Fields" information that appeared in his book.

He responded as follows:

> One of the military reports said that the military alone had killed 60 or so . . . When I was researching and writing On the Laps of Gods, I spent a great deal of time and effort in mapping out—in time and space—the various reports of killings/shootings, etc. And when I put together that map, I felt confident that it was quite accurate. At first glance, the black and white versions of events seem totally disconnected, but once I had this mapped out, I could see how—in instance after instance—whites and blacks were describing the same events, albeit with a different perspective.
>
> I put together the map through a variety of sources: local maps at the time, local newspaper reports, the military reports, reports from the federal agents, and then from close attention to the testimony given in the legal case. What comes clear is this:

The local posses out of Helena, which came that first morning, probably did kill only 15 to 20 blacks. And that became the number they reported in the news, as though that were the total number killed. The killing by the groups that came across from Memphis and other surrounding areas is much harder to count. There are sporadic accounts from whites that tell of various killing events, and I mapped out those best I could. But this part is indeed murky, and this killing went mostly unreported by the white press. Finally, there is the killing by the soldiers called out to put down the "riot." The white newspapers told at the time that the soldiers restored the peace. But if you look at their own reports, they tell of opening fire with machine guns and of a significant number of blacks killed.

It is the documentation for the killing by the military, which I write about in On the Laps of Gods, *that is the best evidence, in my opinion, that the total number of killed was above 100. So, I am confident that the map I drew accurately describes reports of killing fields in time and space. And that map does strongly support a total number killed above 100. I personally believe 300 is too high, however. That is because I think that the numbers reported for some of the killing fields, and, in particular, those where the killing was done by the outside posses, were exaggerated by some of the witnesses."*[10]

In addition to the reasons described above by Whitaker for difficulty in establishing a precise number of African-Americans killed in the Massacre, there are other factors that make a clear calculation impossible. First, an obscurity prevails when such a long time passes between the acts and the search for a realistic record. Second, soon after the Massacre, a sizeable group of African-American families and individuals apparently left Phillips County, taking their recollections with them. Third, no one, at the time, seemed to have an inclination to take responsibility for documenting this aspect of the Massacre. I have no reason to disagree with Whitaker's view that the figure is "above 100" with most of that figure attributable to the federal troops and their liberal use of machine gun weaponry. It is, at least, provocative and interesting to note, however, that the *Encyclopedia of Arkansas History and Culture* and *Blood in Their Eyes: The Elaine Race Massacres of 1919* refer to perhaps "hundreds" of African-Americans having perished in the Elaine Race Massacre.[11]

Even while federal troops continued to "restore order" to Phillips County, African-Americans were being arrested and impounded in the Elaine school building, the Phillips County jail annexed to the court-house, and buildings nearby both. But County fathers had an immediate problem. A large number of blacks and a white lawyer, suspected of aiding the sharecroppers, were now held in the county jail, and a sizeable lynch mob had been forming on and off outside the courthouse during the day on Thursday, October 2.[12] County leaders had a deep concern that a mass lynching would further scar the image of Helena for future economic prospects, but, even more, multiple lynchings would surely cause an immediate, and substantial, exodus of African-Americans out of the county, leading to a major consequence for the white planters— after all, it was harvest time, and cotton needed to be picked. In 1919, cotton was often referred to in the Mississippi River Delta as "white gold" with the run-up in the price of cotton during World War I and afterwards.

The doors of the courthouse swung open in the early evening, and the mob was invited inside with the courthouse doors being locked behind them. At this point, leaders in the county cajoled the mob into foregoing any further violence; in turn, the mob received a promise from county fathers that the guilty parties would be prosecuted and electrocuted with dispatch. Based on these assurances, the mob dispersed and departed. The promise to a mob and the associated judicial and political proceedings in Phillips County and the State of Arkansas set a course that, in less than four years, concluded with a U.S. Supreme Court decision altering and guarding civil rights in the future.

The puissant center of Phillips County was the county seat, Helena. As the principal heart for the administration of justice in the county, the home for many of the white planters, the social and cultural fulcrum of the region, and, at the time, one of the larger cities in Arkansas, Helena had a key role in weaving the tapestry in the aftermath of the violence. The trials of the

African-Americans would be held there, black prisoners jailed there, and speeches by county fathers to the lynch mob were given there that conveyed assurance swift "justice" would be meted out against the black murderers and insurgents if the crowd just let justice run its course.

By the end of the week, the county fathers had another problem. The Elaine Race Massacre (referred to, at the time, by a series of different appellations) started to gain wide interest throughout Arkansas and the country, with many inquiries coming into Helena. What could be said that made sense from the perspectives of the governor and the county fathers? Before leaving Phillips County, Governor Brough appointed a Committee of Seven, composed of the county judge, the mayor of Helena, and prominent landowners, to investigate and decide on the African-Americans to be prosecuted.[13] A cogent story needed to be fashioned and transmitted to satisfy relevant interests; one finally evolved.

On Tuesday night, September 30, the deputy sheriff and the MoPac security agent, not knowing that a union meeting was in progress, had simply stopped next to the Hoop Spur Church to fix a tire and were ambushed by blacks, resulting in the death of the MoPac security agent and a bullet wound to the deputy sheriff. The following morning, posses were dispersed to arrest the blacks responsible for the murder, but the whites had been overpowered by a more significant force of African-Americans with high-powered rifles. Posses from neighboring states and towns came to help, and federal troops joined in the efforts to quell the insurrection; blacks were waging war against whites in Phillips County. According to this story, a written list existed of twenty-one planters to be killed by the African-Americans, and the tale went on to relate that the initial counts of dead blacks had been seriously exaggerated.

Anyone familiar with the facts of the Massacre knew this version to be fabricated. Indeed, the U.S. Justice Department had immediately sent several agents, who arrived on Friday, October 3, to uncover the truth about the deadly conflict. The report that came back to Justice contained a completely different story from the "official," local one: there had been no planned slaughter of whites by the African-Americans, and the number of blacks killed had actually been many times greater than fourteen.[14] However, operating under the Woodrow Wilson administration's policies toward African-Americans, the Justice Department simply allowed the report to be innocuously filed away; a local Justice Department official, involved in the investigation, even offered comments at the time supportive of the local white version.[15]

❖

Now came a difficult phase for county officials and plutocrats: the prosecution of the African-American union and other leaders in accordance with the county fathers' story. Prisoners in the county courthouse, the blacks to appear in court, needed to be "convinced." To that end, city and county law enforcement officers, the black "trustee," and MoPac security agents would invoke various techniques, including conversation, severe whipping, suffocation, and visits to an electric chair with the current increased until pain couldn't be sustained, to persuade the prisoners of the "official," local account. After one, two, or three sessions of treatment, most African-Americans could be counted upon to adhere to the version requested, though some blacks still chose to adopt refractory stances instead.

The legal proceedings for those accused were, as an understatement, speedy. Interrogations of the prisoners started on Saturday, October 4, and a report was issued two days later. Then began the determination of which of the three hundred imprisoned black men should be indicted for murder, but it took just a few days to dispose of those decisions. On Monday, October 27, the grand jury convened, and the trials commenced on Monday, November 3.[16] In advance, county officials and plutocrats developed a list of lawyers who would serve as prosecutors, and the judge, overseeing the trials, decided on defense counsel for the African-American sharecroppers. Though well credentialed, attorneys for the defense often asked questions that reinforced or improved the prosecutors' positions, or they didn't follow up on questions at all. Moreover, the jury box included law enforcement officers and men who took part in the posses that went to Hoop Spur and the areas north of Elaine. The trials themselves were also handled with dispatch, and jury verdicts with even more haste; juries often returned decisions in as little as two minutes.[17] At the end of Tuesday, November 4, having been given a one-day trial, Sheila Walker's granduncle, Albert Giles, was convicted of the murder of James Tappan, a member of a Helena posse that had begun the shooting of blacks in the Hoop Spur area the morning of Oct. 1.[18] While the evidence shows that Tappan could have been killed by a white colleague engaged in crossfire over a slough, the conviction of Albert Giles was more convenient; after all, James Tappan was one of the Tappans, a prestigious and well-known clan in Phillips County. Albert's brother, Milligan, pled guilty to second-degree murder and assault to kill; he was sentenced to ten years.

On November 21, just eighteen days after the first trial began and less than seven weeks after the Massacre, seventy-four convicted black prisoners boarded a train; sixty-two headed to Cummins State Farm for lesser crimes, such as second-degree murder, assault to kill, and "night riding," and twelve sent to The Walls, a prison just outside of Little Rock, where the Elaine Twelve, including Albert Giles, were scheduled to be electrocuted for murder—six on December 27 and the other six on January 2.[19] Thus far, county fathers had lived up to their promise to the lynch mob.

Federal troops impounding African-Americans during the Elaine Race Massacre. Courtesy of the Arkansas State Archives.

At this moment, however, a new figure enters the drama, and the county fathers could not have possibly envisioned the role this black attorney from Little Rock would play in determining the ultimate conclusion to the Elaine Race Massacre.

Scipio Africanus Jones, son of a black woman and a white man, worked his way from the Arkansas fields to become a lawyer before the age of twenty-six. A member of the black power elite of Little Rock early in his career, he developed a reputation for a keen and lissome legal mind and, as an attorney, was well-regarded by both blacks and whites. When a proposition came forth to end voting for African-Americans in Arkansas, Jones organized a strong state-wide group to oppose the proposition, which failed decisively. An accomplished trial lawyer, Jones regularly argued before the Arkansas Supreme Court. He waged battles for the civil rights of blacks, and numerous African-American families named their children after him. In 1901, Jones argued before the state's Supreme Court that his client's criminal conviction should be overturned because his Fourteenth Amendment right to due process had been violated; though Jones lost the case, he would later return to a similar argument to benefit six of the sharecroppers and, more generally, invigorate legal underpinnings of civil rights for the nation's African-Americans.

At the time the Elaine Twelve arrived at The Walls for execution, Jones and several black attorneys in Little Rock knew it was time to start to work on saving the convicted men with Jones selected by his colleagues to lead the effort. They also quickly realized it would be a requisite for Jones to team up with a sympathetic and respected white lawyer; the nod went to an elderly former Confederate soldier, Colonel George W. Murphy. Jones early on decided the initial trials in Phillips County had been manifestly unfair, and, as a first step, a motion for a new trial on the grounds that equal protection had been violated was presented to the local presiding judge, who denied the motion but stayed the executions. While Jones held the opinion that the trials had certainly been unfair, he also believed they didn't violate the Arkansas due process standards; however, upon review of the verdicts, he detected that in the rush to judgment, the Phillips County juries in six of the cases, including the conviction of Albert Giles, failed to specify whether the verdict had been for first or second degree murder;

this group of cases would thereafter be known as the "Ware Six"[20] The names for the two groups of black sharecroppers convicted of murder and sentenced to execution, collectively known as the Elaine Twelve, were taken from Ed Ware, one of the parties in the Ware Six cases, and Frank Moore, one of the parties in the Moore Six cases. In March, 1920, the Arkansas Supreme Court handed down its ruling that the verdicts for the Ware Six were fatally defective, and it granted new trials for those impacted.[21] With respect to the remaining six, the so-called "Moore Six," the Court ruled that they had received fair and impartial trials. Nevertheless, until the results of the retrials for the Ware Six occurred, new execution dates for the Moore Six would be postponed.

For the new proceedings in Phillips County, Colonel Murphy, age seventy-nine, took the lead, but soon after the retrials commenced, he collapsed, requiring Jones to step into the elderly attorney's place.[22] As the retrial progressed, Jones would succeed in altering the story the jury had heard in the first trial; black witnesses recanted stories, telling the local court that they had been tortured to give the previous, untrue testimony. Jones also set a trap for the local presiding judge that he thought would make this retrial appealable to the Arkansas Supreme Court. Predictably, the Ware Six were once again found guilty of murder by an all-white jury.

After the retrials for the Ware Six with new guilty verdicts, an execution date of July 23, 1920 was established for the Elaine Twelve.[23] But, as a result of the legal trap Jones set for the presiding judge in Phillips County during the retrials, the Arkansas Supreme Court also invalidated the second convictions of the Ware Six, and yet another new trial was ordered with the threat of imminent electrocutions again removed. While Jones had, thus far, been able, through legal acumen and tactics, to keep proceedings astir for the Ware Six, it had not gone so well for the Moore Six. In fact, on October 11, 1920, the U.S. Supreme Court denied the petition that had rested on equal protection; coincidentally, Colonel Murphy, who worked well with Jones in defense of the Elaine Twelve, died of cardiac complications the day of the Supreme Court decision.[24] Edgar McHaney, another white attorney, replaced Murphy, but his departure from the team sometime later over money issues created a temporary predicament for Jones.

It had been believed that until legal proceedings for the Ware Six were concluded, the Moore Six would not receive a new execution date; yet, to the defense team's dismay and astonishment, a date of June 10, 1921 was set for the execution of the Moore Six by the new governor, Thomas McRae, who replaced Brough.[25] Political and business leaders of Phillips County applied pressure to decouple the timing for the execution of the Moore Six from that of the Ware Six. Further, after the Arkansas Supreme Court set aside the second trial for the Ware Six, Jones had asked the local presiding judge for a change in venue from Phillips County, but the judge decided not to rule on that request for the Ware Six until after the June 10 execution date for the Moore Six.

Coffins had already been ordered. The promise to the lynch mob by the County fathers nearly two years earlier would now be kept at least for six of the convicted sharecroppers, but the Moore Six continued to believe in Scipio Jones.

Over the previous several months, lynchings and mob violence against African-Americans had been widespread throughout the nation. In Arkansas alone during the first months of 1921, there had been in late January the burning alive of a black man in Nodena; in March, lynchings in both Hope and Monticello; and in early May, the lynching of another African-American in McGehee.[26]

Soon after the Civil War, the Fourteenth Amendment to the Constitution was enacted by Congress. The amendment, in addition to effectively making all former slaves citizens of the United States, stated, in part, that "nor shall any State deprive any person of life, liberty, or property, without due process of law; nor deny to any person within its jurisdiction the equal protection of the laws." In addition, Congress passed a Habeas Corpus Act in 1867, which provided state prisoners access to federal courts to ensure that due process was realized. Notwithstanding these two legal pillars, the U.S. Supreme Court had, following passage of both, undercut their intended effects for the next fifty years by determining that states alone, not the federal government, were responsible for the civil rights of their citizens.

Jones now found himself with few options for the Moore Six. As an act of near desperation, in a frantic search for deus ex machina, on the afternoon of Wednesday, June 8, less than forty hours before the scheduled executions of the Moore Six, Jones and McHaney appeared before an Arkansas judge who had dubious authority to hear the criminal case. Yet, upon hearing the facts for the petition that relied upon the tenets of the Fourteenth Amendment, the judge ruled in favor of the request and stayed the execution. The state attorney general appealed immediately to the Arkansas Supreme Court, asking that the judge's order be annulled, but the state Supreme Court decided to hear arguments the following Monday. After the hearing, the Arkansas Supreme Court ruled, on June 20,[27] against the judge's order with a determination that the execution of the Moore Six could proceed; in turn, Governor McRae set September 23, 1921 as the new electrocution date. The next step would be an appeal by Jones to the U.S. Supreme Court.

In late August, apparently in response to pangs of conscience and feelings of guilt for roles in the Massacre and the local court proceedings immediately following the attacks against the black sharecroppers and their family members, two white, former MoPac security agents, key witnesses in the first trials, now were recanting their stories and telling the truth.[28] With affidavits from these two white MoPac security agents, combined with the affidavits of three sharecroppers who also recanted, the story of injustice in Phillips County to be told in federal district court had become much more credible and compelling. The local court in Phillips County had simply not been independent, for the Committee of Seven, deciding who would be electrocuted and sent to prison and the length of terms given, had taken over the function of the courts. A new factual topography rose for Supreme Court review. Since the State clung to a "demurrer" approach to the facts contained in the Moore Six petition, it was expressing a view that the facts, as stated in the request, did not matter, and, to that point, in late September, 1921, the federal district court ruled against the Moore Six.[29] Jones had thirty days to burnish an appeal to the U.S. Supreme Court, but confusing the situation for Jones was that, surprisingly, the week before the federal district hearing, Jones's co-counsel, McHaney, who had replaced Colonel Murphy, resigned over money issues with the NAACP, which had been funding a meaningful part of the sharecroppers' defense. Nonetheless, with the true story of the Elaine Race Massacre now well-publicized and not challenged by the state, it was clear the state did not wish to return to the courtroom to try the Ware Six, so, before proceeding, the state would first let the U.S. Supreme Court decide on the Moore Six.

The U.S. Supreme Court could not hear the case until, at the earliest, the fall of 1922; furthermore, someone, other than Jones, had been approved to present the oral arguments to the U.S. Supreme Court. Instead of Jones, Moorfield Storey was chosen by the NAACP; Storey, an older attorney, distinguished Boston Brahmin, former secretary to the abolitionist Senator Charles Sumner of Massachusetts and first president of the NAACP, had much experience presenting and debating cases before the Supreme Court.[30] Upon release of the record on appeal as prepared by Jones, it seemed abundantly clear to Storey that the facts for the sharecroppers supported the proposition that the Arkansas Supreme Court affirmed torture and a farce for a trial; indeed, the state process had been a "judicial lynching."

In addition to preparing for the Moore Six hearing in the nation's capital, Jones had been pursuing freedom for the other prisoners; in October, 1922, he successfully arranged to have all but fifteen of the sharecroppers released from the Cummins State Farm.[31]

In advance of *Moore v. Dempsey* being argued before the U.S. Supreme Court, lynchings and the burnings of blacks alive continued throughout the nation. Only a few days before the Supreme Court hearing, a race battle broke out in Rosewood, Florida with numerous blacks being killed and white posses hunting down African-Americans hiding in the woods—a comparatively smaller incident, but still a grim and lugubrious reminder of the Elaine Race Massacre.

On the day of the U.S. Supreme Court hearing, which Jones unfortunately missed—a deep personal and professional loss—as a result of miscommunications with or misinformation from the court clerk regarding the hearing's date, Storey punctuated the point in his argument that if the case before them did not warrant the petition requested, then that portion of the Constitution on which the petition was based should be eliminated for it had no meaning. Importantly, the Arkansas Attorney General could not argue the facts since the State had demurred on the facts earlier in the lower court.

Oliver Wendell Holmes wrote the majority opinion for Moore v. Dempsey, *a case that resulted in a more expansive approach toward equal protection by the U.S. Supreme Court, paving the way for more progressive civil rights decisions. Credit: Library of Congress.*

Oliver Wendell Holmes, the eminent Supreme Court jurist, wrote the opinion for the majority in *Moore v. Dempsey*; he believed firmly the federal court had a duty to provide relief to state prisoners convicted in state proceedings that were grossly unfair. In a 6-2 decision, this point received amplification through Holmes's language:

> *If the case is that the whole procedure is a mask—that counsel, jury, and judge were swept to the fatal end by an irresistible wave of public passion, and that the State Courts failed to correct the wrong, neither perfection in the machinery for correction nor the possibility that the trial court and counsel saw no other way of avoiding an immediate outbreak of the mob can prevent this Court from securing to the petitioners their constitutional rights.*[32]

With this ruling, the federal government became the protector of the basic rights of individual American citizens. Some believed the ruling as important as any event since the Emancipation Proclamation. In retrospect, one could have then envisioned that the days of Jim Crow were numbered.

The Civil Rights Movement in the United States, as the twentieth century would know it, had effectively begun.

The scholar, Megan Ming Francis, characterizes the historical magnitude of the Elaine Race Massacre and particularly the derivative legal case, *Moore v. Dempsey*, this way:

> *The year 1923 is not usually considered to be part of the civil rights movement timeline. It is not etched into our collective memory, like the landmark Brown v. Board of Education Supreme Court decision of 1954, the courage of the Little Rock Nine in 1957, or the March on Washington in 1963. But if the U.S. civil rights movement is understood as an effort to secure the full social, political and legal rights of citizenship, then 1923 marks a significant event. That year . . . the Supreme Court of the United States directly responded to the NAACP's appeal and handed down a landmark decision in Moore v. Dempsey, 261 U.S. 86, which reversed the death sentences of six African American men in Phillips County, Arkansas, on the grounds that these defendants had their Fourteenth Amendment rights violated by a hostile white mob . . .*
>
> *For many, Moore v. Dempsey was shocking—mob-dominated trials and hastily issued death sentences for African American defendants had been widely accepted practices in the South ever since the legal end of slavery. In this context, state criminal trials were typically considered to be immune from federal court oversight. Thus, Moore v. Dempsey marked a turning point in legal discourse about constitutional rights, due to the Supreme Court's willingness to intervene in unjust state criminal court proceedings.*[33]

Richard C. Cortner, who, in the late 1980s, wrote a comprehensive volume on the Elaine Race Massacre and its legal impacts, *A Mob Intent on Death: The NAACP and the Arkansas Riot Cases*, expressed more specifically technical, but similar views about the importance of the *Moore v. Dempsey* decision by the U.S. Supreme Court:

In Moore, the Court began to look behind the procedural formalities of state criminal trials to ask whether, in fact, the defendant had received a fair trial at which there had been an adequate opportunity to be heard. In this case, it had concluded that a mob-dominated trial violated this elementary due process right to a fair hearing in so fundamental a way that reversal of the resultant conviction was the only appropriate remedy.[34]

The Moore Six, the Ware Six, and sharecroppers at Cummins State Farm remained in prison; Jones acknowledged much still needed to be accomplished. The favorable decision by the U.S. Supreme Court, released on February 19, 1923, though precedent setting and historic, had not set the Moore Six free. Rather, the ruling remanded the case back to the federal district court for an evidentiary hearing to determine if the sharecroppers' allegations were true.[35] Upon that affirmation, then Arkansas would be ordered to release the Moore Six. Jones knew that the Ware Six and Moore Six remained inextricably linked, and he could now implement part of a strategy leading to freedom for all the sharecroppers.

Jones had also set another, more momentous trap for the prosecution, which had failed to comply, for the Ware Six defendants, with Arkansas state law. Each time the prosecution requested a continuance of the Ware Six trials while waiting for the Supreme Court decision on the Moore Six, Jones had not firmly objected but nonetheless notified the court that the defendants were "ready for trial." Under Arkansas law, if there were a failure to prosecute criminal defendants for two consecutive terms of court without their consent, they were to be set free. Jones now petitioned for the immediate freeing of those affected defendants. After the filing by Jones of a "motion for discharge" in mid-April, the Arkansas Supreme Court, following the local judge's denial of the petition, ordered the Ware Six free in late June, 1923.[36] With the liberation of the Ware Six, the group that also contained Albert Giles, only twenty-one men, including the Moore Six, of the original prisoners found guilty in the aftermath of the Massacre were then incarcerated.

By mid-September, Jones had received enough signatures to petition the Governor to grant a full and complete pardon to the remaining prisoners.[37]

At about the same time, he not only pushed others to assist in a settlement process, but he also conducted an outreach to the county fathers. Did the state and Phillips County really want a trial to be held in federal court that further disclosed and reprised the manner in which the first trials were conducted? By late September, the mayor of Helena, the Committee of Seven, and other county leaders petitioned the Governor to commute the sentences of the Moore Six and effectively reduce the sentence to time served. A little over a month later, in early November, 1923, Jones constructed the final compromise with the state for the Moore Six; without pleading guilty to any charge, they had their sentences commuted to twelve years (being immediately eligible for parole) and were promised to be released within twelve months.[38]

Yet, the drama did not abate. A few months following the compromise, seven of the fifteen remaining men at Cummins—but not the Moore Six—were released, and then the anniversary of the November settlement also passed, still with no freedom for the Moore Six. On December 19, 1924, Governor McRae, only a few weeks before leaving office, released the last sharecroppers imprisoned at Cummins.[39] At this point, Jones understood that the governor had reneged on the agreement, and since the newly elected governor, replacing McRae, won the gubernatorial election with the backing of the Ku Klux Klan, Jones had run out of virtually all options.

Jones caught a train to Helena. Once he arrived, Jones went to the various offices of the county fathers; since they had agreed to the negotiated deal a year earlier, county leaders should sign a petition in support of the release of the prisoners. In addition to the signatures received in Helena, Jones made sure names of leading citizens from Elaine were obtained. On Christmas Eve, he delivered to the governor the petition of hundreds of names, including those from Phillips County and prominent citizens from throughout the state. Again, nothing happened. On January 13, 1925, Jones visited Governor McRae once more, but, this time, he left with the assurance the men would be freed.[40] As his final act as governor, McRae gave the Moore Six "indefinite furloughs." All the prisoners from the Elaine Race Massacre were now free.

Not only were the sharecroppers, who had been unfairly convicted and imprisoned, free, but Scipio Africanus Jones, African-American, former field hand himself, had also engineered a legal strategy that established a limit on states' rights in legal proceedings against the individual and created a new, forceful precedent for federal protection of the basic rights of American citizens, as guaranteed by the Fourteenth Amendment.

❖

In August, 2012, en route to my fiftieth high school reunion in Monticello, I flew into Memphis to explore, as much as one could now explore, the physical locale north of Elaine where much of the Massacre occurred. A representative from the University of Arkansas, a friend who knew of my continuing interest in and inquiry into the Massacre met me south of Memphis in Helena, and we began our journey back into that patently sad and disturbing moment in American history. Out of Helena, we traveled southwest on Highway 44, a rather deserted, small, but now paved road that shortly brought us to Elaine in less than thirty minutes. While much of the Massacre happened on the outskirts, just north of town, we thought we'd spend a little time meandering through Elaine just to get a sense of the place, nearly 100 years later. The town appeared smaller than I had imagined—a hamlet of a little more than 600 persons (according to the 2010 Census; 861 in 2000 Census).[41] Phillips County had also suffered a depressed economy over the last several decades; its population, which fell nearly 18 percent from 2000, was now less than half of the 1950 figure of about 46,000.[42] With a population decline of about 26 percent since 2000, the performance of Elaine paralleled that of the county but was even worse.

The elevated MoPac railroad tracks that brought Governor Brough, the Camp Pike troops, Lonnie, and others, involved as participants in or witnesses to the Elaine Race Massacre, still ran alongside Highway 44 and were unobstructedly visible from and strikingly close to the center of town.

For film buffs, the town held the abraded look and feel of Thalia, Texas in *The Last Picture Show* with crumbling and solitary, serrated walls being all that was left standing of several downtown (to the extent a downtown existed) buildings. After driving only a few blocks farther south, we eyed a relatively new school with a gymnasium in back; a plaque declared it had been opened in 1984, but the school was now boarded up with a warning sign proclaiming trespassers would be prosecuted. Across the street from the abandoned school stood another relatively spacious, somewhat impressive, but vacant building. We then stopped in at the town library in the center of Elaine and were told the school closed a few years back with students now being bused to Marvell, another small neighboring community. Several women in the library gave us a quick, unsolicited summary of the economic ills of the region, but there was no doubt at all in their minds why we, these strangers, had come to Elaine; others, also curious to sense the hamlet near the Massacre, preceded us. Without prompting, one woman told us they had nothing of interest, but we could possibly find more information in Helena at the County Museum.

On our short trip back to Helena, we walked and rode by and through "the killing fields" and adjacent areas in the fierce and thick summer sun and August Arkansas humidity under a broad azure sky with only a few, high cirrus clouds. Guided mostly by the Whitaker map and with an eerie notion we were surveying a concealed factor in our country's genome, we faced two striking and related conclusions that sprung to mind. First, little change to most of the landscape or along the narrow, dirt roads, off Highway 44, had taken place over almost 100 years, though the sharecropper shacks and some of the wooded areas and coppices, where African-Americans hid themselves from both the white posses and the white federal troops, had completely disappeared, replaced by expanded farmland. In the midst of these modest adaptations, we were still able to fix, within rows of cultivated land, the approximate location of the Hoop Spur Church, where the union meeting had been held, where the automobile that carried the deputy sheriff, the MoPac security agent, and the "trustee" had closely parked, and where the first blood had been spilled on the night of September 30, 1919. Second, no one ever intended to set any historical reminder in that place—a marker of explanation, a monument, a memorial of any kind—so future generations could know, with a degree of certainty, that several whites and more than a hundred (and, perhaps, hundreds of) African-Americans died in these humble and unremarkable fields and in like spaces within Phillips County as part of one of the most important racial confrontations in our country's history.

Portrait of Lonnie on the author's second birthday.

In my quest to sight an existential piece of Lonnie in this theater of the Elaine Race Massacre, I had, after all, concluded history can be doubtless, and too much and too little abided in the fields and fury of Phillips County for Lonnie and me to inhabit any amicable turf there—too much intervening and unsympathetic time, too much dismay as I turned the leaves of record, which bore too much descent and strife and turpitude, too little comity, too little heart.

Numerous people, in and out of Arkansas, had talked about a suitable commemoration for the Elaine Race Massacre. No memorial existed. To be sure, the Massacre and its aftermath pleaded for expanded recognition from the public consciousness across the state of Arkansas and nation. Back home alone in my New York City study but still absorbed in this unassailable context, I cautiously return to Phillips County with a troubling vision—to "the killing fields," to Elaine, to the forlorn and erstwhile violated countryside, and, in this vision, I despair that if historical markers appear along Highway 44 at the former, blood-drenched sites, contemporary variants of the October, 1919 posses will, on some lonely and tenebrous night, obliterate any conspicuous reminders of the unrestrained pogrom. I conjure up an idea that maybe the memorial should appear next to the steps leading into the Phillips County Courthouse or on the grounds of the state capitol, near the statues of the Little Rock Central Nine. At that moment, I wonder why silence and void are too often the preferred resolve to evil and lies; in the background of the vision, which now travels halfway around the world to the outskirts of Kiev in the Ukraine near the Dnieper River and to September, 1941, I then hear the gurgling and groaning sounds along a giant ravine with Jews being indiscriminately shot at the mouth of a pit and haphazardly rolled down the steep slopes, as I involuntarily recall the first two lines of the famous poem by the Russian poet, Yevgeny Yevtushenko: "Over Babi Yar, there are no memorials."[43]

That was the summer of 2012, and much has happened since then. As we edged ever closer to the centennial of the Elaine Race Massacre, I no longer heard the resonance from those two Yevtushenko lines, for after a hundred years without a marker or monument to this tragic event, we could then look forward to the dedication on September 29, 2019 of the Elaine Massacre Memorial, a most fitting, commemorative, and impressive structure, in Court Square Park, located immediately in front of the Phillips County Courthouse, the appropriate placement to punctuate remembrance of torture and unfair, accelerated trials that were performed in that building against African-American sharecroppers soon after the cessation of the violence of the Massacre. Part of this book will tell the story of the memorial, including a recitation of the inspiration, courage, and generosity, demonstrated by a family, the Solomon family, with multi-generational roots in Phillips County, the family that embraced responsibility for the memorial but also took steps, along with others, black and white, to encourage racial reconciliation over the Massacre within the county.

While creation of and observance for the Elaine Massacre Memorial may logically suggest a conclusion, nothing could be further from the truth. It is only the beginning, which begs us all to a long, personal journey for racial reconciliation that will, in so many ways, have no end in sight.

2

THE GENUINELY HUMAN

My Dear Lonnie,

 I do mean "My Dear Lonnie," for I've not had a chance to thank you for the gifts you conferred when I didn't even hold a clue they were gifts: your care, your protection, your constancy, your presence, your love, your forbearance. Lonnie, you, of course, could summon the very beginning. Alas, I was too young to remember, less than two years old when my father died in Arkansas three months after being diagnosed with cancer in Texas, while my mother, your daughter, then enjoyed few options, so I became for years your ward, if not in law, certainly in practice and by your simple and big-hearted acts of mercy and fidelity.

 You took this grandson into your home to live in August, 1946, and for years thereafter that's where I belonged, now recalling you most, for you were there most of all. You, Lonnie, habitual thereness that you were, seemed to welcome and devote yourself every day all day to this grandson more than you had for your own offspring, seven of them—so, it was said along the anecdotal line circulated repeatedly through your sons and daughters. Me, your retirement project, some rumored. I arrived later when you had retired from the Missouri Pacific Railroad and finally enjoyed time to spare with no job to hoard your energies and circumspections. Apparently, you were eager earlier to leave the house, returning to the tracks wherever the train took you in those days, staying clear of home.

Here and now, I need to talk about an imperative subject we—certainly, I—cannot evade or avoid, for race shaped us both as much as any and much more than most. Notwithstanding those plenteous expressions of goodwill you spread over your grandson, I'm writing this missive to bring to light the moment in your life when you participated in the 1919 Elaine, Arkansas Race Massacre, an horrific onslaught by whites against black sharecroppers and their families in Phillips County, Arkansas along the Mississippi River Delta—attacks by white posses, white vigilante groups, and white federal troops against blacks, an event largely misplaced by American history but which resulted in the deaths of over a hundred, and perhaps, hundreds of African-Americans. You took part in possibly the worst racial conflagration in our nation's history.

One of your other daughters, one of my aunts, once instructed me that your forebears, our forebears, owned slaves. As a young teenager, I also heard you were a regular, practicing member of the Ku Klux Klan. Apparently, it was no secret you belonged to the KKK with stories hidden well within family troves how you rose some nights, putting on your sheet and hood, returning several hours later, never recounting what transpired. Surely, social and economic pressures in the Arkansas Delta and at MoPac may have been exerted on you to be part of the Ku Klux Klan and the Elaine Race Massacre, but I have learned nothing from the family over the years to signal you somehow didn't carry endemic and pervasive racial animus from your damaged heritage.

Why do I choose you, Lonnie, to accompany me in the writing of this chapter? For you are a backdrop in so many ways to the arc of concepts and impressions forming a sort of codification of my response to race relations twenty years into the twenty-first century. From your part in the Massacre to your nights within the Ku Klux Klan and to your very last home, standing only three blocks away from Little Rock Central High School where major political resistance to the integration of public schools happened after the U.S. Supreme Court decision in *Brown v. Board of Education*, which eviscerated the separate but equal doctrine, I often think back to you, your history, your inclinations and deeds, as a counterpoint to my own bearings on race.

What impelled you into the ways of racism? Was it only the times in which you lived and had your being? A prominent figure from my early life, you are observed and examined as a constant archetype over what I have come to acknowledge and comprehend as inherited racism in our country, a problem foisted upon us by damaged heritage, so prominent among white Southerners, but also among numerous other white Americans. While there is nothing natural about racism, you had nonetheless assimilated damaged heritage, just as others will inherit trauma—both of these passing from one generation to the next. Lonnie, you must have been inebriated by flow of the legacy which you ingested and for which you had been nurtured through racial prejudice, possibly hatred, human inequities, and a disbelief in the genuinely human—damaged heritage, so intimate and so thorough as your mother's milk.

That which one abuses, one loathes. The various reminders of the abuse one practices can be mortifying and agonizing unto deep anger over one's self and the object or target of that anger. Ethnic and racial hatred exemplifies this curse. In the extreme, complete elimination of the object of one's abuse (e.g., genocide) suggests that the motive behind the abuse can then also simply disappear with the absence of the object or victims, but this process never squelches the motive. At the same time, in addition to serving as an outlet for abuse, if the object provides some value, such as the blacks' unquestioned contribution to the production of cotton, destruction becomes impractical. White Southerners could not exonerate themselves from the abuse leveled at African-Americans so that the anger persisted and the loathing formed expressions that could not be denied. The illusion that loathing only exists because the object deserves hatred has led to violent outbursts reflected over time through lynchings or brutalizations, such as the mutilation and murder of Emmett Till.

Children and adults infected by this inheritance have had virtually no option or choice—no exit, no escape—without some form of epiphany or illuminations by increment, for that multi-generational phenomenon and character of damaged heritage with its ravages and communal temptations probably feeling as wont to you as the heat of the sun or the coolness of a breeze. Damaged heritage had no beginning or end. It just was, is, and will be. Only by an individual's highly willed and fulsome rejection of this metastasizing disease can one be rid of its consequential and malevolent virus. Whites who break with their damaged heritage turn and conclude, only on their own, that all forms of inherited racial prejudice are the opposite of the genuinely human.

Yet, Lonnie, you are hard to dismiss, and your notions on race cannot be left behind; they are all too well suited for the topic at hand. So, I cannot leave you alone with peace in the midst of this commentary, for your name was surely invoked anytime members of the family conversed about race and associated forks in the road: you of a different era, you of different centrifugal social and ethnic forces, you of different persuasions and tactics, you of different junctures with African-Americans, you of a different geography, you of the land and railroads and a different America, you of different loyalties and affections. Nonetheless, I have often speculated and hoped that your rescue and attentive treatment of me so long ago may have possibly somehow been part of a search by you toward atonement for your role in the Massacre.

I think of you in my own context and along my own journey, for I cannot oust this fixation on all you served and prized. While I have unreservedly written here and accepted that you are part of me, you cannot be in fact and in sum, for consciously and unabashedly, I abhor that part of you who pursued a massacre of blacks, you who could mortify, terrorize, burn, or lynch, and then claim the rightness of it all with an allegiance to the proposition of superiority for a white coterie. Maybe, by calling you forth into this commentary and galvanic air, I can for once and conceivably for all time expose, divide, and disperse those sectors of the past that mythologized insufferable delusions of memory.

In the truest sense and purpose of my words, whether you, Lonnie, have passed on or not is hardly pertinent, for as William Faulkner once wrote, "The past is never dead. It's not even past."[1] Thus, dead or alive, you belong here with us, author and reader, as we traverse the hiatus of then and now, you and me, touching both the past and the present, which cannot be severed.

Germane to these sentiments, let me introduce Sheila L. Walker and tell you she and I committed to reconciliation as legatees from the two inherited sides of the Elaine Race Massacre—she, a descendant of African-American sharecropper victims, and I, your grandson, who separates himself from those whites who inflicted mayhem and terribly violent acts of murder and despoliation on our black brothers and sisters. Sheila has said more than once she is more forgiving of you for what you did than I am. She may be right, for I admit I have difficulty grasping how freely her merciful and effusive forgiveness emanates for you. She frames her attitude by declaring that "People aren't bad. Circumstances make people do bad things." And yet, I know there is something much more sinister, blood lustful, mad and ferocious, demonic, and sinful that has run through our white blood lines for generations, belying the rationale for such forgiveness.

At the same time, my own forgiveness of you, Lonnie, is far from complete. My recalled experiences with you are all so very intrinsic, tender, and familiar, but then there is this personally non-contextual, foreign event, the Massacre, in which you were involved. I often realize how far away I am from truly forgiving you, but I know that I should forgive you for no other reason than for myself, as I grieve over my inability to entirely forgive. I've talked with Sheila and her son, Marcus, about these shortcomings. Then, two days following the dedication of the Elaine Massacre Memorial at the end of September this year (2019), Sheila sent me a truly remarkable note about my own lack of capacity to forgive you fully for your participation in the Massacre; a part of that email is below:

> "I continue to look and see you have inherited the best parts of Lonnie. Loving and compassionate. For the path you have taken throughout your life without knowing this about him is no mistake. I pray you find some forgiveness and peace in your heart. You have acknowledged his sin, and you can't change it, but I believe you are what Lonnie wanted to be but didn't know how . . . genuinely human."[2]

Sheila saw you, Lonnie, as a prisoner of your time and envisioned you as a man who demonstrated his inherent love and compassion in the ways you treated me as a grandfather, a man possibly struggling to be more than his past but failing.

It is also possible my inability to forgive you fully reflects my own individual anger at the way blacks have been treated in this country by whites over generations. In a recent review of my latest book of poetry, *Now And Then: Selected Longer Poems*, Melinda Thomsen discovers this anger in my quasi-fictional poem, "The Mixer," which demonstrates the treatment received from a small town in southeast Arkansas by a mixed couple (black woman/white man) who fell in love, creating a family against the mores and shibboleths of the time, a time that just preceded and continued during the onset of the Civil Rights Movement:

> Reading this book more as an autobiography and less as a historical account helped me connect directly to this time in history. By understanding a reason why Johnson wrote long poems on these topics helped me pinpoint his outrage, an outrage introduced in "The Mixer."[3]

Lonnie, we come, for many generations now, from a most racist and cruel region for African-Americans—southeast Arkansas—along the Mississippi River Delta, where, less than a hundred years ago, lynchings and the burning alive of African-Americans happened in small towns, a region referred to by the scholar Nan Woodruff as the "heart of darkness"[4] after a term, coined by Joseph Conrad, for an inferno of unrestrained violence and odium—southeast Arkansas, an area the NAACP had come to call "the American Congo,"[5] meaning its characteristics and history resembled those of the African Congo, where brutal labor conditions, murders, and terror against blacks routinely prevailed. At a certain point (I do not remember when) I decided that the adhesive element for our typical white family there that kept the white family together as a unified whole came from a consensus commitment to white supremacy and the degradation, both verbal and actual, of blacks. Otherwise, it is much more difficult to explain the considerable, internal dissonance and separation affecting white families there when differing views about race and racism are held and overtly expressed among family members.

I think I speak for you and others when I pose that we whites of a damaged heritage somehow knew we could never save ourselves: the traditions, the customs, the evil, the gratuitous acts of violence and repression reflected in our history against African-Americans were too ingrained and too intertwined with our own special original sin for us to cleanse ourselves. We always knew we could only be cleansed by those we had made our victims, black brothers and sisters among us. Over the seven decades of my life facing racial division and white subjugation of blacks, I have witnessed time and again the unwanted reason we whites have little capacity to cleanse ourselves, for the execution of continuous harm by whites against blacks built up so much scar tissue over the years and generations that it became impossible for the perpetrators to penetrate into their humanity through those layers of tragedy whites inflicted. Indeed, although it was not publicly articulated this way, the Civil Rights Movement nevertheless relied heavily, in its non-violent tactics, on this very presumption.

I hear you asking the inevitable and legitimate question: what is meant by the "genuinely human"? For every generation, the challenge exists to accept and advocate willingly that the commonality between humans far outweighs any differences in custom, history, background, skin color, language, dialect, manners, and rituals; unfortunately, however, these very minimal differences suggest to many whites the perfect reason for exclusion, separation, and isolation of others. So, in turn, racism in America for every generation repeats itself in varying degrees for the simple reason too many white Americans have shown little desire to accept, continuously and committedly, the genuinely human in another. It is truly remarkable how we learn and routinely embrace customs, laws, habits, traditions, and all the rest from a previous generation but cannot embrace, in our own time, the genuinely human which underlies and strengthens the way one can authentically and fully care for, love, and behave toward another. Affinity for the genuinely human curiously resides in the amplitude of those who can just love another above any of those marginal differences. Two children are reared in the same family; one absorbs and inculcates without reservation the customs, laws, habits, traditions, manners, and punitive racial culture that precede her or him, while the other child extends beyond those traits and seeks to express to those of a different color caring and loving ways of behavior, constantly in direct opposition to inheritance. The mystery of this dichotomy still flabbergasts the best of minds.

An obstacle to higher moral achievement in this country, Lonnie, through those expressions toward one another, generation after generation, consists of invasive racism that will rise recurrently, continuing through four hundred years and still going strong. Why don't we learn? Why can't we learn? Why won't we learn? Why do the repetitions of racist moments and episodes occur?

Rosanna Warren, daughter of the famous Southern writer, Robert Penn Warren, and a renowned writer in her own right, sent me a note on the relevance of attention given to the unsolved nature of our country's white racism against African-Americans: "In the face of our monstrous amnesia, we need to keep refreshing our sense of the human . . ."[6] In a very much related comment, the philosopher Soren Kierkegaard wrote 170 years ago that one generation does not learn anything genuinely human from a past generation; in other words, we have to learn anew for ourselves that which is genuinely human.[7] Kierkegaard's view that one generation cannot rely on a previous generation to learn the genuinely human tells us that filiopietism will inevitably embrace racism since that revered past, in this instance, would observe African-Americans mostly in a perpetual state of human subjugation. I've come to believe that both Rosanna Warren and Soren Kierkegaard are right, for we alone can open ourselves to the genuinely human, not bound by those who come before or after us, but we alone can open ourselves to the genuinely human—that is what we can do, that is our grace. Otherwise, we are continually plagued by the eternal NO, which we sometimes call "evil" or "sin," if you will, of which racism is a vicious, elemental part.

In the Judeo-Christian tradition, there exists an overarching tenet that the individual "will" must express itself morally, that is, in one form or another—good, bad, or indifferent. In this respect, the most immediate and abiding form of expression for that morality lies in the social dimension of our behavior toward each other, not because our neighbors are simply ciphers for God, but because we are all individually worthy of love and because we are all individually integrated into an elaborate composition that calls us inevitably into interaction.

It is the interference with that interaction that makes damaged heritage so corruptive, for whites, Southern whites especially, were fed damaged heritage without our agreeing to be fed—we simply had no say in the matter. In both spoken and unspoken ways, that heritage imparted a whole universe, involving the treatment of folks of color, the inculcation of an attitude toward blacks, and an expectation of the ways that blacks would wish to treat whites. This is not to say we who were recipients of this tainted universe and tradition didn't have an ability to abrogate the spoiled milk, but it took a significant effort and, often times, many years or a special epiphany to obviate the effects. It is remarkable how some whites adhere throughout their lives to bequeathed notions about African-Americans in the course of that interaction without any desire or hint toward adjustment while others will show a special resolution for change to inherited persuasions. Through readings and Rosanna Warren's description of her father's passage from his own damaged heritage to racial enlightenment and an acceptance of the genuinely human in African-Americans, I found an example that underscores an ability for the human being to reject inculcated racist beliefs.

For the 1930 book, *I'll Take My Stand*, consisting of essays written by a number of white Southerners, having various associations with Vanderbilt University, who took strong positions against industrialization in favor of agrarian life, Robert Penn Warren, in his mid-twenties, authored an article that in retrospect is quite shocking in its espousal of constricted and prejudicial views about African-Americans, reminiscent of a *Gone With The Wind* portrayal of and attitudes toward black Americans, associated with Southern campestral and farm life:

> *The Southern negro has always been a creature of the small town and farm. That is where he still chiefly belongs, by temperament and capacity; there he has less the character of a "problem" and more the status of a human being who is likely to find in agricultural and domestic pursuits the happiness that his good nature and easy ways incline him to as an ordinary function of his being.*[8]

Thirty years later, Warren would cast aside such damaged heritage views, echoing the sentiments of Martin Luther King, Jr. that black and white lives are so inextricably joined that blacks can free whites from a permanent death of the spirit created by racial subjugation and segregation. In this excerpt from *The Legacy of The Civil War*, Warren pictures a white male member of a mob in demonstrable opposition to integration:

> *Does he ever consider the possibility that whatever degree of dignity and success a Negro achieves actually enriches, in the end, the life of the white man and enlarges his own worth as a human being?*[9]

Robert Penn Warren was "increasingly drawn to the civil rights movement by the late 1950s."[10] According to Rosanna Warren, as her father traveled through the South to interview civil rights leaders and activists in the early 1960s, "he was often in danger (long rides on country roads in cars with no headlights on; hiding in farmhouses with all the lights off, the blinds drawn), and our house in Connecticut was targeted by the KKK, as I vividly remember from my childhood."[11] A good friend since the first grade followed a not too dissimilar route to the genuinely human response to African-Americans. In college, this friend authored an essay that was decidedly anti-black in its written characterization on collecting rent from the town's blacks for the family business; within a few years, his ideas and actions stood in impressive counterpoint to that college composition. While the examples of Robert Penn Warren and my friend of many decades are noteworthy and heartening—alas, from my perch, there are still too few such stories, illustrative of an affirmative disavowal of damaged heritage.

No easy explanation describes why some whites experience an adjustment in racial attitudes through an epiphany while others must face a transformation over time, but whether such change occurs as a result of an epiphany or by crucial increment, it is an intensely personal journey.

Facing the concept of the genuinely human from a somewhat different angle and cribbing a bit from the prophet, Martin Luther King, Jr., it is less important to know who commits racial injustice, but it is very important to know what is responsible for racial injustice. The what forms the obverse of the genuinely human. In response to the obverse, it is certainly not possible to attain racial reconciliation between individuals of a different color without finding the genuinely human both in others as persons and in the community of individuals whose history, background, accents, customs, and traditions may be different, possibly radically different from one's own. Vast elements of mutual humanity that reside between most individuals, excluding the patently evil, undergird and claim that commonality.

Lonnie, I will spend a moment on the fact that Sheila Walker and I have relied from the very beginning of our communications on the rubric of "truth and reconciliation" in that word order. She emphasizes a reliable coda in her Foreword to this book with the following words, which I will now restate for you: "The message Chester conveyed stood out, not as a selfish release of 'white guilt,' but as an accountable acknowledgement of the truth. Chester's writing was able to allow me, a descendant on the 'other side,' to relate and empathize with his perspective."

So, without even conversing about the relevance of our mutual alignment with the history surrounding the Elaine Race Massacre, we realized, from the start, that, in the absence of this agreement on the facts of history, our capability to proceed toward reconciliation was destined to fail.

From a true accounting, we empowered our journey with the genuinely human as a steadfast election on which we depended. Without even articulating the steps that led us, Sheila and I readily resolved to treat each other in contradiction to those characteristics that were an unrestrained presence during the fall of 1919 in Phillips County, Arkansas at the time of the white attacks and in the near-term aftermath of the Massacre. We chose respect over degradation, goodwill over control, friendship over pressure, truth over mendacity, comity over manipulation, and compassion over torment. For a broader purpose, we also felt that our racial reconciliation, which moved rapidly to authentic friendship, also stood in sharp contrast to the surge of white nationalism and white preference that had gripped the country soon after the election of Donald J. Trump as president.

She and I held goals for which we could together exert our time and energies. We foresaw the need to expand known facts about the Massacre locally and elsewhere. We also began to feel that our own story toward reconciliation should be shared in Phillips County since we realized the local community still had not come to terms with the Massacre; we found that various residents not only adhered to a discredited rendition of the Massacre but were also reluctant to visit factual accounts documented in recent years through books by Grif Stockley and Robert Whitaker.

I should acknowledge that Martin Luther King Jr. did not use the phrase, "genuinely human," to express one's ability to reach beyond another person's public characteristics—her or his customs, language, accent, skin color, history, and the like—to recognize and thoroughly accept that greater commonality existing between and among people. Rather, he referred to this heightened feature as "the weapon of love." The term, weapon, seems conspicuously out of place associated with the other prominent word in the phrase, but bear in mind that the entire phrase meant to express the manner by which African-Americans were to respond to whites opposing an action or position the Civil Rights Movement pursued at the time in the 1950s and 1960s. To answer one's opponent with the weapon of love posed a remarkable alternative to the universal methodology of confrontation, battle, or war, to put it conventionally, for to love your enemy, though it be one of those concepts from the Sermon on the Mount, alongside the beatitudes, concepts that usually get tossed aside for virtually every conflict, will have the distinct power of acceptance, a surprise acceptance for another, who had wished harm and ill will.

It is not anticipated the other person or party will immediately and fully accept the weapon of love, but if freely given, the act of expressing the genuinely human cannot be totally discounted by the recipient, and over time, the effect can engender modified, more favorable behavior. This process is not an easy one and may be slow, but King believed it would essentially yield better results than a resolution formula that relies on old-fashioned responses consistent with an "eye for an eye" and similar measures that inevitably lead to more violence. He believed the approach eventually struck at a preferable side of human nature and at the greater desire to be loved than to be feared.

So, there is a well-grounded consistency between King's "weapon of love" and a surrender to the genuinely human in each other, regardless of the recognizable differences that can, for some, serve to separate us, recognizable differences that are often selfishly and cravingly adopted to define others in obdurate ways that leave little room for either an expression or receipt of the genuinely human but sow those conditions that entice, satisfy, and help to shape inveterate racists among us.

King never intimated that racism somehow exhibited an innocent flaw in a white person's perception or appreciation of blacks; rather, he knew racism to be simply an evil manifestation and treatment of African-Americans that plagued American whites. Not buying the argument that past generations of white folks had just a wrongful notion that blacks were somehow not fully human and not deserving of equality, I realized at some point that the evil causes of racism, reflected in nefarious acts against African-Americans, called for whites to admit their damaged heritage and their need for forgiveness from those who had been victims historically of that heritage. The need for forgiveness from African-Americans became a revelation for me, and I finally realized what I think King had meant by the "weapon of love."

Being white, it is simply difficult for me to envision Sheila's progressive steps toward reconciliation with me or any white person for that matter, in the absence of her having discovered a tolerable mode of forgiveness for the evils of slavery, racial isolation, and segregation, and yet, she conducts herself in a way that indicates past evils inflicted on African-Americans by white persons hardly affect her at all in her dealings with whites. My experience with Sheila suggests that, through her indomitable positivism, she learned to separate her past associations with white culture and its concomitant gravity for tragic history from each white person she encounters.

Somehow, she is able to accept a white individual without the imposition of the legacy of racism affecting her judgment; rather, damaged heritage that is otherwise tethered to that white person melts away and disappears through friendship. I do not believe she even thinks about that part of the entire constellation bearing on her engagement with a white. I find it remarkable that with Sheila, there does not need to be even a conversation about either generic forgiveness or a shared rumination on how the topic of forgiveness for previous white treatment may affect her desire or feelings toward reconciliation with someone who is white. This attitude means she sees me completely separate from my family's undeniable racist past, and I'm deeply grateful and humbled.

Racism and its multitude of tentacles into the lives and souls of whites had been insidious from the start and realized as such, viewed retrospectively long ago when a former slave trader, John Newton, wrote the words of "Amazing Grace" in recognition of and repentance for the evils he had wrought . . . and then on, in America, to the Emancipation Proclamation . . . and then on to the words of Ida B. Wells when she wrote in 1887 that "I have firmly believed all along that the law was on our side and would, when we appealed to it, give us justice. I feel shorn of that belief and utterly discouraged, and just now, if it were possible, would gather my race in my arms and fly away with them. O God, is there no redress, no peace, no justice in this land for us?"[12] . . . and on to the present. I cannot be convinced that whites, for generations, didn't comprehend the evil nature of slavery and subjugation of blacks, but they could not help themselves from following the well-worn path, clearly marked without ambiguity which grandfathers and grandmothers, mothers and fathers also followed, so that encroachments on the past and departure from traditions simply became a form of heresy.

To put this reliance and reverence for living and deceased family members in context, it is helpful to look far in the past, as reflected in the words of the Oxford University scholar, Larry Siedentop:

> At its origin the ancient family was both the focus and the medium of religious belief . . . The circle established by religious belief was exclusively domestic . . . Clearly, the family—past, present, and future—was the basic unit of social reality . . . Nothing could legitimately violate its domain.[13]

Admittedly, we've come a long way from the days when ancient Roman and Greek families worshipped, through rituals, prior family members as gods. Not-too-modest vestiges of that persuasion still remain, however. Some white folks, with a compelling kind of veneration, a filiopietism kind of veneration, can be found, even today, to adopt explanations of history, such as the Elaine Race Massacre, with little, if any, basis in fact, reflecting confidence in exculpatory rationale for past conduct by antecedents and endorsing the idea that ancestors always practiced good and acceptable behavior. We saw this approach in explanations for the event among whites in the Arkansas Delta, who discounted and discarded incontrovertible evidence.

In support of my argument that our forebears, both near and distant in time, should have corrected much earlier the evils of black subjugation, I take much satisfaction in the historical record that the father of our country, George Washington, in his last will and testament, prepared only a few months before his death in 1799, made provision for his slaves to be free. Without a keen and acknowledged awareness of the evils perpetrated by slavery and subjugation against blacks, would he have executed such a provision some 220 years ago? At the same time, Thomas Jefferson would probably today be dubbed a "limousine liberal" by some Americans, for he obviously talked, through his writings, a good game about liberty for all, but he fell well short of his words by his unwillingness to implement a course of action leading to freedom for African-Americans who were slaves at Monticello, Jefferson's plantation and estate.

Adding also to the certainty that those in the past who practiced subjugation of African-Americans knew that it was surely wrong to do so is the fact that filiopietism has existed for many generations; simply put, there would have been no need for excessive veneration of tradition in the absence of the guilt and shame associated with recognition that racial tyranny against blacks was evil and wrong.

Over multiple generations, while our ancestors realized the evil nature of slavery and subjugation of blacks, they couldn't stop themselves, for the availability of free or inexpensive labor and the allure of white supremacy, as a way of life, were much too appealing to oppose. It ordinarily proved more convenient for a white to lie to oneself about those who were adored by white progenies and those who adored white progenies than to forge ahead with a rejection of damaged heritage. But all knew (and our forebears knew) that sins and evil had been committed, and that cannot be denied.

By becoming racists and embroidered onto that history, so many white Americans were destined to become mere ghosts, wraiths without a will to pursue the consequences of the genuinely human. For ghosts pass over landscapes without touching the fiber around them, and so much is lost as personhood degrades, and only thinness and lightness of form and substance reside in a gossamer of intricate webs with inertia or worse toward both equality and justice for those without white skin. We have learned the ways of racists, the filiopietistic storytellers whose tales grow in exaggeration and excessive loyalty until the storytellers are no more than the stories they tell, who devoutly resist the genuinely human existing between and among those people, black and white, white and black, who alternatively stand firm, cohered and co-inhered, original together, unhaunted and undaunted by racial rigidity and racial tyranny.

Of course, racial reconciliation between blacks and whites requires more than a single act of forgiveness. While Sheila's forgiveness of you, Lonnie, is more than a beginning, racism can be defeated only by a much wider reconciliation that involves a context of black forgiveness and the expansive adherence to the genuinely human for African-Americans by white America.

In conclusion, my dear Lonnie, there is a very old adage that the dead shall rest in peace; unfortunately, in the spirit of William Faulkner's view that the past is not even past, your rest must be postponed a little while longer, for I have brought, by unequivocal intention, the racism entwined in your life and history forward into this immediate conversation. Certainly, I wish with all my might and being that the racism drawn from the past shall finally be put to an end, and yet, it will not be in my lifetime nor in my children's lifetime, but I do believe that someday, the genuinely human shall prevail in all its love and glory, and the past shall then rest in peace with replete contradiction to Faulkner's credo.

With love and determination for racial equality and racial accord,
Your grandson, Chester

3

FIRST STORIES

n the early days of calendar 2014, Robert Whitaker, author of *On the Laps of Gods*, the story of the 1919 Elaine Race Massacre, casually asked if I desired to talk with an African-American woman, a descendant of several people who endured the Massacre up close and lived to tell about it. I had written a long article on the Massacre circulated in 2013 for a four-part serialization by the literary journal, *Green Mountains Review*, and Bob not only examined my article for accuracy prior to publication, but he also meaningfully contributed to it by providing key data in response to questions I posed to him. For these purposes, Bob and I exchanged emails several times, and we had gotten to know each other.

Bob described Sheila Walker in glowing language, as someone who learned about the Massacre over the years mainly through snippets from family members until Sheila received copies of books on the Massacre written by Grif Stockley and Bob Whitaker. After deep absorption into Bob's *On the Laps Of Gods*, Sheila researched, on her own, several familial aspects of the conflagration and then reached out to Whitaker, who coincidentally spent time in his book on the experiences of Sheila's family members during both the assaults and the historically important aftermath. At some point, Bob concluded Sheila and I should reach out to each other based on our connection to the Massacre: those of Sheila's family as victims and my maternal grandfather, Lonnie, as a contributor to the onslaughts.

I did not know what Bob had in mind by establishing a dialogue between Sheila and me. Of course, I'm thankful to him for arranging this special nexus, but I never discovered the specific goal Bob foresaw, and he never once opined either to Sheila or me the rationale for bringing us together. Someone once told me that good fortune usually needs a little human ingenuity and goodwill to put the right pieces together.

I did not wait very long to contact Sheila. Once securing her phone number, I delayed only a day or two. Of course, part of me felt apprehensive. What if she speculated that I somehow carried views aligned with my forebear who participated in the Massacre? Would she voice out loud on the phone concerns and reservations about talking with me? Would she expect me to carry the conversation alone? If so, what should or shouldn't I say about Lonnie? Should I tell her the long story of my unearthing the facts and personal history which brought the well-founded realization that Lonnie joined in the Elaine Race Massacre? Would she even want to hear such an analysis? What would be the outcome of our conversation? Could we have future calls or emails? These questions carried merely passing, inconsequential reservations.

It was clearly not just curiosity that enticed me to search out Sheila. I realize that. Rather, even then, I recognized my inclination, my desire for a connection that dealt with a mutuality in history. We were both returning to a place where our ancestors met in absurd, terrible circumstances, where death sprouted prodigiously all around, conjoined within the fructuous, full-grown cotton rows, readied for harvest in southeast Arkansas of early fall. It was a place that mattered, certainly to me and undoubtedly for Sheila. How could it not matter? Our respective stories remained incomplete without a circle being tied: progeny of victims and perpetrators meeting, talking, metaphorically salving the wounds and bitterness which led to the attacks, our arrival in rectitude to revert the ending sequence, the ending claim of a hundred years ago for white vanquishment of blacks.

The initial phone call with Sheila proved much easier than I had feared. We spoke for over two hours, and we covered smoothly a myriad of subjects, all of relevance, including crucially the best-known facts about the Massacre. The conversation proved the wisdom, for potentially sensitive discussions, of dwelling first on agreed upon facts before grappling with more personal and delicate topics. So, we talked over the versions of the assault, beginning with the one posited at the time of the Massacre by the white planters: maybe fourteen or so African-American sharecroppers died on the first full day of attacks, October 1, 1919, when local white posses were amassed and released to squelch a black insurrection, and those were the only black deaths that occurred during the Massacre; further, according to this account, white federal troops were brought to Phillips County to restore order, and that's all the military did—restore order orderly. Some descendants of the 1919 Phillips County whites and a smattering of other white citizens apparently had adhered to this or an approximate rendition of this story, notwithstanding the more credible version that subsequently surfaced in several, well-documented books on the subject.

Without any difference of opinion, Sheila and I reached concurrence on our understanding of the several pertinent facts surrounding the toll of African-American deaths from the white onslaughts. There had also been five whites involved with the Massacre who died at the time, but two of those white deaths possibly came by way of whites.

We additionally settled on the causes for the rampage leading to all those killings: the infectious and dilating fear of white planters and county plutocrats that black sharecroppers were taking effective actions through unionization to receive better general market prices for cotton that these sharecroppers sold locally. The motive to unionize reflected the remarkably increased cotton prices that had been evident across the world during and soon after World War I. The sharecroppers wished to use part of the larger income to extinguish debt that they constantly owed to white planters who often charged African-Americans exorbitantly for staples and goods purchased on credit at local farming commissaries in advance of harvested cotton being brought to market for sale. The continual incurrence of this debt by black sharecroppers kept them strapped to the land they farmed; as long as debt remained outstanding at the commissaries, sharecroppers could not leave the land. The African-Americans had already hired an attorney from Little Rock to confront the planters over numerous and various disputes existing between white planters and black sharecroppers in Phillips County. Many whites also feared a broader and imminent uprising by the black community in the county, where African-Americans substantially outnumbered the ruling white social and governing hierarchy. The simmering burn had now ignited between the sharecroppers and local law enforcement, flaring late in the evening of September 30, 1919 at the Progressive Farmers and Household Union meeting being held at Hoop Spur Church, a flare that spread into murderous wildfires of black death over the next several days.

Sheila and I each took a deep breath, for we could now start to settle into the more personally consequential features of our individual stories. But our agreement upon the above facts served Sheila and me well. Each of us had completed our respective homework, and we had no debates. The facts were clearly set, based on all we had learned. In so many ways, there was no reason at all ever to return to our understandings of these details of the Massacre we had just recounted unless new information somehow brought into question any of the general conclusions we shared. On our own, we discovered the reason many approaches toward reconciliation, racial or otherwise, begin with a determination of, and agreement upon, the truth. She and I quickly breached through that obstacle, and we had faith in each other's conclusions about the root causes for the Elaine Race Massacre.

Sheila began to tell her own story scrupulously. On occasion, her grandmother Annie, who witnessed the Massacre as a youngster in 1919, attempted to convey her recollections of the killings and bedlam to Sheila, who, as a young person at the time, sat and listened. However, during these moments, Annie did not finish her declarations she meant to impart to her family, so that the story had a chance to be passed along to future generations. Most often, Annie's voice just stopped soon after the attempt started, and then Annie sobbed and trembled. The trauma of memory took its toll; the event in recall expanded into an indomitable beast Annie could not disgorge; the Massacre, notwithstanding her desire to relate its diabolical features to the family, continuously won out. I could hardly imagine the compounding sadness Annie felt from her inability to report those moments in her life that were so real, so consumptively real and potent that she was powerless to vent to those she loved, to those who needed to know. Apparently, these seizures blocking her voice occurred in varying degrees, so that other family members, who heard more from Annie at other times, could convey to Sheila that the story Annie wanted to tell had been Annie's own experiences during the Elaine Race Massacre.

Sheila also recounted stories, directly and indirectly, from her great grandmother, Sallie Giles, and Sallie's two sons, Albert and Milligan—all three of whom, along with Annie, had found themselves within the Massacre's killing fields. Only luck or Providential good fortune saved both Albert and Milligan. At fifteen, Milligan had been shot in the face by Henry Smiddy, security official with the Missouri Pacific Railroad, the same company then employing Lonnie and the company that supplemented, at the time, local law enforcement for the purpose of protecting extensive facilities of the railroad company in Phillips County and for safekeeping passengers and client goods as they passed into and through the county. Smiddy's bullet had lodged in the back of Milligan's neck. Members of a white posse pursued Albert, the older of the two brothers, and shot him several times with bullet holes showing on each side of his head—and yet, he survived. Both Albert and Milligan spent time in the hospital before being transferred to the Phillips County Jail, an annex to the County Courthouse, to await trial. According to Sheila, Sallie frequently visited her two sons in jail before court proceedings started to tend to her sons' wounds and to try to lift their spirits and attitudes as much as Sallie could keep her own self strong and affirmative.

Following the Massacre, the accelerated trials of the African-American sharecroppers moved rapidly through the Phillips County Courthouse. Many of the prisoners were tortured so that the white story would be the sole narrative, dominant in the local courtroom; some sharecroppers refused to adhere to the features of the white story, but others acquiesced in response to the torture doled out in beatings and electric shocks, among other measures, in advance of the trials. The prosecutor charged Albert with murder of one of the five white victims, a crime for which he would be convicted and sentenced to death by electrocution, expected within weeks of the verdict. He would also be counted as one of the historically important Elaine Twelve, African-American sharecroppers who had been active in the Progressive Farmers and Household Union and were all found guilty of murder. The serpentine elements of the litigation in which the Elaine Twelve were involved gained attention throughout the country at the time, especially from the black press.

Milligan joined the sixty-one other sharecroppers, convicted of various, lesser crimes evolving out of the Massacre, who were sent to the Cummins State Farm. The facts that led to freedom over five years for the two brothers and their seventy-two fellow prisoners are explained elsewhere in this book, but for now, we should let Sheila continue.

Upon Albert's release from The Walls, he decided to leave Arkansas for fear the Ku Klux Klan and other Arkansas whites might wish to take the law into their own hands and complete the job of executing Albert and other sharecroppers whom the law had failed to put to death, as promised by the Phillips County officials and plutocrats back in early October, 1919. Both Ed Ware and Albert went to Illinois—Ed to Chicago and Albert to Springfield, where he set up a business and resided until his death.

Sheila never got to know Albert, but she had fond memories of Milligan, whom she described as thoughtful and empathetic. Her family, including Milligan and her grandmother Annie, settled in Hot Springs, Arkansas, where Sheila was born. Hot Springs, one of the larger cities in the State, is located approximately 170 miles west of Phillips County and some sixty miles southwest of Little Rock. At about six years of age, Sheila left Hot Springs with her mother and moved to Chicago; later, she resided in New York City and then Syracuse, N. Y., which she and her husband, Ivor, called home at the time of our telephone conversation. Looking back over the past, Sheila unquestionably believes that the Massacre infused fatalism and trauma into the family fabric of which she was part. An event of such savage proportion as the Elaine Race Massacre could not be sustained by victims who survived the onslaughts without anguish of recollection being a constant shaper of behavior and attitudes, passed down in subtle and not-so-subtle ways to future generations. Undoubtedly, the curtain to a view for the family of the Massacre had been open for an impactful glimpse.

At this point, I now returned briefly to those modest concerns I held before the call and posed this abrupt question to myself: is everything OK? Yes, it was OK; it was more than OK. A certain inexplicable commonality of purpose, of acceptable and relational infrastructure, of comprehension and strength resonated in the exchanges between Sheila and me, reflected in constant and immediate, elemental trust that occurred unsurprisingly for some earnest and natural reason. Our words rested easily on our collective credibility.

Lonnie then came to mind. While Bob Whitaker had, of course, explained to Sheila a few salient points concerning Lonnie and me and Lonnie's engagement in the Massacre, I felt it necessary to divulge my own perspective on this story to Sheila. After all, she generously transmitted to me her unique views about her family members who withstood the Massacre's killing fields—family members, some of whom faced momentous legal and personal challenges after the conflagration. I could be no less open in counterpoint.

I went on to tell her that Lonnie was employed by the Missouri Pacific Railroad, a major economic force in the region, for his entire working career, and based on all I knew and have been told, he loved the job. I suspect the mobility and travel by train from place to place delighted, if not seduced him. Until Lonnie joined MoPac, his world's radius had ever been situated just north of McGehee, Arkansas on a farm close to Tillar, Arkansas, south of Phillips County and Elaine, with that radius being rural and arranged for farming and with neighbors and everyone all around him involved in aspects of agriculture. But Lonnie disliked farming and abrogated the family farm to his brothers, although he retained an economic share, even after being hired by MoPac. He lived most of his adult life in McGehee before being transferred to the larger MoPac complex in Little Rock, where he resided with Hattie and several of their children and grandchildren until his death.

The railroad trained a keen eye on the towns and cities it served and kept an attentive ear to the ground in order to understand politically, socially, and racially those places in Arkansas. Indeed, the first person to die in the Elaine Race Massacre had been W. A. Adkins, a local MoPac white security official, who, on the night of September 30, 1919, joined Charles

Pratt, the Deputy Sheriff for Phillips County, and Kid Collins, a local black prisoner trusted by law enforcement, traveling in a Model T Ford to Hoop Spur Church, located north of Elaine in the southern part of the county. We do know that either Adkins or Pratt or both fired into the church that night, most likely with an intent to disrupt the proceedings. We also know they were fired upon by African-American guards protecting the union meeting. Adkins died in the exchange, and the Deputy Sheriff was shot in the knee. Unharmed, Collins simply walked away to a nearby community. Thus began the Elaine Race Massacre.

By the next day, responding to calls for assistance from Phillips County officials, white men from Tennessee, Mississippi, and neighboring Arkansas localities started to arrive to help resist a black insurrection. Around this time, my mother likely gleaned that her father Lonnie would participate in the Massacre. I suppose it was this first full day, October 1, when Lonnie joined in the attacks against the sharecroppers, for the propinquity of Elaine by train amounted to about sixty-five miles; ready access was available from McGehee, MoPac's southeast Arkansas hub. I also assume the death of a fellow MoPac employee, Adkins, the prior night further inspired railroad workers from McGehee to go to Elaine to combat the African-Americans. When a young teenager, I heard my mother describe the place of attacks as she had heard it detailed by Lonnie.

The story of Lonnie's juncture with the Elaine Race Massacre had been buried deep in my memory vaults for many years after I first assimilated allusions to the event from Mother, who referred to it as a "well-known race riot." I had no reason at all to associate her story with the Elaine Race Massacre until I came across the long treatise written by Ida B. Wells. I then became immersed in the onslaughts and killing fields close to or within cotton rows near the MoPac train tracks, and the sizeable number of black deaths. Of course, there had been lynchings of African-Americans in southeast Arkansas around the general time frame of the Massacre, but none so significant, none of this size. I then conflated the "well-known race riot" my mother had alluded to with the Massacre.

At the time of Mother's narrative, I did not think she had discovered whether Lonnie actually killed any of the sharecroppers or their family members. She never said, and I doubt whether Lonnie told her one way or another. Moreover, I couldn't conceive of Lonnie killing another human being. That simply wasn't in Lonnie's nature, was it? My grandfather, my constant companion during the earliest years of my life, remained a singularly adoring and devoted figure. The image of a killer and the flood of emotions I felt for him could not coalesce; the two images were all askew and detached from one another. For in those early years with Lonnie, he kept me close, and I always sat next to him or on his lap. We ate together, and I napped in his arms. I was his 24-hour a day project in retirement, chortled adult family members at the time. We had long silent walks together, just the two of us, and from him I learned early the gift of silence, the impervious silence that rested comfortably upon us. He taught me the grace of silence residing as an inseparable part of affection and love between, in this case, grandfather and grandson, Lonnie and Chester— Lonnie who died within months after we were permanently separated once Mother set up her own home in Monticello.

Yet, I would now have to learn to live with two Lonnies: the one I recognized, even from a distance, and the one I didn't know.

At this point, I thought two hours had tried Sheila and me enough. Even good intensity can drain and enervate the best within, but still, we, each of us, did not wish to relinquish this common achievement, this step of disclosure. The milieu and ethos of conversation felt as though we together could have virtually neutralized the venom released during the Massacre across unremarkable cotton fields in an unremarkable place a century ago.

Almost simultaneously, we each asked the other what we should do next. Sheila recommended we meet face-to-face for our next exchange. To resurrect and rekindle what we had finished today? Maybe, Sheila and I could adjust the dialogue so that we share more about who we are and then be better able to understand why we spoke in the tenor we had. Was it possible for us to gain a receptivity that led to a modified universe where conversations did not include an inference of race, white or black? Of course, that's the direction to take, and yet, an almost incomprehensible saga from the past spread over our words and notions that could not be denied. The beginning had begun, and we were both better today than yesterday.

Sheila then pointed out that she and Ivor were scheduled, in a few weeks, to visit, in Boston, their son Marcus, daughter-in-law Franzi, and two grandsons. Since she had become aware that I frequently traveled to New England and Massachusetts from New York City, Sheila asked if I could possibly meet her in Boston to spend several hours together. Maybe, Bob Whitaker would also join us from his home in Cambridge, Massachusetts. Immediately, I agreed. I would be there mid-March.

4

MARCH 15, 2014

O ver the intervening weeks between the telephone call with Sheila and our face-to-face meeting, a variety of thoughts floated as constant companions for my pending, increasingly unresolved and proximate questions. My conversation with Sheila had unearthed unquiet compulsions not only about the Massacre, but also more extensively about my racial past and inheritance, including the relevance of Lonnie's experiences and, even more broadly, the general influence of race from additional members of my own family—compulsions I could not release even as I readied myself for this first close-up time with Sheila.

I wondered if Lonnie ever gave a short minute to misgivings about racism or had he gratuitously accepted his views and behavior without any hesitation? Lonnie possibly absorbed his attitude and violence toward African-Americans as second nature, like another cup of coffee or a normal shave he faced each morning before embracing with compromised willingness, sanction, and occasional resolution the mundane choices and routines that came so naturally and perfunctorily day after day.

I did not presume that his conjectures or ambivalences were ones I understood or appreciated, for time had made our differences so opaque, or had it really? Was this assumption too easy? To submit to time-honored traditions encouraged a thoughtless process with generations conforming to this practice in order to distance themselves directly from culpability. A submission to time meant that Lonnie and other white folks took on practices of prevailing eras, including a conveyance, an inheritance of racism, and were excused from probing further.

Bob Whitaker met me at South Street train station in Boston late morning on Saturday, March 15, 2014. In some respects, he had, at this point, become a kind of benevolent intervenor between Sheila and me. She recommended the hour and place for this face-to-face, and Bob would not let it fail to happen. He constituted an enabling broker, the person who kindly put Sheila and me together, and his reward could possibly be a story on top of his story. It was an extension of the Elaine narrative that he had laid out so effectively for the reading public in *On the Laps of Gods*, but how could the next chapter be written and be intoned with more current features? To the three of us, the ending didn't terminate with a recital of unadulterated facts about the Elaine Race Massacre and a momentous Supreme Court decision; no, something more personal, contemporary, and illustrative impelled itself from the past toward a possible reckoning. Something else had to be said beyond prime facts, describing a racial conflagration of a hundred years ago. Did that prospect form a specific mission for Sheila and me?

We three realized that both Sheila and I had been affected by noteworthy moments and instants surrounding the Massacre about which we knew little or nothing at all. History is told through those who come after and who receive only the reverberations and perturbations that time imparts in its solitary discretion. The acts that formed Lonnie and my mother also flow through me unrecognized as though they were told in a foreign language, and I accept them mostly without discovery as they construct parts of me for which I can only speculate as to origin. Lonnie and my mother's behavior passed through to a next generation implying

we nonetheless experienced the same episodes. The human being appre-
hends inheritance in the physical so thoroughly that he or she neglects to
acknowledge other sculpting aspects that fall to succeeding generations as
naturally as the color of the eyes or the architecture of the forehead. Still,
there is repeatedly a refusal to acknowledge the influence of terrors and
outcomes abiding so ineffably in legatees that we dare not or cannot believe
they even exist until they propel themselves into the present with forms
of mystery and absolute manifestations so apparent we think some nether
wraith must have foisted these considerable and diabolical consequences
upon our flummoxed worlds.

Racism consumed all small towns in southeast Arkansas where I lived
my young life in Monticello during the 1950s and 1960s. Its contour and
apparatus held each town in their clutches. With whites always first in line
regardless, where could blacks appear morning and night? How public could
a black be? How could blacks even think about entering an eating establishment where whites ate? Blacks couldn't be seen in white sections of town
after dark, except at their peril. Everyone—black and white—monitored
compliance with the racial taboos and shibboleths, and I mean everyone:
children, teenagers, adults, and the elderly. Even at death, separation
between blacks and whites remained de rigueur in a divided cemetery. As
a child, it was impossible not to observe everything racial in our midst.
Seldom did one speak of the efficacy of racial rules, though I can remember
white declarations that if one small rule were discarded, the rest could come
tumbling down without warning. In those days, the town had been literally
swallowed by the racial apparatus with everyone and everything consumed
by race and related behavioral guidelines.

Nevertheless, only infrequently did family discussions and comments
actually dwell at length on these matters, and yet, in each white family, there
were the talkers and eager oracles who imagined black heresies at the slightest
turn where there had been none or where speculations ran amok at the suspected desire of blacks to break ironclad codes; precipitate signs of danger
were what white oracles always foresaw. In white families, there was always
someone who talked openly about black motivations and the degree to which
whites must continue to fear African-Americans, and he or she applied base
terms in calling out black actions. Somehow, from the words of many and

in the minds of many, the use of base terms seemed to help keep blacks in their place, even if no African-American heard each time those comments had been applied by a speaker. For my family, there were uncles and aunts who accepted the role of oracle for these purposes. My mother wasn't one of them, thank God, although she occasionally employed base appellations upon conjured, absent black violators when she felt a consensus for the use of such words abounded in conversations among our white family.

Before commencing on the matriarchal environment surrounding my early life and the associated impressions it had on the racial context in which I was reared, it should be noted that both of my grandfathers had died by the time I reached the age of seven. With my father's demise occurring before I turned two, women shaped the ambit against which my world would be played out until the time I entered organized sports, at which point male coaches served as mentors and occasionally as crucial father figures, especially football coaches in a sport I enjoyed immensely and in which I proved to be adept through high school and even into college until an injury ended the joy of it all.

After Lonnie passed away, his widow Hattie soon became a regular, if not constant visitor at our home. If she weren't with us, we seemed to be with her in Little Rock on weekends, leaving Monticello when the last school bell rang Friday afternoons. Over the years, I sensed Hattie's presence meant to make life easier for my mother, which seemed unusual to me at the time, for after all, Hattie had six other children and a passel, if not a virtually innumerable set of grandchildren located from the Atlantic Ocean to the Pacific who routinely and randomly circulated through Hattie's house and life. I wouldn't call her obese but decidedly overweight, though she still scampered through her home and ours at a light-of-foot pace. Perpetually engaged, she compensated for her noticeable speech impediment by continual motion in service of others: family, friends, and friends of friends and family. For racial commentaries and allusions that inevitably fired through our house and hers from time to time, I don't recall a pejorative racial term about blacks exiting her lips. Looking back over the years, it now seems doubly ironic that Hattie eschewed those family discussions, considering the overt acts her husband Lonnie had managed to demonstrate by his own predilections in favor of racial animus and worse. This is not to say Hattie represented a strong alternative to the views expressed by so many others of her family when it came to racial bias. She was clearly not that by any measure. Rather, I just don't recall that she voiced agreement or disagreement with the prevailing sentiments of racism filling the hours when I was a youngster, even before I became a teenager. Hattie kept those thoughts and expressions to herself—at least for the years I knew her, which extended well into my college life when she died at the age of seventy-nine. I loved Hattie for her strength, her regular clarity of service, her generosity, and endless sacrifices.

Although I do remember, more than once, my mother's articulation of racial bias among family members, friends, and acquaintances, she very seldom, if ever, voiced slurs or epithets about African-Americans around me when we were alone. The only other person in the family who approximated the approach of silence that Hattie adopted about racial terminology and language was my father's sister, whom all the grandchildren called, "Sister," caretaker of the Johnsons, three branches of whom, including our small family of three, resided in Monticello at the same time. White Southern families at the time often had someone like Sister functioning as caretaker, who never married, who openly acknowledged her commitment to the immediate and composite rings of the family, who attended to the family's old and aging, who served as confidante for the grandchildren, who constantly operated as the disciplinarian buffer between child and parent (meaning if one were expelled from school for a day or so, the young culprit would first confess to Sister and then seek advice before confronting a parent) whenever punishment was involved, and who carried family stories from one generation to another with exaggerated good and righteous being part and parcel of the narration (later, a grandchild realized that he or she had received a morality play from Sister as the story morphed into a lesson about behavior, courage, judgment, or wisdom).

When I walked home during my grade school and even later school days, I frequently stopped off at Sister's house, which she shared with her aged and sickly mother, to corner some advice about one or two professedly insolvable problems (as a youth would see them) I faced at the time in advance of some admission that confronted me when I got home.

Sometimes, these conferences with Sister simply represented a pause in the action allowing me a little time to gather my thoughts and plan my tactics.

Sister also talked about black persons who had previously worked for the Johnsons on the farms or in the Johnson household, recounting the talents and proclivities of those African-Americans whose familiar names I then knew by heart. I have no recollection of mean-spiritedness or blanket indictment against any blacks she relayed and evaluated.

❖

So, what caused these reflections on my extended family this morning on my way to meet Sheila face-to-face for the first time? Perhaps, they consisted of flashes I sensed about Sheila that reminded me, in a mostly inexplicable and esoteric way, of moments of cognition that I had stored in my memory vaults and recalled mainly about Hattie, but also, though to a lesser extent, about Sister—that airiness, that open field given to others without regard to consequences or reprimands. It was safety, I guess, that had been inculcated by Hattie and Sister, even if not emphatically spoken. Sheila had also realized the traits people need—no, require—in order to feel like they do not have to ask for forgiveness. This quality spread so generously from Sheila that she could say she forgave Lonnie more for his role in the Elaine Race Massacre than I had forgiven him.

Was this commonality the reason that brought these women into recollection this morning? It was well-known that women—black and white (even if wontedly unintentional for most white women)—facilitated success of the Montgomery Bus Boycott in 1956, and it was black and white women shortly thereafter who helped to mute the demagoguery of Arkansas Governor Orval Faubus in the Little Rock Central school crisis, but wasn't it also a white woman who slapped Martin Luther King, Jr., in an Atlanta department store for accidentally stepping on her toe, when he was only eight years old, an experience he recalled for the rest of his life? And, of course, I heard some of the most virulent verbal attacks against blacks being voiced by white women. Still, the symmetry coalescing this morning for me among Sheila, Hattie, and Sister cannot be discounted in my memory banks, forming racial recollections that carry me to this point of meeting

Sheila today, who would have likely understood, better than I do, the discipline and reticent courage shown by Hattie and Sister.

During the drive from South Station, Bob admitted to his excitement for Sheila and me to meet and converse about our respective reactions to heritage from the Elaine Race Massacre. He also posited that Sheila had contacted him a few times in advance of the day to learn more, as much as possible, about me, my background, my opinions, anything he may know in addition to my comments in the article, "Evanescence: The Elaine Race Massacre." Apparently, Sheila reacted positively to the contents of the piece, for the attitude and history in it comported with hers, and I had not exploited any mea culpa significance in the writing of an honest portrayal with its unfettered depiction of the role Lonnie played by joining in the furious and murderous onslaughts. Sheila had also responded favorably to my true feelings of affection and care for Lonnie, notwithstanding my genuine disgust and abhorrence at his role in the Massacre.

How I respond to Sheila will likely reflect an engagement in pursuit of honest conversation and disclosure for similar circumstances, as probably could have occurred with Hattie or Sister. Nothing forced. Nothing dramatic. Nothing unexpected. Nothing that somehow could betray the genuinely human between Sheila and me. A gesture, a moment, and motif on which something else is built and expanded that allows us to explore and expect a return to the fall of 1919 in the cotton fields of Hoop Spur, just north of Elaine, Arkansas, but that opposes and seeks even to rectify the manifestly inaccessible history.

When Bob pulled up in front of the house where Sheila's son and his wife and their small children lived, I inadvertently peered at the windows of the second-story structure, and my eyes met those of the person I knew would be Sheila. How long had she watched from the window for us to arrive? Sheila obviously shared in her own special way the searching exercise I too practiced in anticipation of this day.

Once Bob and I entered the house, Sheila and I embraced for a very long time. I do not know what she thought, but I didn't occupy myself at that point with any single, factual piece of our Elaine story; rather, the moment meant a promise Sheila and I could have then worthily imagined: the silencing of rifles and of screams in pain and terror; a silencing of orders and pejoratives; the omission of coverture and escapes into Govan's Slough, the coppices, and never-ending canebrakes; the deletion of trauma and the deluge of hatred and fury; a lapse of fear and vengeance; and the lapse of old grudges and all violent forms. A moment apart from the rest, a moment when confounding rifts had been mended for all time, as we may have sensed them, and the future was amended by goodwill, and our own histories had also been altered by a freedom from race, as menace, threat, or defect, and we were removed from the inference of arbitrary separation, and we could actually believe in oneness for ourselves and those who follow.

Sheila and I agreed to bring photographs of relevant family members to the day's event. I remember the pictures she shared at the time of her grandmother Annie, her granduncle Milligan, and her great grandmother Sallie. Absent from those pictures of family members who had endured the Massacre was one of her granduncle, Albert Giles, of the historically crucial Elaine Twelve, who were found guilty of murder and sentenced to death by electrocution, but who were ultimately freed. Whether Sheila purposely excluded Albert from the rest of the images or no picture of him had been available as part of her collection, I did not know nor did I inquire.

The photographs I introduced were limited mainly to images of group shots of Lonnie, his wife Hattie, and me. The picture which captured more attention than any other I shared depicted Lonnie and me in front of my grandparents' home on my second birthday with the two of us affectionately staring at each other, a lit cigarette wedged comfortably between Lonnie's lips while I stood perched a bit precariously on a small table hovering over a birthday cake that displayed two candles. Lonnie, jacketless, wore a tie with a white shirt and buttoned sleeves—a man properly dressed to be an attentive grandfather for the celebration of his grandson's birthday.

Sheila and I spent much of the afternoon together, elaborating on stories each of us started during our previous phone conversation. Bob spent much of his time talking with Franzi and Marcus, whom Bob had formerly gotten to know well, based on the ease with which the three effortlessly and enjoyably passed the time together. Ivor, Sheila's husband, along with Marcus when he wasn't with Franzi and Bob, took care of the two boys. Also, following and recording the dialogue between Sheila and me was Franzi, an Emmy-award winning video documentarian, who had established a cooperative project with a few other video documentarians to produce a piece on the descendants of both victims and participants in the Elaine Race Massacre and the various ways our generation responded to the Massacre's recurrent effects; the video had been preliminarily dubbed "Bound By Blood." The conversation between Sheila and me constituted material, pertinent to the documentary's theme, that Franzi planned to employ in the film. Indeed, Sheila and I were bound by blood—not retained blood, but blood that flowed profusely through the affected families, the affected history, and in this instance, also through the affected and future cases relying on *Moore v. Dempsey* and associated decisions to foster a multitude of advancements in equal justice and the furtherance of black liberation.

Throughout the course of the afternoon, it seemed the natural and right thing for us to do, as Sheila and I periodically reached to grasp each other's hand. On occasion, Franzi caught the moment on film. At one point, someone asked me to describe the purposes for a path to reconciliation. The answer would be long and complicated and not conducive to sound bites. In many respects, a more than partial answer was simply that I had no other conceivable option given Lonnie's malevolent participation in the Massacre and my own avowed words and stances on racial matters; for once I reached the determination that my grandfather had been part of the onslaughts, I could not leave the fact alone, as acknowledgement leads to circumspection, and circumspection leads to broader examination, and broader examination forms redoubtable guidelines for moral and ethical conduct, and yet, reconciliation and love then finally take control. Could I explain this remarkable migration succinctly? Among the options of which I availed myself, reconciliation felt the most honest and direct route to arrive at love. Non-acknowledgment or betrayal of the facts just leads to selfishness and pretension, and adherence to white traditions cannot progress beyond simple denial. Similarly, marginal interest in true history indicates a preference for abiding ignorance, and whoever charts that path is of no use to anyone.

So, my choice, apparent from the outset, remained a road to reconciliation that recognized imperative history, which made sense of all we learned from beginning to end, discounting none of the most intrusive facts, regardless of how uncomfortable. A recital of all the personal implications from the events beginning at Hoop Spur Church about 11:00pm on Tuesday, September 30, 1919 could not rely on mere sound bites from me or even a short, bearable paragraph spoken deliberately but calculably. Sheila provided a blessed outcome from the impulse to reconciliation, for she realized the limitations for whites to address the past with self-forgiveness or self-instituted redemption. Maybe, that was the reason Sheila said she could forgive Lonnie more than I had, or probably ever, could. Maybe, she knew that for me to forgive Lonnie meant I had found a way for whites to forgive themselves for their past, and she was much readier to do that for us than most whites could possibly attain, certainly more so than I had envisioned.

Maybe, the inability of whites to fully forgive themselves and even others is simply a function of being white. Maybe, that reverence of the past, that filiopietism, has insulated whites more generally from having to feel the need to forgive. Maybe, white supremacy and white privilege have given whites the prerogative, even arrogance, to be less than munificent in their forgiveness, so that whites are more devoid of that facility when it really counts. Maybe, therefore, forgiveness is something whites just do not do well. Yet, we all (black and white) should acknowledge the exceptional power and infectious impact of forgiveness.

There can be a multitude of renditions associated with the concept or word, reconciliation. These may begin with the more formal, diplomatic notion of simply understanding the other person's position with an implicit decision to let any future act be guided by that understanding. This approach does not bother to extend to love or even empathy, for it merely recognizes with respect another point of view, and assurance is given that this respect will guide acceptable behavior in the future. At the other end of the spectrum, we find love or co-inherence, which can underlie a more spacious, abundant relationship. In between the two, one can find human hope, sympathy, and the like. Thankfully, in our expression and experience of reconciliation, Sheila and I found our way into agape love and, I believe, co-inherence. While we apprehend agape love to be that multiple love, love outside oneself, love shared with other humans, it is the construct of co-inherence, which is a bolder and broader framework that I suggest Sheila and I found as part of our journey.

The idea of co-inherence formed out of a theological lexicon, and the thrust of its power goes back many centuries. For example, we condense from the Book of John of the New Testament, "We in him, and He in us."[1] From his *Paradiso*, Dante further refines the concept, but in more humanist terms: "did I in-thee myself, as thou dost in me thyself."[2] In other words, co-inherence is not limited just to the relationship between God and a person, but rather, considering racial reconciliation, it can extend to the human community and, more specifically, to relations between and among individuals, including the bonds between African-Americans and whites.

The British theologian and writer, Charles Williams, one of the Inklings, along with C. S. Lewis and J. R .R. Tolkien, and one of the strongest and more earnest proponents of co-inherence, considered the human community as "the City," which, to Williams, was "Union," and any exclusion from "the City" or "Union" was hell: "It is the doctrine that no man lives to himself or indeed *from* himself . . . We are, simply, utterly dependent on others."[3] I would argue that co-inherence constitutes the epitome of racial reconciliation, for race goes away entirely as a feature or element of abiding human relationships through co-inherence.

More precisely, the attitude toward the genuinely human with co-inherence as the venue, according to Williams, becomes: "your life and death are in your neighbor; they in Me and I in them."[4] As we enter the third decade of the twenty-first century, with white nationalism marauding over the American countryside displaying a villainous intent to separate "the City" further, we would be wise to take to heart the words of Charles Williams, from eighty years ago, in adopting co-inherence in racial matters, black and white relations, at this time for our beloved United States: "It (co-inherence) might find that, in this present world, its labour was never more needed . . . its concentration never more important."[5]

So, how did the modality of co-inherence advance the reconciliation for Sheila and me, one for the other? For my reconciliation was in her, and her reconciliation was in me. Toward this end, we believe each other, we believe in each other, and we believe for each other. We trust each other, and we are in trust for each other. As I witnessed and benefited from her generosity, Sheila's personal and public forgiveness of Lonnie created a two-way path in trust, leading to a combined acceptance of and quest for the undisguised truth, as we discovered and dwelt together with the Elaine Race Massacre. Each for the other, we did not stand in contrast; we rather stood together in union, in communion as we brought into focus the history, the familial history of the Massacre, and that history—one for the other—brought us closer through a more illuminated past that our respective backgrounds shared. We have now claimed our way back to Hoop Spur, black and white, and convene together in contrast to the killing fields in ways we could never accomplish alone. We define this journey, this racial reconciliation, not alone and separately, but in and through each other, and it is that definition, captured by our co-inherence at that final place for so very many under an Arkansas sun and very near the mighty river without lingering traces of either black or white.

When Bob and I departed Sheila and her family late in the afternoon, I realized my homework had become much more extensive than the magnitude Sheila had to address as we together grappled with questions of racial accountability, both black and white, toward each other in light of the Massacre. Clearly, Sheila stood well ahead of me in understanding why she could forgive Lonnie more than I could. She realized, better than I, how so many whites were less free in coming to terms with forgiveness of the past than those who were victims of it. By so many measures, we whites must depend on African-Americans to help guide us in the direction that will allow us to forgive the who and what that have defined us in ways we often do not yet admit. The who and what, by whites not fully seizing the relevance and influence of accepting the genuinely human in African-Americans, still maintain a hold of incalculable power we whites again and again quite conveniently and ineptly surmise no longer shrouds or collects us.

Bob and I also had our own reasons to commiserate that Saturday. In my article, "Evanescence: The Elaine Race Massacre," I referred to Lonnie's role in the Massacre as "likely," which conditionality reflected my own reluctance to declare, in an unqualified fashion, that Lonnie had indeed participated. So, during dinner that March evening, Bob and I reviewed several of the factors that led to my conclusion over time that Lonnie had indeed been a part of the Massacre's white attacks. Bob and I previously concluded that it would be constructive for the two of us to scrutinize the evidence together. Toward this end, I reiterated that Mother recounted to me the fact that Lonnie had been part of a "well-known race riot" when he worked for the Missouri Pacific Railroad in McGehee. Both Bob and I knew emphatically that MoPac was a corporation "up to its eyeballs" in matters linked to the onslaughts; indeed, the first deadly casualty on the first night of the Massacre had been W. A. Adkins, a security official with MoPac. In turn, MoPac, during the Massacre, sent a caboose loaded with men through the area several times a day.[6] Other acts of involvement by employees of MoPac included the acknowledged shooting of Milligan Giles by Henry Smiddy and the torturing of black witnesses in advance of the trials so that the white narrative could exercise control over the local court proceedings.

During my first visit to the scene of the killing fields during the summer of 2012, which I have previously discussed, I recalled the topographical description Mother furnished many years preceding that had been relayed to her by Lonnie: white attacks rose along dirt roads leading through the primed-for-harvesting cotton rows nestling west to east finally against the elevated railroad tracks that bore trains leaving from and returning to McGehee. As I gazed across the August vista in 2012, I then found the landscape shockingly accurate as embedded in the description conveyed by my mother to me, a young schoolboy at the time, listening to the critical details. In fact, I could close my eyes and recollect how I had originally pictured the killing fields, when depicted by her, where many of the black deaths took place; in a strange and surreal manner, my authentic view a half century later agreed inordinately well with my first, imagined panorama of the terrain. How many places were there in southeast Arkansas where killings transpired similar to the Massacre with the same topographical features, both imagined and real? As I relayed these thoughts to Bob, a fanciful encounter enveloped the moment as though I saw the location that night through my imagination again, and the scene had remarkably come alive like a poem or a psalm whose words reflected my own experience in such a way that the words became my words and the poem or psalm became my own. Bob sensed the mystery of a young boy's imagination transmuted into a man's factual observation.

Bob also heard from me again about the proximity of Lonnie's farm to Winchester—no farther in miles than the number of digits on a hand.

The home of Robert Hill and the headquarters of the African-American union, Winchester was situated in the extreme northeast corner of Drew County, on top of the border with Desha County, and approximately thirty miles (point to point) from Phillips County. Drew County was my home, where the papers creating the Progressive Farmers and Household Union had been crafted by lawyers from Monticello, and directly south of Phillips County, Desha, before Lonnie's move to Little Rock, was Lonnie's home, where his family farm and the hub for MoPac in southeast Arkansas had been located.

Robert Hill was a black veteran of World War I, who found upon his return from fighting for his country that nothing had changed or would change for black sharecroppers in southeast Arkansas without an aggressive labor movement in the form of unionization. The white planters in the region reasoned that black agrarian workers, including especially sharecroppers, proposed taking a more incursive tactic and approach toward the protection of their economic interests than had previously been the case. After all, to African-Americans, they went to war to defend the nation and should now be beneficiaries of greater freedom, more respect, and higher cotton prices, higher than anyone had, a few years earlier, ever realistically projected. Lonnie and his brothers who farmed the land knew these black sentiments and associated white fears gripping the rich Mississippi River Delta, including not only Phillips County but also Desha County, where Lonnie and his brothers enjoyed land holdings for cotton and where they would have envisioned the African-American economic threat as a clear and present danger.

Among other pieces of evidence, I could not fail to mention to Bob the family's acknowledgment of Lonnie's racial activism of intimidation and worse through the local Ku Klux Klan in McGehee.

After reciting these factors that had led me to the precipice of an unqualified admission of Lonnie's role in the Massacre, I realized that I had another hurdle to traverse, and that would be the removal in the future of conditional language surrounding Lonnie's participation. In my own way, I had found rescue in denial; the use of "likely" kept open the possibility that Lonnie acted differently than other whites around Hoop Spur in the fall of 1919. As I walked away from dinner with Bob Whitaker on March 15, 2014, I conceded it was now time for me to remove my conditional account of Lonnie's role; all that was circumstantial nonetheless simply aided in evincing and confirming the truth and facts of what he himself had repeated to family members at the time of the attacks, and my mother had, with courage and without reservation, passed that certainty along to me. I was clearly no hero. I had merely been a conduit. A level of forthrightness held a place of consequence in the continuing narrative of the Elaine Race Massacre, as I felt an obligation to respect my mother's courage that spurred the truth about Lonnie from one generation to another. For my own legacy, I would have a mission to transfer at least an equal response to that which I received from my mother, relying on the words and conviction that set me free to do so—no, not in some sort of likelihood, but in certitude at this time for that other time and place I had come to know as the Elaine Race Massacre.

5

MONTICELLO, ARKANSAS

I n 1949, while the country moved toward the new decade of the 1950s, my mother, my older brother John Maxie, and I moved into Monticello at 308 East Shelton. Our home was a small, modest house literally "on the other side of the railroad tracks" but with an ample backyard, which my brother and I, over time, put to good use as a vegetable garden, a dirt basketball court, a short track and field lot, and a few additional plats evolving out of our imaginations. Mother always remained malleable about adjustments to this outside space.

East Shelton ran exactly parallel to the next street, East Jackson, one block south. African-Americans in Monticello resided both across town at the western end of Jackson in an enclave known as "Vinegar Hill" and toward the other end of Jackson, beginning approximately behind our house and running east for a few blocks across and along South Connelly, unpaved once it intersected with East Jackson. For the time my brother and I grew up there, beyond an open field on the far side of our backyard stood the homes of African-Americans. Whites lived on East Shelton, African-Americans East Jackson—within a few yards of each other.

Cotton and the rich alluvial soil that draped along the Arkansas side of the Mississippi River Delta caused African-Americans to be placed in southeast Arkansas and East Jackson:

> *From 1800 to 1860, cotton production provoked human and territorial expansion at a blistering pace. . . . During this period, the lure of cotton and the anticipation of wealth generated a significant internal migration into the new cotton states—Alabama, Mississippi, Louisiana, Arkansas, and Texas. The scope of the slave migration was enormous.*[1]

While the Delta attracted most attention for cotton and black labor—the two being inextricably linked—immediately adjacent areas, such as Drew County and its county seat, Monticello, also benefitted economically from cotton, as white gold with its associated demand for African-American hands. Poised some thirty miles west of the Great Muddy, Mississippi River and forty miles north of Louisiana, Monticello stands at the cusp of the Mississippi River Delta, meaning soil around much of Drew County near Monticello does not enjoy the same rich, earthen deposits that distinguish Delta land. If one drives the short distance east to west, away from the Mississippi River to Monticello, it will be evident that the town received its name, not as an homage to Thomas Jefferson's home, but as an accurate derivation from Latin for "higher land," as just east of town, an ascending ridge starts to emerge and proceeds west from the more valuable, choice soil.

And yet, the vicinal land in Drew County contributed to profitable farming that relied on African-American labor. In 1890, nearly 60 percent of the population of the county was African-American, but this percentage would decline, so that around the time of the Elaine Race Massacre in 1919 and the lynching of Philip Slater, an African-American, on the Monticello town square in 1921, about one-half of Drew County's population consisted of blacks.[2] The proportion of blacks reflected in Monticello's population also fell, but continued to be integral, illustrated in the 2010 level, with 36 percent of the town comprised of African-Americans.[3]

When I first moved away from Lonnie and Hattie, I discovered there was no one with whom to play on East Shelton in Monticello. I had cousins several blocks away, but Mother wasn't especially close to that part of my father's family at the time, and I was simply too young to walk the distance. A number of children around my brother's age lived on East Shelton, but none my age nor even within a couple of years, so I spent a lot of my time on the back porch. I'd put on a towel made up like a cape to jump from the top of a shed in the backyard à la Superman, or I'd climb up and down a pear tree next to the garage with its low-lying branches smoothing my ascent and descent. Much of every day was to be spent in the backyard contriving games on my own and visualizing all kinds of eerie creatures hidden away in the large oak, sycamore, or pine trees in the backyards of the houses on each side of our own, houses where only old folks dwelled. Television had yet to arrive on East Shelton.

That spring, frequently in the early mornings and later in the afternoons, I spotted black children, boys my age running, yelling, and just gamboling in the open field on the other side of the backyard fence. At first, I waited and watched. On occasion, an older African-American boy, about my brother's age, appeared, and he always commanded awareness and amendment by the younger black boys. I didn't venture through the fence, though I wanted to, from the outset. After some time acknowledging and observing each other through the back fence, the African-American boys found reasons for reducing the proximity between us—a ball came within a few feet of me or one of the boys ran near where I stood inside the fence.

Mother never instructed me not to crawl through the wire barrier, and a natural opening appeared at about my chest level so I could pull down that part of the fence and let myself through whenever I desired; no barbs, top to bottom, amplified the danger. So, I eventually chose to include myself in whatever the four or five African-American boys about my age were doing out in the field. I don't even know or remember the game they were playing, but a ball much bigger and lighter than a baseball had been involved. In a matter of minutes, I flowed right into part of the tossing and throwing, even talking and later yelling at play.

Mother must have monitored the process and effects from the back porch, but I don't think she ever once said anything about my climbing through the fence or embarking on those new friendships. And more, I don't think she ever cautioned me about anything related to the field or the games.

This is the way it started in early spring and all summer of 1950 before I began first grade, and as it continued throughout that whole first school year in the afternoons since I, like all other white students, attended classes only half a day. The next year for the second grade, I attended a full day, leaving school at three o'clock, which altered everything.

But for now, soon after routines kicked in, I quit thinking about whether I should or shouldn't crawl through the flimsy wire fence behind our house separating the backyard and the field beyond. I never learned the owner of the field, which was "bush-hogged" from time to time so our games could be played without interference from high weeds or overgrown grass. With the exception of colder weather, which in southeast Arkansas ran from late October to February or early March and with many intermittently warm or tolerable days, even in the colder period, and with a blessing of no rain most days, we'd be found in the field each afternoon—and during the summer, in the mornings as well.

At our age, we played at playing baseball. Someone brought a real bat or a big piece of wood, and someone else a baseball or something like it. Older African-American boys often joined us to play real baseball, but they unfortunately imposed rules and skills. My brother, some seven years older than I, entered our games now and then, but the older players never remained as long as we younger boys did. Maybe, they were just too busy or too distracted. We younger players liked the idea of fostering new rules as we went along, so we didn't mind it much when the older boys departed. We had our own style.

Once in a while, we'd point out our own homes from the vantage point of location on the field. No grownups from either street ever tried to interrupt our times on the field except to call us home for meals or bedtime, and yet, there were oddities about it all. In retrospect, the field seemed isolated from everything else around us. The field established itself beyond the parallel streets we felt would never invade us. Still, we arrived from separate worlds and later returned from where we came, never sharing each other's interiors on East Jackson or East Shelton. The field became uniquely our own somehow, but we already realized that I should not return to their homes, and they were not to return to mine. As young as we were, we already perceived the steadfast, impermeable rules governing the riven ways to conduct ourselves. Race as the great separator had inserted itself, and we acted through obeisance to it, even at our tender age.

We were friends, and we acknowledged that declaration each time we reached the field to be together. I was the only white boy, but it didn't matter while we stayed anchored on our field.

At the end of an indeterminate stretch, our ardor and confidence manifested themselves in a desire to expand the territory for our games and play. The logical next venue would be Godfrey's sewage ditch, located about seventy-five yards east of the field among dense thickets, coppices, overgrowth, and underbrush, where we could be hidden within the protected confines set along each side of the ditch. It was a perfect spot for hide and seek. The only vulnerability for those in our game consisted of thin stalks, which waved to and fro when anyone hid in their midst or when anyone moved slightly from one location to another; if anyone kept deadly motionless, he could be caught only by a seeker actually stumbling over him. One could stay undiscovered for a long time with the promise that brush gave maximum cover while he waited cautiously and still.

A certain day alongside Godfrey's sewage ditch sticks out more than others. A small sandbar rose appreciably higher than the rest of the narrow embankment, and we occasionally reclined on that sandbar between rounds of hide and seek. The sandbar's disadvantage was its exposure to walkers above us on East Shelton Street and houses with their short porches on each side of the ditch. We could easily be spotted.

On this day, I grew a bit thirsty and decided to drink from the ditch, for after all, I had no idea about the purpose of a sewage ditch, which seemed like any other stream to facilitate spirited escapades. Just as I cupped my hands and took a full gulp of water, I heard a woman's voice scream out, and by some means, I instantly knew the scream was meant for me. "Stop that, young man. You'll get very sick."

That flash in time now endures as clearly as yesterday. The white woman appeared from nowhere and slid down to the sandbar in a short second, talking quickly all the time in one harmonious motion. Grabbing my elbow, she spoke louder than she needed, "You go home right now, and tell your mother you just drank water from this ditch." I could tell she meant business, so I didn't ask any questions. By then, my black friends had scampered back into the overgrowth or underbrush, and I imagined they were probably halfway home by the time I climbed up the short incline onto the road and began to walk at a faster-than-normal clip to 308 East Shelton.

Needless to say, Mother reacted angrily and got me straightaway to the family doctor who administered a battery of shots and inoculations over succeeding days. While nothing terrible happened to me from drinking water out of Godfrey's sewage ditch, I had gained the rather glaring point. I believe I returned to the field and my friends in short order, maybe within a couple of days or so. Whenever I did something that carried a reprimand or whipping in those early years, Mother normally added that I must also stay inside our house for a specified period, although she never allowed me to miss school applying her punishments; routinely, this element of her discipline got progressively smaller over time by virtue of my incessant inquiries and by my orchestrating too much ambient noise. After a while, Mother often facetiously remarked, "John Chester, why don't you go out and play in the traffic?"

As I look back on those days, I wonder why white adults looked upon my play with African-American friends without any concern or horror at all. Adding fifteen or twenty years to our ages, combined with our conspicuous friendship and daily and extensive nexus, would have caused a scandal in Monticello in 1950, a spectacle to mandate intervention or worse. Why the nonchalance for these black and white friendships? Was separation observed as an inevitability? Did adults simply rely on the inevitability to do its traditional job, and adults were wise not to interfere beforehand? I think so. Such friendships could never weather the preponderance of institutional forces poised to inflict intervention at the times and in the magnitude necessary to make things the way they had mostly been and would continue mostly to be. The ability of these friendships to sustain themselves faced too much historical momentum and opprobrium.

Was my own mother part of this cabal or conspiracy? I have usually viewed her laissez-faire attitude toward those childhood friendships a definite mark in her favor, and yet, over the years, a suspicion about her benign neglect took hold, for it was reasonable to conclude that she intuitively expected the ineluctable termination to take care of our young friendships. At the same time, could I have realistically done more to curtail the inevitability? This gradual, compulsory, and institutional separation from my African-American friends became my very first, serious exposure to the peculiar consequences of racism.

By the time I entered the second grade, the additional hours my white schoolmates and I spent at the segregated school assisted in a codification of white fraternity, although almost never did these newfound brotherhoods result in trips to my home on East Shelton. My mother now allowed me, for the first time, to walk approximately ten blocks back home from elementary school; as a first grader, I'd be picked up by her after class around noon every day. On occasion, some of my early white acquaintances that eventually turned into long-term, dear friends subtly or not so subtly conveyed that I lived too far from school and in a more undesirable part of town where houses were smaller or more dilapidated or too close to African-Americans. Almost instantly all adventures with my African-American friends ceased as I now returned home each day from school much later in the afternoon, having been delightfully distracted both by afternoon pick-up games or by invitations for cookies and milk at homes where my white friendships were burgeoning. Since Mother declared that our family always sat down to the evening meal at 5:30 P.M. sharp, I had little time to go into the field.

On weekends, our family routinely traveled to Little Rock to see Hattie, or I'd meet my new white friends at their homes; only later, these newer friends and I gathered on the town square. I do remember that while in grade or "grammar" (as locals often vernacularly referred to it) school, which ended with the completion of the sixth grade, my black friends and I, on Sunday afternoons following Sunday school and church, would now and then convene again in the field for games and play, but these reunions happened more infrequently, and then they disappeared entirely.

Looking back on experiences with my African-American friends, a question continually arose for which I still did not have an answer many decades later: why was the power of separation or, let's call it, segregation so prohibitive and enormous that those friends simply couldn't come to my house and I couldn't go to theirs? What persuaded me at that young age not to ask my mother if I could bring those African-American friends home for water, a meal, or a bathroom break? Were the patterns so overpowering that, even at my young age, I buckled weak-kneed and mute? Somehow, my African-American friends and I heard the incursive voices of tradition forbidding any visits more personal than those the field allowed between blacks and whites. Whenever I got thirsty, which was often, or sought a bathroom, I chose to run home during a break in the action, and they did the same, back to East Jackson.

Probably by the time I reached the fourth grade, we never saw each other anymore, except for an episodic, short pick-up baseball game, but for those rare moments as we had gotten stronger and older, a few non-racial dangers mounted. For example, one of us hammered a baseball from the field to the back of a house facing Gabbert, an adjoining street, and the ball crashed through a back window with all of us then running for our lives back to our respective homes. The next day when I arrived from school, Mother handed me the baseball that had been delivered by the older white woman residing alone in the house with its window smashed. Mother asked me to apologize for the breakage; all I remember from my apology is being told by the older white woman that she knew the damage to be an accident, and she already had a new pane installed. We never broke another window.

The final time I spent with any of my African-American friends took place somewhat later when I belonged to the white Boys Scout troop, and a couple of my black friends belonged to the black troop. The two scout masters decided that because of the racial mix in the town's population, it would be a good idea if the troops merged for one project of delivering advertising circulars to all the houses in Monticello. I was paired with one of my black friends from the field. Though the joint task spanned only a few blocks in our part of town, we felt comfortable and furtively inspirited by the reunion.

Whether there was any connection, I cannot say for sure, but I do recall that as an avid Little League baseball player (I don't believe a black Little League existed in Monticello at the time), I always chose to use a bat with its signature of Larry Doby each time I went to the plate. As the first African-American baseball player in the American League, Doby broke into the major leagues only a few months after Jackie Robinson to become a star with the Cleveland Indians. While not determinable, I want to think that I constantly turned to my Larry Doby bat back then as an homage to my black friends, my fellow baseball zealots from the field, located between East Shelton and East Jackson.

Less than two decades later, after the assassination of Martin Luther King, Jr., I would leave New York City and be back in Monticello again, this time teaching sixth through twelfth grades in the all-black public school before integration of the local education system. While the connection between my African-American friends and my return to Monticello may seem mildly oblique, I'm certain the decision to teach at the black Drew School before school integration rested, in part, on the memories of those unending and incomplete games we found to be so accessible and natural when our field did not let history and tradition be a completely countervailing force for racial separation.

I have often ruminated, especially in recent years, on that period when my African-American friends and I found our way together. I've often wondered did they somehow open my perspective or consciousness in ways I could not define but ingested without reservation? Through a fabulous twist of fate, they were me, and I them, a co-inherence, and they taught me an unmistakable accord, which could not be abandoned or exchanged. It could not leave me, for I claimed its empowerment and inference, and it expressed itself beyond understanding to capture a world yet to be, a world contemplated and admired but not yet fully designed nor enabled. Still, I know, and maybe we knew, it would exist someday with simplicity in its certitude and continuity. On the basis of they in me and me in them, I could believe in a promise unfilled, but a promise intact that would inflect into something more we together knew had partially started with us on a sun-sharpened, sun-drenched, and refulgent field anxiously awaiting our return.

Monticello ineffably, but redolently in subtle fashion argued that it had been much different from other small towns in southeast Arkansas with local folklore holding the town to be more genteel, more enlightened, and maybe even more tolerant than sister communities within the region. No evidence existed to affirm this claim. In fact, from the book *A Corner of the Tapestry*, the story of the Arkansas experience for Jews, we learn that a certain Jew, Louis Bloom, attempted "to open a store at Monticello in

Drew County but was told Jews were not welcome there."⁴ Considering my wife's ancestry is Jewish, this behavior is not exactly how I care to remember the town of my youth, although apparently, a Jewish merchant, Joseph Mayer, had in 1860 opened a small store in Monticello after having peddled for some time within southeast Arkansas.⁵ At the time of my growing up there, while no Jewish families resided in Monticello, a host of towns in southeast Arkansas benefitted as home to numerous Jews. Further, in the 1950s and early 1960s before I left for college, few Catholics lived in Monticello either, and those who did were so thin in number they simply could not support their own house of worship, which meant Catholics were obliged to travel on Sundays some twenty or more miles to nearby communities.

Within the white world I experienced, Monticello was hardcore Protestant. In fact, beyond the absence of Jews and only a smattering of Catholics, the Episcopal Church, which has been, historically speaking, one of the more liberal Protestant denominations, did not have a place of worship in Monticello until well after I departed for college. A Monticellonian, who noticed and followed such trends, once told me when I was a high school student that fourteen Baptist churches then existed in Monticello and on its outskirts, ranging from the First Baptist Church to a Free Will Baptist Church, with all shapes and sizes in between.

One of the more visible and vocal religious controversies in dogma during my high school years dealt with dances for students from the white school following every Friday night home football or basketball game. Because dancing was considered a high-level sin among some Baptist sects, a significant number of Baptist students boycotted our dances. Even among the less severe Protestant denominations, pressure abided for congregations and others in town to stay within narrow bands of conservative, if not nearly puritan behavior. For instance, commercial establishments were and are still prohibited from selling liquor in Drew County. Apparently, when a preference for a dry county initiative passed within Drew County, the First Methodist Church of Monticello, which I attended for most of my school years, had constituted the bulwark and spearhead for temperance in the county. Of course, there was—and still is, no doubt—an ever-flowing stream of automobiles from Monticello and Drew County during the day (except for Sunday) and especially at night on the highways to the nearest "wet" county to stock up on happy juice.

We will spend time shortly on the consequential relevance for Arkansans of the integration of Little Rock Central High School. Before turning to that critical moment, I'd like to recount an associated event pertinent at the time to Monticello's religious attitudes toward racial matters. In September, 1957, at the beginning of the Little Rock Central High School crisis when nine African-American students sought to attend and integrate the largest high school in the state, special concern existed for the safety of those students hounded by white mobs that routinely showed up to harass the African-Americans as they attempted to enter Central High. As a result of the fear that something terrible could happen to the nine students, a call went out to white Arkansas clergy to come, in their clerical garb, to Little Rock and walk in front of, alongside, or behind the black students as they made their way into the school building. Two white members of the Arkansas clergy responded to the call: one from Little Rock and the other from the First Presbyterian Church in Monticello.[6] Apparently, the decision to stand tall and serve as an escort for black students at Central High didn't sit well with several elders of the First Presbyterian Church in Monticello, while others supported the white pastor who left Monticello about a year after his demonstration of courage and adherence to Christian principles.[7]

As a child, I always noticed stores were closed in town all day Sunday, encouraging families to remain at home after worship services, although more, it seems, took the opportunity to visit, entertain, play golf, hunt or fish, do what sweethearts do, or drive (it didn't matter where or how slowly).

For many years, little did I, as either denizen or former denizen, know or learn of the several episodes dramatically illustrative of the town's deadly racial past. I previously heard about one such incident that happened on the town square a few decades before my birth, when a very large segment of white men in Monticello and the County turned out to participate in and witness the lynching of a black man in 1921.[8] I discovered much later, on my own, the ostensible excuse for the extralegal killing. I do remember growing up in Monticello that the telling about that lynching held a certain secretive allure for many white people through near whispers and indirect allusions inferring that listeners only needed to be reminded of a mere thread, and the whole fabric of the incident would then fall into place.

Following my discovery of the Elaine Race Massacre, I concluded it was crucial I explore violent attacks against African-Americans that took place in the town of my youth, located one county removed from the site of the Massacre. Toward that end, I began further research focused on lynchings of black Americans in Monticello.

I should pause at this point and explain two, measurably different versions of the meaning for lynching between a number of black and white writers. These dissimilar attitudes have led to some misunderstandings and a bit of confusion. It's been my experience that whenever the word, lynching, is raised, a white person writing about the subject will often limit the mental vision to death by hanging—of course, of a black man. On the other hand, a black person writing about the same subject will normally put a broader cast on the meaning of the word to include not only death by hanging but also death through shooting, burning, choking, drowning, knifing, etc., by whites who execute one or more African-Americans in such an extralegal act.

In my opinion, this difference in the interpretation of what constitutes "lynching" derives from the way Ida B. Wells applied the meaning to her studies, particularly through her tabulation of the number of lynchings of African-Americans whites committed annually in the latter part of the nineteenth century. In those studies, Wells routinely included as lynching the extralegal deaths of African-Americans from shooting, burning, choking, drowning, knifing, and other forms of murder in addition to hanging.[9] And why shouldn't she? At the recent opening of the lynching memorial in Montgomery, Alabama, more formally known as The National Memorial for Peace and Justice, lynchings are memorialized that include, for example, the onslaughts against African-Americans from a more comprehensive meaning, including the use of machine guns by federal soldiers who inflicted the most deaths on blacks during the Elaine Race Massacre.

Returning to the topic of lynchings in Monticello, defined as Ida B. Wells would have, I decided to begin my expanded inquiry, relying first on documentation contained in the *Encyclopedia of Arkansas History and Culture*. As soon as I chose "lynching" for my subject and perused information that explained lynching's history before and after the Civil War and the primary perpetrators in Arkansas, such as the Ku Klux Klan, "whitecappers," "baldknobbers," and "nightriders," this source, to my surprise, next immediately dealt with, as an extreme example, the gruesome killing of two men, one black and the other white, in Monticello in 1868 soon after the end of the Civil War. Apparently, sheriff William Dollar, viewed as progressive in his relations with African-Americans, was kidnapped by fifteen masked men and tied to a black man, Fred Reeves. The two were then dragged together for three hundred yards and shot. According to this source, "to signify the sheriff's attitude on racial matters, their bodies were posed in an embrace and left in the middle of the road to rot in the sun."[10]

As I read and researched further, the Monticello I prized from childhood didn't look like the one depicted by this history. I discovered six lynchings in Monticello but found no recorded lynching prior to the 1868 double murder. It doesn't mean there weren't any; it just means the several sources I examined didn't report any such killings. On the other hand, the 1890s proved to be a grim time for the town, with three recorded lynchings during the decade. In July, 1892, an African-American man, Eugene Baker, was accosted by white vigilante bands in Ashley County, just south of Drew County. "Nightriders," who were known at the time to attempt to drive African-Americans from employment or off land desired by members of the white vigilantes, came to Baker's place and demanded he open the door. Upon his refusal, the "nightriders" attempted to break down the door, at which point Baker shot and killed one of the invaders. After being arrested, Baker was then taken to the Drew County jail in Monticello. Later that night, when the jailer had been overpowered, Baker was removed from the jail and taken outside of town where he was tied to a tree and killed by gunfire. Six years later in July, 1898, two African-American men, James Reid and Alexander Johnson, living in Monticello, were lynched on the same day, but little is known about the grievances against them or the circumstances that preceded or precipitated the lynchings.[11]

More than two decades then passed before the Slater lynching occurred in Monticello. It is reported that on the night of March 15, 1921, a white woman (the name was not part of the record) and her three children took a shortcut to neighbors through the woods outside of Wilmar, the small hamlet about eight miles west of Monticello. As it started to rain, two sons took cover under a tree. Soon after, the mother heard one of her boys crying and saw him struggling with an African-American man. At that point, the woman fought with the assailant, who then ran away. On March 22, a week later, the white woman identified Philip Slater from a lineup as the person who assaulted her and her son. That evening, the Drew County sheriff and his deputies faced an expanding mob that surrounded the Monticello jail. When the sheriff surrendered keys to the jail, Slater was removed by the mob and taken to the town square. At that point, the mob consisted of approximately 1,000 persons. Once a rope had been placed around Slater's neck, he was hoisted up a telephone pole, and more than a hundred shots were then fired into his body. When Slater's family did not come to claim the body from the undertaker, he was buried in potter's field.[12]

Apparently, no lynchings have been recorded in Monticello since Slater's death.

But as I moved from the second through the sixth grades, I focused on few matters spawning a connection that involved race. My narrow world during that time embraced mainly three separate purposes. First, I committed myself to friends—white friends—of my own age and of my own school class. Of course, the school was segregated, and while I did know the location of the black children's school, I didn't think much about it nor did I find reasons to visit or learn more about it. In hindsight, I can see the effects of segregation encouraging de facto acceptance of racism.

So, engagement with classmates of my own age and gender held a crucial mission, and I poured myself into the pursuit of four special friendships. All five of us have left Monticello. We're still friends many decades later; I usually see them every couple of years if not more often, and we sometimes call each other on birthdays. I would daily go to one of their homes after school throughout most of my grade school years, especially to those whose homes were located right on or right off Main Street and only a stone's throw from the schoolyard.

During the latter part of grade school, a secondhand bicycle became my own and afforded an independence no other asset acquired later in life could readily match. When this gift swept into my daily regimen, freedom of movement then conveyed a completely new meaning, and, being white, I luxuriated in that Monticello of the 1950s with its census population of 4,501 and its milieu of extensive places for play, available for my personal enjoyment. If friends were otherwise involved or away, I often then pedaled to the largess of the local library, located across the street from the First Methodist Church on one corner and also across from Sister's house, which she shared with her elderly and infirm mother, Ora. Within another fresh and animated universe, I explored and meandered through library stacks that seemed without end, although I always stopped at one book or another before arriving at the end of the volume-laden shelves. Around this age, on most Saturday mornings and every day over each summer, I would eat breakfast rapidly and jump on my bike by no later than 7:30 A.M. and off I wandered through the world I fathomed without reservation or radial limitations for the remainder of the day, returning home unscathed by 5:30 P.M. in the late afternoon for dinner.

Traveling along Main Street with stops at homes of friends or over tributary roads wending without uniformity off Main Street, white children were controlled by a loose net of zone defenses. An unwritten, but emphatic code abided that if children passed through one's yard, grown-ups of the associated home should take responsibility for instruction and instant discipline of the children. Sandwiches and sweetened ice tea were always available at every friend's home, and pick-up games of tree climbing, baseball, basketball, even semi-tackle football were also regularly available. Toward the latter part of grade school, I'd journey to athletic facilities and fields on the outskirts of Monticello at one of the town's two orphanages (Baptist and Presbyterian) to sharpen my skills. Girls around that age had their own tribal rituals, and rituals of the two sexes overlapped some afternoons, especially on Saturdays at the one indoor movie theater or at another convenient spot, such as Jolley's Sandwich Shop, the town square, or someone's house for an ever-increasing gaggle of boys and girls. By living on the other side of the railroad tracks, out of the way and well off Main Street or prominent arteries, I never worried about arrangements for friends, like me, who'd pop in with no warning.

Throughout my childhood growing up in Monticello, I felt I was a little less white than my white friends. I don't know how to explain it. Maybe, it had to do with where we lived in town or maybe, it had to do with my solitary, long walks or long bicycle trips here and there, to and from various locations in Monticello, that caused me to separate myself somehow from the normal, routine comradery of social gatherings and mixing among friends. This detection, this discovery, this interpretation never occurred to me while I lived there. Only later did I come to realize that I had never felt as white as my closest friends.

There was, at all times, of course, the other side to Monticello for African-Americans who experienced and undoubtedly observed prevailing attitudes and racism in ways I certainly didn't appreciate—surely, not then. Over the years, however, in periodic retrospective, I realized that my naive way of contextualizing myself within the white culture and environment of Monticello could hardly have been mirrored among the lives of my African-American friends from the field between East Shelton and East Jackson. Early on, they would have been cautioned about the town's peck- erwoods, those unruly enforcers of white privilege and supremacy, and the omnipresent suspicions among whites about even very young blacks, so that the safety of their own neighborhood around East Jackson would have encouraged those African-American children to return home and remain there. The older they became, the greater and starker were the divisions between white and black children: whites had little league baseball teams and a swimming pool, and at the movie theatre, whites could sit in the front sections, but blacks were cordoned off to the balcony. And still older, black children would notice the difference in the condition of roads and the handling of waste and sewage and the deference blacks had to pay to whites, always deference to the whites, and separate waiting rooms at the doctors' offices, and the exclusion from restaurants and white parts of town after dark, no football teams, no school bands, and the isolation with no part-time jobs except for yard work, no track and field teams, dated and tattered books and ancient facilities at the segregated Drew School, and, of course, the repetitive degradation of their mothers and dads and their brothers and sisters, and the carloads of white boys looking for black girls for one purpose. All too old, too close, too much, too soon.

Of the three commitments I had made then, my second consisted of time and effort at school. The Johnson family, notably Sister and Ora, communicated high expectations for educational achievement by the grandchildren. Early on, Mother adopted the Johnson views on education—Lonnie and Hattie hadn't instilled in their own children the degree of attention and intensity for studies the Johnsons promoted. Getting homework completed and receiving high marks weren't enough. Simply put, grandchildren shouldn't disrupt classrooms or disobey instructions. I failed badly to honor the latter dicta, being kicked out of grade school classes more than once for fighting in class and on or off school property. Still, from my perspective, my teachers took this conduct in stride, giving me low marks in deportment and reporting it was an area that needed improvement, and yet I never sensed a strident or repressive backlash from teachers for my behavior.

The third area of concentration during my five-year, second-through-sixth grade phase dealt with church, the town's all-white First Methodist Church, which presided impressively over a busy and consequential intersection across the street from the County Courthouse and town library. The architectural stature of the church also ruled over the distance of about fifty yards between the Methodists and Sister's house, once she and her mother had moved to Monticello from Wilmar. I found it to be a fun time at church both during weekdays and on Sundays whenever our small family didn't visit Hattie. On Saturday nights, the fellowship hall with its concrete floors could be transformed into a frenetic, but exciting roller rink for skaters. Scout meetings and choir practice happened at church. A place to enjoy. For white students, school and church frequently overlapped in those days. For example, I, along with several other fifth grade school students at the First Methodist Church, were requested with some regularity to memorize and recite without notes for main Sunday services favorite passages from the psalms or other scripture. My fifth-grade teacher was also my Sunday school teacher, and she let a few of us stealthily slip out of school class now and then to practice in an empty classroom an upcoming recitation for church. Whenever we weren't with Hattie in Little Rock for the weekend, I also had a duty to pick up any money gathered at the various Sunday school classes that ranged from the very young through adult. Members of the congregation who didn't plan to attend the main Sunday service normally left money for the church at Sunday school, and I was expected to collect and deliver these funds from each of the Sunday school classes to the Church's treasurer immediately before the beginning of the principal Sunday service. I took this responsibility very seriously.

So, I eagerly acceded to the reality that two pairs of hands shaped my world then: school and church, probably in that order, but I wasn't sure. I moved between the two with facile amusement and focus. New discoveries at each kept me wanting and pursuing more, and I had no way of predicting from day-to-day, month-to-month the next exciting installment at either place.

And yet, neither of those sets of hands—church and school—could have prepared any of us, toward the end of my third-grade year, for the arrival at our elementary school of African-American prisoners from the Arkansas penitentiary system. How could I then have ever envisioned these inmates coming for a long stay in our town, to be at our school? But there they were, right outside our school window, working like mad to dismantle an old part of the elementary school complex.

Nonetheless, after a short time, we all got accustomed to the prisoners' presence, as I was especially drawn to one African-American prisoner on the project, who performed like an overlord, sitting imperially and immovably in his director's chair, surveying the incremental deconstruction of the old elementary school building in advance of the erection of a brand new one: the W. C. Whaley Elementary School. The deconstruction of the old commenced at the end of my third grade and was followed by construction of the new, over the summer before and through much of my fourth grade. Each time I talked with this prisoner trustee at the end of a school day, I couldn't keep my eyes off his teeth; laid into his two, upper, prominent incisors were gold stars glistening each time he opened his mouth to speak or smile. I'm sure he observed my eyes locking into an uncompromised stare straight at those two teeth every time we conversed. In addition, he probably realized that when I stopped by to talk with him, a crucial part of the motivation involved my desire to get one more gander at those star and gold encrusted "beauties."

The Arkansas prison system, like those in many Southern states, contracted out, for money, convict labor that would demolish existing buildings, such as the old elementary school structure in Monticello, or provide low-cost labor for a multiplicity of purposes. A Pulitzer-prize winning book in 2009, *Slavery by Another Name*, authored by another writer who had also lived in Monticello, Douglas A. Blackmon, details a series of similar practices in Southern incarceration and penitentiary systems for contracting prison and local jail labor to private and other enterprises.[13]

The prisoner trustee and I didn't converse for very long every school day, but our talks, though brief, became a sort of ritual. I didn't feel like I could leave the schoolyard without dropping by and spending a few minutes with him. Somehow, I believed if I ceased to visit with him, he'd have missed our time together. Maybe, that impression formed as a figment of my imagination, but I knew I'd certainly lose something without a few minutes of his presence.

Although prison guards were always near, they wouldn't surround the trustee; they acted as though they never doubted where he would be at any given point in time. He was simply left alone. An off-white hat, loosely worn, with sweat stains everywhere and a short brim protruding all the way around the tubular circumference sat lightly on his head. I had no idea how old he was, but lots of scars blanketed his muscular forearms and face. I don't think I ever saw him in a standing position; of course, he'd have to move sometime during a day, but I was never there when it happened. Typically, I sat in my classroom imagining my next conversation with him. He never told me his name, though I'm sure I passed on mine along the way. I recall he had been in prison a long time, but he didn't impart anything about the offense that landed him there in the first place. I did receive an inkling he had accepted that the prison system was now his home forever.

The trustee once mentioned he'd always lived in southeast Arkansas, and all his prison work assignments were to places in the area. Since he anticipated home would always be the prison, then he had understood he'd live his entire life in southeast Arkansas. But if he never left, then how did he come to acquire those teeth? Pine Bluff, yes, that must be it. Pine Bluff, the biggest city in the region.

Sometime during my youth, I had heard a story from my father's side of the family about a black man who worked on my grandfather's farm, close to Wilmar, and who had been arrested many years before for allegedly stealing a hog, though the Johnson family held a strong conviction that the evidence against him was thin and dubious. According to the story, this black man, who enjoyed a reputation around Monticello as an excellent cook, kept getting his prison sentence renewed and extended, for he'd be contracted out to prepare food at Arkansas deer hunting and duck hunting clubs without any expectation of ever being released from prison. Maybe, the trustee with the star and gold teeth had a related story. Maybe, it had been another case of slavery by another name with African-Americans being placed in prison or local jails on minor offenses—or not so minor—to be conscripted out on lease, never to be released permanently to loved ones again. A thing like that happened to black people in southeast Arkansas, and it was accepted and acknowledged.

Even though our conversations transpired a very long time ago, I remember the trustee telling me that for a building like ours with classes being held at the same time a new building was going up, the tearing down of the old could be just as tricky as constructing the new. I didn't know exactly what he meant, but he seemed pretty sure of himself about everything. I wondered where he and the other prisoners spent their nights in Monticello—probably in the local jail. I wondered about a lot of things in their lives. One day, the entire crew, including the trustee, just disappeared. No one in class said anything, but I remember I missed him for a long while. They went back to prison, I guess, or to another job in southeast Arkansas. I had no one else so interesting to talk to about the usual and commonplace.

The Civil Rights Movement did not exist for me until 1955 with the Montgomery, Alabama bus boycott, which ended, almost to the day, a year after it had begun. The wide-spread publicity about the boycott, including television and newspaper coverage, brought the outcry of black voices for change close and reached my consciousness for the very first time. I had entered the sixth grade three months earlier. My mother purchased a television set when I was in the fourth grade, so by this time I had become familiar with the news broadcasts communicated through the medium of television, and I, in turn, learned of the remarkable Martin Luther King, Jr. Like the African-American trustee, I had known only southeast Arkansas, but no one—black or white—spoke like King. He said things like equal treatment and fairness and the need for integration and the unwillingness of white people to respond to black grievances. I never heard words and phrases like those put into sentences the way he did. Sure, I recognized separation and segregation of the races; my black friends from the field were unable to attend my school, and I didn't attend theirs. No bus service existed in Monticello, but the Little Rock bus system, I was told, had already been integrated, which expanded the complexity of the discussion. What was happening? How could white people in Arkansas call King all sorts of names and yet what he requested had already been put in place for the biggest city in Arkansas? So, why all this anger among white people in Monticello? I didn't understand, and I think most at W. C. Whaley Elementary School didn't understand either.

Mother often shut off the television channel covering the news of the Montgomery bus boycott. Somehow, by intuition or mere impression, I foresaw at the time that a movement, a major discussion, major decisions faced young people around my age, black and white, in the future, for blacks and whites looked at racial matters differently, and blacks were already prepared to bring their views into public display in a process that didn't align with the approach whites argued or I heard. A most startling part of the white response consisted of the vociferous and recriminating language numerous whites employed to characterize African-Americans generally and King particularly. The recriminations by whites in town and among certain family members about black initiatives and efforts rose to nearly an invocation of violence I hadn't previously heard. As diatribes could burst into the open, I feared that if someone spoke her or his mind, whatever that might be, which skirted even a modest departure from the words whites had said, or if a black person simply joined in the conversation, it could have gotten worse very quickly. But for the patent, white invective, it was obvious that repetition of silence for a response had been preferred.

During those early stages of the Civil Rights Movement, nothing happened yet to impose adjustments onto the rigid way of life in Monticello and among our extended family members, but that was hardly the point. By the alternate world envisioned in the words surfacing out of Montgomery, whites were threatened in a way even sixth graders could foresee, a form of life challenged and tested. What did it all mean? Maybe, I didn't feel well.

The Montgomery bus boycott ended in the latter part of December, 1956 with the goal of desegregating the public buses having been achieved. Then, only nine months later in early September, 1957, the Little Rock Nine, African-American students, took steps to integrate Little Rock Central High School, an event that sparked a significant challenge to federal authority and law in the aftermath of the Brown decision when the U.S. Supreme Court unanimously rejected the separate but equal doctrine of *Plessy v. Ferguson*. While the Montgomery bus boycott set the stage for white Arkansans anticipating a challenge to their segregated way of life, the crisis that surrounded the integration of Little Rock Central High School became the play itself. From the start, the crisis moved to a federal versus state confrontation, as Arkansas Governor Orval E. Faubus repeatedly refused to comply with federal requirements or to provide continuous and adequate protection for the African-American students attempting to integrate Central High School. White mobs, often consisting of persons from outside the state, besieged, sometimes violently, the campus daily to oppose school desegregation.

The Little Rock Central crisis, coming on the heels of the Montgomery bus boycott victory for the Civil Rights Movement, enflamed the blood and quickened the pace for many segregationists throughout the South to resist any further integration of Dixie. Indeed, the Montgomery success hardened positions of diehard segregationists who did not intend to allow a victory for civil rights to be reprised in Little Rock.

To secure safety for the African-American students, President Dwight D. Eisenhower called in the 101st Airborne Division to place the federal government between white mobs and black students, thus assuring integration of Little Rock Central High School. In addition, individual soldiers of the 101st walked the African-American students from class to class to reduce the prospects for violence against the Little Rock Nine. At the end of the 1957–58 school year during which the African-American students endured continuous harassment from a group of white students intent on tormenting the blacks, Ernest Green, the only senior among the Little Rock Nine, graduated from Central High; among those attending his graduation ceremonies was Martin Luther King, Jr.

The next school year proved to be a disaster for Little Rock high school students, both black and white. Rather than comply with the desegregation ruling, Governor Faubus and his supporters convinced Little Rock voters through referendum by a margin of more than 2.5 to 1 to close completely the city's high schools. So, during the 1958–59 school year in Little Rock, over 50 percent of black students and 7 percent of white students attended no school at all.[14] In fact, one of my roommates during my sophomore year at Harvard College was a white student affected by that closing of the Little Rock high schools.

For the people of Arkansas as a whole, Little Rock whites were not alone in being impacted by trauma of this kind during the late 1950s. Unaccustomed to the national and international spotlight, Arkansas whites felt the external and internal pressures to go through a self-examination process, and the outcome for each white family proved to be unpredictable and frequently surprising. In the years following the Central High crisis, members of white families often split over racial attitudes. Friends were regularly shocked at the evolving viewpoints of other friends over race. Of course, Arkansas being Arkansas and a Southern state, most white Arkansans held to views they inherited, and yet a discernible shift among many young whites in support of integration altered the landscape, and numerous young white Arkansans would choose to be exiles and emigrants from their state over time.

Looking back, the Central High crisis served as a dividing line for racial consciousness among many of us living in Arkansas at the time. Before the crisis, it would have been easier to deflect, as a young white person, the moral consciousness and imperative associated with racism in our lives. Blacks and whites resided in separation, but the consequences for blacks of that immured separation had not been forced upon whites to acknowledge and certainly not to address. The reality of Little Rock Central exemplified the plight and grievances sustained by black students in particular, but also by all African-Americans. The fixed separation of the races insulated whites from a broader admission to the pain and degradation inflicted on blacks by the system under which we all lived. That simply would no longer be the case. Arkansas could no longer continue in the luxury of its obscurity and insularity. The nation and the world fell upon us, and there was no place to hide our sins, our damaged heritage. The novelty of this disclosure and palpability fell on the young disproportionately. For myself, I didn't discuss much of this momentous adjustment confronting attitude and action with my white school friends. Because our parents didn't actually know how to frame and shape conversation on race, a subject that remained deep in inarticulation and implacability, how were we white children to talk about the events unfolding in front of us in our own state? We were learning. So, we whites didn't talk much about racial matters among ourselves, and the region's segregation apparatus did not afford us an opportunity to talk about such issues with young blacks, but that didn't mean we weren't thinking and reflecting on the implications and challenges.

The searing pictures in newspapers and on the television screen created a special, personal effect, for I could more emphatically imagine precise spots where the Central High events were being revealed. After all, the last home for Lonnie and Hattie once he was transferred from McGehee to Little Rock stood on West 18th Street, just off South Park, the main roadway directly in front of Central High and where the Little Rock Nine were trying to enter the school, only three blocks away from where my grandparents had lived. I walked those sidewalks that led to Central High School with Lonnie and later alone, after he died and when Mother, my brother, and I visited Hattie. The corners of the streets I had traveled in preoccupation looked the same on television but they bore an entirely incongruous message and angle from the pacific strolls taken along South Park on many a day and early evening in the years before anger and indisputable intolerance of roiling crowds took their place.

I couldn't condone at all, even then, the manner by which so many white people treated Elizabeth Eckford, separated from the other eight African-American students that fateful morning of September 4, 1957—the taunting and physical threats as she confronted her confusion, vulnerability, and uncertainty in the midst of a white mob, yelping at her like hyenas before a kill until an older white woman, Grace Lorch, who had all the features of a grandmother, stood between the student and the white mob and then helped Elizabeth Eckford onto a city bus. The images of those mostly feigned, but nonetheless menacing attacks and vicious dudgeon divided many white Arkansas children from those whites portrayed on the television sets. Indeed, a moment for a different heart arose as some white children differentiated themselves from the "criminally white" aggression we saw representative of white skin. I know I thought of my former black friends from the field and how I, nearly thirteen, could simply not treat them in the way whites behaved toward this lonely, solitary, totally exposed black girl near Central High.

Clearly, something was happening, not just at Central but in Arkansas, and elsewhere in America. We could not speak of it yet. We could not form the words to voice the consequences. We could not even confess these shortcomings to those whites older than we were, but in some way, maybe in many ways, nothing would ever be the same again in Arkansas, in Monticello, or for me as I watched the news reports each night on Channel 4 in September, 1957.

Mother always struggled describing suitable race relations. In later years, well after the Central High crisis, as she acknowledged my views on race which departed meaningfully from the ones prevailing in Monticello during my youth, she didn't dispute my conclusions, and yet, I can still remember distinctly the times she sided at family gatherings with one sister and one of her brothers, who were quite virulent and spiteful with their racist reprovals. Mother was a product of her age and milieu; she lived amid a world she did not fight nor feel obliged to protest. And yet, in years following the Little Rock Central crisis, her comments and replies to my questions sometimes implied a direction that told a different story than the one professed by her damaged heritage.

Nevertheless, whenever Mother attempted to rationalize and explain away the tyranny and arbitrary nature of racism against African-Americans fostered by family and traditions, I often heard arguments that, in the future, resembled economic ones espousing the spirit of some form of

Darwinian capitalism; that is, the strongest, the best educated, most knowledgeable, and the most prepared with the best tools always survive and prosper the way whites had survived and prospered. Absent were acknowledgments that the system had always been stacked against blacks; it was like running a quarter-mile race with one runner already three-quarters of the way around the track before the race began. Whether Mother believed her arguments I'll never know, but I realized along the way that racism never intends to explain itself rationally, and it never does—over the years, it has mostly supported the status quo in silence to enjoy corrupt benefits.

Still, all is not so cleanly attested or verified, for Mother had been the one broaching with me, around the time of the Little Rock Central crisis, the subject of the Elaine Race Massacre and Lonnie's role in it, though she didn't apply the words, "Elaine" or "Massacre." Rather, she simply used words, such as "a well-known race riot," while we drove along a highway one day, probably on our way to Little Rock or on our return trip to Monticello. My brother had left for college, and Mother and I therefore had more time to talk, which proved especially crucial in the midst of Little Rock Central creating history before our eyes. Once she began to tell the story of Lonnie and "a well-known race riot," Mother had no qualms about deciphering, as best she could, all that she had been told and could remember about the "riot," echoing the descriptions of the cotton fields, the railroad tracks nearby, and all the rest.

For years, of course, I did not know what to do with the information, which I undoubtedly buried, for I had little to which I could attach the story, even as she referred, in the same breath, to Lonnie's association with the Ku Klux Klan. And yet, I know now her intention, in the contemporaneous context of Little Rock Central, that I carry the knowledge for a cause she could not then project or foretell. Maybe, her desire had just been to tell a related story while we discussed the Little Rock Central crisis. Maybe, the crisis had wrenched her from a past ethos and acceptance of damaged heritage to look at her own father's participation in the "well-known race riot" in a way that forced her toward disclosure—at least to a son who kept asking questions about race. Maybe, it was an adjacent and familial history to pass the time on our car ride someplace. Each of these choices is probable, but I prefer to believe that part of her legacy to a son who conceived of an alternative to the status quo had been to tell of another, former, pertinent season that needed refinement for the coming, inescapable changes to Arkansas and to America.

With the unsolicited addition of biographical information about Lonnie and the Ku Klux Klan, including family insights about his comings and goings on those nights with the KKK, Mother perhaps had unwittingly exercised a right to exorcism from her received damaged heritage, that implanted racism, the endemic disease that white people took upon themselves for generations without a reprieve or termination from the trappings of southeast Arkansas. Perhaps, the integration of Little Rock Central High School had proven to be for her a catalyst for a partial verbal disgorgement from a storehouse of visions and behavior that often separated herself from herself and separated her from what King might have called her own freedom, but which she had not yet defined or called her own.

Fourteen months following the integration of Central High and only a little over three months after Little Rock voters cast more than enough ballots to close their own high schools rather than adhere to the court-sanctioned desegregation plan, I arrived in Washington, D.C., as a page for the U.S. House of Representatives, having been appointed to the position by the local congressman, whose house stood only a few blocks away from our own and who had been a family friend going back to my paternal grandfather. Being fourteen at the time meant I was a bit young to be a congressional page, but the representative who granted the appointment informed my mother that he favored a page at my age over an older one who more easily discovered good reasons to get into trouble in Washington, D. C.

Feelings in the nation's capital about the Little Rock situation experienced over the preceding fourteen months had become demonstrably raw and vocal against my state. Adding insult to injury—at least as far as people in D.C. were concerned—was the recent, successful write-in campaign for a resolute segregationist to replace Brooks Hays, a congressman from Little Rock whom most people in Washington supported as a moderate on race issues. A large part of Washington believed the wheels had come off the wagon in Arkansas, no thanks to Governor Faubus, seen as the one person who mendaciously engineered local circumstances so that President Eisenhower had no other option than to invoke federal authority to resolve the federal-state confrontation, to bring stability in the fall of 1957 to the Little Rock Central High School crisis, and to furnish protection for the Little Rock Nine. Washington also, in turn, disliked Faubus for his manipulation of conditions that led Little Rock voters to close their own high schools for the entirety of the 1958–59 school year, which history dubbed the "lost year."[15] Little Rock and Orval Faubus were hot topics all the time I served as a page in the U.S. Congress. Even a page from the State of Mississippi, about which Roy Wilkins, head of the NAACP, would say, "There is no state with a record that approaches that of Mississippi in inhumanity, murder and brutality and racial hatred,"[16] harangued over the racism existing in Arkansas. The white Mississippi page seemed to enjoy using Arkansas for this purpose a little too much.

In these circumstances, it would be natural, at fourteen and white, to feel that I was being treated as though I were somehow individually responsible for those monumentally racist and chaotic events that transpired in my home state. While these impressions seeped into my consciousness quite a bit, I meant to deflect them throughout my time in Washington, D. C., for I recognized that little productive result could come from submission to such unfair and internalized self-guilt distillations.

Two matters, one historic and one personal, served to divert my preoccupation with the Little Rock Central crisis and the way it came to be viewed by my fellow pages and other contacts I had while I worked at the U.S. Capitol. First, at the very end of 1958, Fidel Castro and other revolutionaries in Cuba successfully overthrew the Batista dictatorship, which caused a mammoth stir over several months for governmental and political types in the nation's capital. Second, one day as I sat in the page pool on the Democratic side within the House chambers, a call came for one of us to go immediately to the majority leader's offices; John McCormack, who eventually rose to be Speaker of the House replacing Sam Rayburn, occupied the position at that time. After being chosen by the dispatcher to fulfill this request, I arrived at McCormack's office and was requested by the majority leader to describe to a group of Japanese legislators the daily life of a House page. Thereafter, whenever the majority leader wanted a page, he always asked for me. In turn, I began to work on weekends in his office and got to know him. Later, near the end of my time as a page, I again happened to be in his office, and he asked if I wanted anything as a memento, and I presumptuously asked for his elegant wooden nameplate with a small eagle carved above his name, which he immediately handed to me, a possession I still proudly retain. These two meaningful distractions—the Cuban revolution and my fortuitous assignment to assist the majority leader of the House of Representatives—helped ease my otherwise constant absorption with impacts from the Little Rock Central crisis in a place far from home.

Nonetheless, as I listened to the regular and unquenchable voices in Congress and throughout the nation's capital attacking Little Rock particularly and Arkansas generally, I was forced to consider the nature and truth of those accusations. It was only logical, however, for a certain defensive and chauvinistic response to rise in me from time to time as I listened, but still, I realized even then I had to digest the relevance and truth of the words, whether targeted for Arkansas or not, about race, racial tolerance, racial brutality (physical, social, and subtle), racial privilege, racial indifference, racial intimidation, and more. In the late 1950s, the national public seemed to view the race problem with narrow geographic boundaries; indeed, at that time, some Northerners exercised a certain arrogant impression that racial division reflected itself predominantly in the South. We later came to realize racism had no real perimeter within our nation—only less or more racial prejudice.

On my return to Monticello later in the year, I recognized a persistent and mammoth gulf in the dissonance between the attitudes on race I heard in Washington, D.C., and those expressed in my hometown among white adults whom I overheard at church, at school from teachers, or during restaurant discussions and monologues. The distinctions between the two congealed not simply as two points of view, but they were rather much deeper and more intrinsic than a mere difference of opinion. The comparison brought to mind the story I heard at the U.S. Capitol about a fight that broke out in the halls of Congress before the Civil War: the caning of Senator Charles Sumner, an abolitionist from Massachusetts, by Representative Preston Brooks of South Carolina that nearly killed the senator, an encounter characterized as reflecting the inability of parties to continue civil discourse on the subject of slavery. I had reason to feel that the differences between the two sides in the early stages of the Civil Rights Movement were only a little less acute, could not be closed by debate or understanding, and would be resolved by fiat or will or just plain supremacy. A defense for the Faubus resistance to integration soared in most parts of Arkansas, including Monticello, from a fear of change so profound that it couldn't or wouldn't be tolerated, and those who felt this outrage vehemently let fury be their license and order.

Even though I had heard similar rhetoric before, history was now at stake, and lives could be lost (and would be lost) in the breach between the two, and notwithstanding my age then, I sensed more collisions. It was the beginning of a phase of dissonance I had no ability to deflect from myself. I knew enough to acknowledge change was upon us; it was coming, and coming at an unpredictable clip, and change would have its own shape and final provenance. To what extent I would have any association with it at all depended on incidents and conditions I could not yet imagine.

The remainder of my high school years continued apace with few local surprises. There were excitements, of course, that involved school and sports, many of which could not be predicted or planned, but in the context of this book, they are hardly relevant. For we in Monticello continued to feel the tectonic shifts that eventually would impact even small towns in southeast Arkansas, but for now, they were merely headlines in newspapers or pictures on television screens. Little Rock Central shocked the citizens of the state, and there were multiple and disparate decisions and values that emerged with unforgettable and, in so many ways, seemingly unresolvable immensity to be pondered and refined but never to be dismissed—no, never would we, who inhabited the moment, have the luxury to dismiss. Little Rock Central set a stake in the ground, and we were present, and what happened before did not traverse through to the other side—that is, to the period following Little Rock Central—without a reconstruction for all active witnesses and participants. Nothing then felt as it had in August, 1957.

The year following my time as a page in Congress, I was a sophomore in high school, and in February, 1960, we heard about a student sit-in in Greensboro, North Carolina to integrate lunch counters. Shortly thereafter, more than a hundred similar sit-ins popped up across the country, including one in Little Rock in March, 1960, only a month later than the one in Greensboro, and another in Pine Bluff in southeast Arkansas, still closer to Monticello.[17] For many in my hometown, it was like waiting for distant fires; one could virtually feel the heat lapping over some imaginary ridge, as the streams and occasional billows of smoke came rushing in our direction, north from Little Rock and Pine Bluff. And then, an even more imposing dilation of the impending combustion emerged for those who feared change, a tactic that took more courage for those seeking integration—through Freedom Rides. In the summer of 1961, buses with Freedom Riders dispersed out of St. Louis with destinations for Little Rock and Pine Bluff, and after only a few months, by November, 1961, the Little Rock bus terminals were desegregated.[18]

The state newspapers also reported that the Student Nonviolent Coordinating Committee (SNCC) had operations in southeast Arkansas, and as I packed for my freshman year at Harvard College, news commentators revealed that James Meredith, with the backing of federal courts and the power of the federal government, would attempt, the following month, in September, 1962, to enroll at the University of Mississippi.

6

AFTER FREEDOM SUMMER

During the summer of 1964, known among civil rights workers as Freedom Summer, I sat in Quincy House along the Charles River at Harvard University. I frequently sat that summer in the same place re-reading newspaper articles about the remarkable events, remarkable in their turbulence and impact for anyone participating or observing near and far the Racial Revolution of the American South. I watched the unfolding from a Massachusetts perch.

In June and July that summer, hundreds of mostly white northern students descended on the State of Mississippi to register black voters, to upset the state's racial norms, to open schools and political operations—all this cumulatively designated as Freedom Summer. While the target of this northern advance was the institutionalized racism arrogated by the state as a whole, the geographic area holding the most promise, northwest Mississippi, would be given most attention, where freedom workers expected staunch resistance, the area of the state conventionally known as the

Mississippi River Delta, where blacks often outnumbered whites, the sister locale across the Great Muddy from the counties of Phillips, Desha, Drew, and all the rest in southeast Arkansas. No wonder, then, that I dwelt repeatedly on reported newspaper accounts originating some 1,500 miles away.

Shortly after this initiative began, three civil rights workers associated with Freedom Summer were murdered near Philadelphia, Mississippi in Neshoba County; as a result, over two hundred federal investigators and other personnel flooded the county and surrounding area to find the bodies of the three: James Chaney, Andrew Goodman, and Michael Schwerner— a search that the nation followed with intensity and sympathetic anger.

Then, toward the end of July, seminal civil rights legislation was enacted into law by Congress and the president around the same time that the Harlem race riots erupted as a harbinger of internal combustions and infernos for succeeding summers when ghetto riots spread like viral wildfires through American cities, one after another. In the summer of 1964, the United States embarked on a racial reckoning, a battle beginning with the South as the target but flaring into a national outrage for racial grievances everywhere. With black and white players frequently bearing a Southern accent, one heard ancient outcries for— and against—rectitude.

I decided to attend summer school to study under the eminent theorist, Rollo May, who normally didn't teach at Harvard and whose writings I admired. I cannot say that incipient racial and civil rights avowals alone dominated my thoughts that summer as I sat in Quincy House while the invasion from the North resonated with other outside pressures to impose change on white Southern ways and culture. No doubt I wondered whether the 1964 events would finally open the threatened long-term revolution that so many believed should have happened without interruption soon after the Civil War in conformance with the passage of the Thirteenth, Fourteenth, and Fifteenth constitutional amendments, meant to ensure the economic, social, governmental, and racial freedoms for African-Americans in the South. Alas, these consequential, constitutional steps didn't impact blacks in the region the way that had been anticipated. Would freedoms flower for African-Americans this time along the Mississippi River Delta, a place I then still called home?

Should I continue to observe from afar in Cambridge, Massachusetts or encounter for myself a turn to the other side of history that Freedom Summer presaged? Looking back over time, I don't think I had a choice—an option didn't actually exist. Subsequent to the summer of 1964, I often wondered why the judgment to return to the South at the close of that summer drove me so formidably, naturally, and irrevocably. An Arkansan I respect proposed, attempting to characterize the rationale for my decisions and conduct during this historic period, "to my way of thinking, Chester, you seemed more interested in pursuing an education than a degree."

For over three and a half years, I returned to live in the South, but in an increasingly different white South, one that constantly felt itself under growing and unsympathetic threats on manifold sides, a white South that recognized its many vulnerabilities but did not have an inkling how to combat or address them except through either outright surrender, which was unlikely and not part of the white South's DNA, or perilous anger that frequently translated into unencumbered demagoguery and violence, the residual legacy of the region's damaged heritage.

My mother had purchased a small Plymouth Valiant for me to trek back and forth between Cambridge and southeast Arkansas, but I would now employ it to travel roads, byways, and highways to towns and cities in the region of the South, hearing reactions to Freedom Summer, the incipient Racial Revolution, and how both blacks and whites responded to the historical dictates that a people, African-Americans, would now be free, even in the American South with its codified Jim Crow regimens and habituations. I worked at a carpet mill and at organizing periodic pulpwood, hardwood, and pine timber cuttings off the family's tree farm. Now and then, I attended classes at the University of Arkansas until I accumulated enough course work, together with my Harvard credits, to graduate.

Notwithstanding the seemingly hodge-podge nature of the exploration, I now conclude that this period probably constituted one of the most, if not the most, important and formative times of my life. While painful and uncertain to be sure, I learned about individual and societal adaption and reconciliation and forces affecting racial accord and discord I may not have acquired in any other way. It was filled with a multitude of challenges and storms, a journey that many friends and family members did not understand or condone, a journey that eventually took its course change for north toward home, to New York City.

On occasion, I've used the phrase in this book, "north toward home," the title of the book by Willie Morris.[1] However, I'm using the phrase differently than he did. North toward home has meant for me the time spent and objectivity procured in the Northeast and especially New York City to formulate and express, in my own remembered context, the racial turmoil and struggles that existed for the region of my ancestry and blood lines, which are unalterable and with me always. That past I inherited informs and continues to shape parts of me. Nevertheless, it does not lessen the force I see as an obligation to examine and thereafter describe my own individual propositions on a region of the nation that has uniquely suffered, a suffering of its own making, yes, but a suffering also from external defeat, international economic dynamics, and conducive soil over which the region's races have had little control. I faced the fact decades ago that this individual view, my individual view, could happen, blossom, and be harvested only outside the place of my birth and breeding, a place I cannot deny nor from which I can fully distance myself; for so much of what I've had to say about these matters embodies my own journey of "north toward home."

My attention to race during those years back in the South after Freedom Summer ultimately evolved into a series of compositions on elements of the subject, both in expository and poetic forms. Several of these pieces are now contained in the J. Chester Johnson Collection at the Civil Rights Archives of Queens College in New York City, which is the alma mater of Andrew Goodman, one of the three civil rights workers martyred by white supremacists near Philadelphia, Mississippi at the beginning of Freedom Summer.

Growing up in southeast Arkansas, I often heard the expression, "Thank God for Mississippi"; otherwise, Arkansas could have ended up at the bottom of a national list for various economic, educational, or other rankings and indices. While a page in Congress and a student at Harvard, it occurred to me that there was a sort of "Thank God for the South" syndrome on race for much of the rest of the country as the egregiously overt racism in the South allowed other white Americans to point at the region with a sort of "tsk, tsk" for its flagrant acts of racism, relieving those white

Americans outside the South from fully examining their own manifest or more subtle, but often no less acute, expressions of racism within their own front—and backyards—a sort of deflection from home sins that temporarily succeeded. We learned in the decades following Freedom Summer that finger pointing at the white South concealed more than enough racist traditions and practices outside of Dixie. With this pandemic thought in mind, I should emphasize that while many of the comments appearing in this book are aimed specifically at white Southerners, of which I am one, an extrapolation of even modest proportion of my words is apropos beyond the contours of the white South to those towns and sections of the country that not only sympathize with the white South but have also conducted their own special brands of racism.

Leaving Harvard after Freedom Summer, I initially based myself in Monticello, though I traveled extensively, mostly through the South but not exclusively. I traversed beyond as well—west to California and Arizona, north to Chicago and Kansas City, east to Washington, D. C. and more. I lodged with family, friends of family, and friends while occasionally sleeping in my Plymouth Valiant, which I had, by then, dubbed "Little Car," for after a time, a name of affection appeared to be completely suitable as the machine became my sole companion for my indefinite pilgrimage. It's an anthropomorphic transcendence the way an inanimate object can appropriate, through our own mythical projections, human traits and a personality in circumstances when friends and family are no longer present. The South was my destination, but not as a defined, final location, but rather as a circumstance for recognizable behavior where a place simply becomes part of the message. Of course, a hamlet, town, or city would have their coordinates on a map, but the place contained more of what I truly sought—its attributes, a character, a speech, a context, even an army and weaponry, that were well-hidden until piqued or pricked.

I knew what I was looking for, and I knew where to find it without a dot on a map or a sign on a highway. It would simply appear, this South, these shades of the South that Little Car and I longed to uncover, which we also feared, but which also feared us, a native son now always suspicious with an undevoted and completely suspended obeisance to the white South's damaged heritage. The South was my destination, but the country also served as a reference point against which I explored the subject of racial conduct and the prospects for racial freedom in its various and protean expressions.

A brand-new Civil War had emerged for Southern whites. Whether it emanated mostly with Freedom Summer or earlier with *Brown v. Board of Education* or from the savage mutilation and murder of Emmett Till, no one could really know. Still, another invasion of the region had taken hold.

The South was different and the South knew it; the white South cherished its distinctions, for many a white Southern family was, for generations, unapologetically racist in each aspect of daily life even, if not especially, following the prior invasion during the first Civil War. The new aggression during Freedom Summer had all the earmarks of the first one a century earlier: to the white Southerner, the armies looked different, and the armaments were different, but it was a seismic invasion nonetheless.

The South was different; certainly, the white South was different. It had been that part of the Union which was a little less part of the Union than the rest. By custom, the white South's loyalty to nationalism consisted of its desire for national agendas that fostered regionalism or promoted a national laissez-faire attitude for local control to facilitate the continuity of racism with white Southerners doing more as they pleased. The white South relied on that separation from the rest to justify itself and its traditions; the region carved out its own versions culturally, economically, even linguistically, and most assuredly, racially—that is what the white Southerner knew in his or her soul and had known for generations, and the white South's desire for this separation bred exponentially whenever invasions befell Dixie.

Of course, not all white Southerners or white people living in the white South could fit the broad references contained here. However, this characterization depicts the dominant culture in the white South, and persons representing that culture are white Southerners. To put a finer touch to it, the white South and white Southerners would have been those who elected Orval Faubus, Ross Barnett, George Wallace, Lester Maddox and who would have supported the white citizens' councils or who thought Martin Luther King Jr. was moving too fast or who believed in private, white educational institutions to circumvent court-ordered integration. More particularly, the white South nurtured, directly and indirectly, by various ways and efforts a culture of white supremacy and the inequality of African-Americans.

The incursions against white Southerners had now taken many forms. First, if not foremost, schools: *Brown v. Board of Education* in 1954, integration of Little Rock Central High School in 1957, and James Meredith's enrollment at Ole Miss in 1962. There were attacks from national spotlights: Emmett Till in 1955, Birmingham in 1963, The March on Washington in 1963 with King's rhetorical assaults on the South; and the intrusions on Southern culture and norms were felt to be severe: the Montgomery Bus Boycott of 1955–56, the lunch counter sit-ins of 1960, and the Freedom Rides of 1961. Most apparent of all: support for integration from the Federal Government by prevailing administrations or the U.S. Supreme Court, singling out the South. And then Freedom Summer of 1964, as each state in the region focused on Mississippi, for every Southern state acknowledged its own impotence to various forays suffered by the Magnolia State: a national focus on the assailment by Northerners against Mississippi, the ridicule of Southern ways with Southern blacks and Northern whites mixing socially, the promotion of black activism through African-American voter expansion, the establishment of Freedom Schools, the protection of blacks through Federal investigations, and the unearthing of the bodies of James Chaney, Andrew Goodman, and Michael Schwerner. The white Southerner watched as all the instruments for the invasion were borne on the back of the State of Mississippi, which made Freedom Summer a magnified storm against the entire white Southern population and the wider Southern way of life—with the Civil Rights Act in July, 1964, conveying its additive insult.

A second Civil War had come, and coincidentally this war transpired one hundred years following the first. Within the region for the centennial, white Southerners went to suffusive lengths to commemorate the glories and perceived integrities associated with the great cause of the first Civil War: keeping African-Americans subjugated. All kinds of acclamations and memorials sprung forth throughout the regional lands, saluting this battle and that skirmish, this burial ground and that encampment. But many white Southerners in the 1960s had been seriously peeved and incensed by an epigrammatic expression that circulated at the time, composed, at least in the minds of white Southerners, by some blasphemous Northerner that "the North may have won the Civil War, but the South won the centennial." The terseness and eloquence of this sarcastic witticism obviously tore at many a white Southerner's deep sense of traditional honor and respect for "the great cause."

Still, judged from the long span of history, it is, in so many ways, striking, amazing even, that white Southerners had been so successful for so many generations in keeping black Southerners in subjugation, considering the nation's underlying testimonies and articulations for individual liberty and personal freedoms. This assertion is doubly striking when the relatively small population of white Southerners is factored into the equation. How did this modest number of persons hold the nation at bay for so long, even into the twenty-first century, on such an important political and socially determinative issue for the national image and self-identification.

The practices of the white Southerner in the subjugation of blacks survived while outside pressures for change remained. Paradoxically, extrinsic contempt created a firmer solidity and stubbornness that made this regionalism even more definite and enduring.

The South, as codified by the white Southerner, has been more into itself than it has been into the rest of the country, reflective of its obsession with national college football championships, its adoration of beauty pageants, its special food, its remarkable and mostly endemic music, its prideful dialect, adulation if not deification of its white writers like Faulkner, Welty, O'Connor, the Percys, Capote, Harper Lee, Robert Penn Warren, among others. Not so revered by the white Southerner have been black writers from the region such as Eldridge Cleaver and Richard Wright.

Part of the regionalism and insularity, which exist even to this day, results from a conviction that much of the rest of the country did not appreciate white Southern ways notwithstanding the deeply cultivated timbre many white Southern writers put on those manners and ways. This non-acceptance and often contempt the white Southerner felt from certain other Americans magnified a defensiveness the white Southerner often learned to turn to his and her advantage from generation to generation. And yet, "Why do people live there?" became an age-old question for which an answer was not always immediately available. Of course, a racially privileged social and economic structure has more than several attractions for those benefitted, enough for many to cherish residence there.

Within a few years following Freedom Summer, Richard M. Nixon exploited a political opportunity to harvest white Southern votes for the Republican Party through a strategy that leveraged the region's racism, fundamentalist religions, and conservative policies to inure to his benefit and for future Republican politicians, who maintained the strategy with some variation from time to time. The strategy gave respect to the white Southerner, and that respect compounded a Republican hold on the solid South. In fact, many would say it has all gone too far and too long. One can surely now make an argument that this strategy, first formulated by Nixon and endorsed with little qualification by Republicans then and later, and even further inculcated by Trumpism, has over time actually come to mean much of Republicanism with its own not-too-subtle racism, its exclusionary, nativist tendencies, and its wide and various attempts at voter suppression, having their very roots in white Southern political practices. Indeed, Republicans from the rest of the country frequently looked south for guidance. Over time, the white Southern mouse ate the elephant.

So much to be repudiated and dismissed by the white South coalesced in the Freedom Summer moment; "nerve-racking" for many, the white Southerner was now convinced that the "new day" exalted characteristics reminiscent of the frightful history of a hundred years earlier. The Republican Party's southern strategy relied on this fear for anticipated real and imagined adjustments to a preferred style of life. For some white Southerners, a recollection of Reconstruction had even been evoked.

Freedom Summer held firmly to its Northern mission, joining the phalanx of individuals who assaulted Mississippi's social and racial fabric. Some have called this nexus the fulcrum or lever of the Civil Rights Movement, for the combination of the maneuvers set much of an activist nation against the white South, and the ramifications would be felt for another fifty years. Freedom Summer illuminated and foretold unprecedented change for the region, change I recognized then to be inevitable, but change that, for some very explicable reasons, most white Southerners were in no frame of mind to make. Even at that age, I realized in every ounce of my bones that this was a revolution, a second Civil War, if you will, that the white South could not prevent, and yet, in so many respects, the white South would not, could not apprehend that inevitability, that justified inevitability. Little did they know or expect that very shortly, they would be dealing with the greatest codification of emancipative legislation and administrative procedures for the actual freeing of African-Americans since the advent of slavery.

Within a few years, the South saw its local public school systems integrated. Moreover, the country witnessed, after the Selma march to Montgomery, the protection of the blacks' right to vote, which would have considerable influence, especially in places where blacks matched or outnumbered whites. Fair housing, an aggressive affirmative action initiative to make up for past grievances, and equal employment opportunities, among other programs, became realities. To confirm that these inordinate legislative and administrative efforts weren't frittered away, an elaborate enforcement system by the federal government came into existence to protect the interests and rights of African-Americans. Most of these actions were specifically targeted with the white South in mind.

Even before King's murder, the course had seemingly begun in recent years to consolidate gains achieved earlier during the 1960s. While the Federal Fair Housing Act of 1968 was enacted on April 11, 1968, a week after MLK's assassination, much happened even earlier to be solidified during the last half of the 1960s. In southeast Arkansas, SNCC, which entered that part of the State around 1962 to lead voter registration drives among African-Americans in places like West Helena, Pine Bluff, and other communities where especially active leadership existed, left southeast Arkansas after 1967.[2] Monticello apparently didn't have the organizational infrastructure or wasn't a prime target for black voter registration. For some places in the Arkansas Delta, SNCC achieved considerable success, increasing local black voter rolls by a large percentage. It should not be surprising though that SNCC chose to concentrate efforts in that region of Arkansas since the social and economic demography of southeast Arkansas, in many ways, constituted an approximate, mirror image of the areas just across the Great Muddy in Mississippi, where Freedom Summer had concentrated many of its goals. When I began to teach at Drew School, SNCC had already pulled up stakes in Arkansas.

Time rolled forward, and the days resembling the past were numbered. Nothing could stop the rolling forward of the inevitability, and yet, I still sensed that the revolution would occur like trench warfare, an inch by inch territorial, jurisdictional, legal struggle, a struggle that still has not ended. Periodically, even after all the savage history that Southern racism produced, the struggle still, from time to time, reverted back to earlier, more brutal periods. We always knew, but we now recognize with more transparency that the vehement white Southern racism gave voice to other Americans outside the South who felt likewise and who would behave, often in concert with the South, in acting out those views.

Traveling through the South after Freedom Summer, I kept passing through towns resembling the towns I had just visited. The similarities were astonishing—an aged similarity with a related conclusion that if life itself were to remain like earlier lives of previous generations—and the social and racial milieus had a sort of mandatory relevance to stay as they had been for generations, then, of course, why shouldn't the towns look much like the past, aged and reflective of the preferred history? Why can't one construe that the racial codes and strata system dictated such adherence and held that all would be sort of frozen in deference to one supremacy? For if a town's energy and priority were preponderantly dedicated to the single measure of keeping one race dominant and of subjugating another, then little else could prevail to inspirit innovation and the future.

At this point, I discovered an aspect that arose as part of the threat from the Civil Rights Movement that puzzled me. Many white Southern families fractured over the matter of black liberation, and I struggled to formulate a fully encompassing reason. Family members proffer diverging points of view all the time, so why did this topic create such a dividing line that if one or another family member crossed it, that part of the family often broke off from the other? One clue to this otherwise imponderable conundrum resides with the composition of one's own image. If someone has decided that her or his own definition of selfhood includes race as a principal element setting her or him apart in a beneficial way from a member of another race, then I get an inkling of a divide by that person from a family member who has determined race to be less pertinent to her or his membership within the larger human community.

White Southern families that split around this time or even later, including my own, centered on the criticality of race as a differentiating factor in the worth and non-worth of another human being. The distinctions in the way two individuals view this fundamental matter, especially those of the same family, are hard to resolve as all related relevancies are then brought to bear: why people choose the lifestyles they do, love the people they do, admire the people they do, defend the people they do.

During this time, a number of Southern blacks described to me their preference for the appellation "black" (and a little later, "African-American"). The rationale went like this. The category of race in which blacks fell had been, over the centuries, "negro," a European word of Latinized derivation. However, the dialect employed by white Southerners routinely pronounced "negro" as "negra," which can quickly, through an intermittent stage or two, descend into the most offensive term, the pejorative "n" word. I often thought of these conversations with blacks when I passed a table or two of white Southerners venting their anger at the prospective changes through a growing and louder use of the pejorative "n." It seemed that as the threat of expanded liberties for African-Americans manifested itself, many white Southerners reacted with a more prodigious employment of the "n" word, representing a sort of retaliatory weapon that could be launched toward blacks who were known to be offended by it. Not only did I hear a more regular use of the pejorative among whites, I heard it repeated more often within earshot of blacks as well.

Late on June 21, 1964, the day that Andrew Goodman arrived in Mississippi as one of the Northern students participating in Freedom Summer, he, James Chaney, and Michael Schwerner were murdered. The manner by which James Chaney, a 21-year-old black Mississippian, was killed differed from the deaths of Goodman and Schwerner who were white and who received close range gunshots. While Chaney had been shot, his skull was also crushed. Over time, I decided that this contrastive and particularly savage treatment of Chaney had its idiosyncratic and perverse reason. Of course, the additional, special violence meted out to James Chaney could be simply a demonstration of the flagrant anger that those white Southerners held for black Mississippians, especially those who aligned themselves with Northern students engaging in the summer invasion. On the other hand, one can imagine the high dudgeon those white supremacists harbored for the white students, Goodman and Schwerner, who were set on amending the racial fabric of Mississippi.

Rather, I decided that those who murdered the three civil rights workers meant to send a message, a singularly harsh message, to black Mississippians, a message that echoed the fiendish manner Emmett Till had also been murdered outside Money, Mississippi nearly a decade earlier. Till, only fourteen at the time, was also shot, but first was brutalized callously and mercilessly by having his skull crushed, apparently through repeated blows, probably with the butt handle of a pistol, before being shot.[3] I do not believe that the parallel way these two young African-Americans, Till and Chaney, died was coincidental or accidental, for the similarity meant to convey a message and a warning.

In small towns, blacks had always shared with each other bits of knowledge and experience about racist firebrands to be avoided. And now, following Freedom Summer, the caution would be redoubled for African-Americans to give local "peckerwoods" a lot of space and to try to stay away from confronting them. Blacks and whites together recognized the peckerwoods, those of the same ilk that tore fourteen-year old Emmett Till apart before shooting him and those who murdered Chaney, Goodman, and Schwerner. Most every small town in the South had their peckerwoods, the pitiless whites, who seemed to be authorized to enforce violently, if necessary, racial codes and who always seemed, especially to blacks, to be on some kind of prowl. Southern blacks now had real and special incentives for walking on the other side of the street from a gathering of peckerwoods and for letting them take a favored parking space, as white law enforcement officers in small Southern towns often gave peckerwoods a long leash from the law. With blacks threatening advancement everywhere in the South, peckerwoods had reason to lash out at close reminders of those threats. So, blacks woke up cautious and slept cautiously.

Once I started the extension in travel and observation following Freedom Summer, it seemed that black-white relations in places I knew from preceding years had been altered, probably forever. A different prism had been put in place, one unfamiliar to both sides in many and obvious respects. The daily human windings between the races were careful, especially for

Southern blacks, who questioned how the news items on civil rights that occupied a segment on television every night would be received by white employers for domestic black help or by white employers for any black help, for that matter. Southern whites then had reason to wonder whether they recognized the actual attitude of black employees or the dissimilarities, if any, which existed between those publicly touting massive adjustments in the Southern way of life and those African-Americans who had come to work at the same place every day for years. Because the answers to those questions were not readily apparent, doubts and lack of assurance crept more into black-white relations that carried a new kind of mounting edginess; of course, a certain degree of edginess had always been there, but this was quite different. During these years, white Southerners were also much interested in what was being said and preached at local black churches.

In some towns and more populated communities, blacks felt emboldened to press on with their own liberation agendas for electing candidates who proposed more equitable treatment of African-Americans, for accelerating school desegregation, and for progressing toward better black employment opportunities in cafés, stores, and other commercial establishments. In southeast Arkansas, for instance, SNCC set up operations to maintain pressure for the implementation of changes that were seen as available or would soon be available as part of the civil rights agenda. Here and there, Ku Klux Klan chapters or ad hoc groups of revanchist whites took aim at black activists through menacing intimidation or worse.

White police officers scrutinized license plates more intently now, particularly out-of-state ones. Routinely, automobiles with out-of-state plates would be pulled over for no reason at all by police who inquired about the purpose of those occupants being in the jurisdiction. Depending on the whims of the police, more extensive interrogations were conducted on the side of the road or, less frequently, at the local police station. Suspicions reigned supreme in much of the white South. They were in the air people breathed. Folks who had known me for the better part of my life behaved differently toward me, and being treated that way, I presume I behaved differently toward them.

History gave the white Southerner the life he or she claimed, but the present was in rebellion against that history—rather, the present and, in conjunction with it, the future had declared war against that history. Those who sided with history could not afford to be less than fully vigilant against the agents of change. For so many white Southerners, myths and inherited lore assumed an influence the present just could not match, so that those whites, especially those located in counties or parishes where the black population rivaled or exceeded that of whites, openly feared a return to the semblable time of Reconstruction when blacks enjoyed the power to hold public office in Southern states. What would that mean for Little Johnnie or Little Susie wondered white parents and grandparents? What would it mean for the family business? How could whites trust African-Americans who received control of the levers of power? Do whites move? Where? Do they go North or West? How? Resistance at all costs was the only answer.

A steadfast commitment to no change; that had to be the code of honor. The white Southerner would fulfill his or her commitment to tradition and history by being dug in. No adjustment at all without a fight to the end. Grudgingly. At the same time, white Southerners began to challenge themselves with these thoughts and questions: How in the world did we allow this Civil Rights Movement to happen in the first place? It was solidarity that helped protect our way of life for so long. How did we betray the cause? Was it our loss of commitment that let the inherited system slip away? We just didn't pay attention as our forebears had for generations to keep the blacks under our thumb, under our control. Violence and commonality of purpose and focus were inspired ingredients to the long survival of this legacy, passed along with an obligation attached.

This self-incriminating interpretation did not account for the many legal suits that percolated through and altered the justice system over several decades: *Moore v. Dempsey, Powell v. Alabama, Brown v. Board of Education*, etc. This self-incriminating castigation also understated the passion and ability of African-Americans to gain, to obtain more influence over their own lives. The white South had presumed for a very long time that its passion to keep blacks denigrated and in chains (hardly metaphorically speaking) somehow transcended the passion of a condemned people, once envisioning the advent of freedom for themselves and their children. In other words, those who had been condemned can normally draw on a special courage to challenge a sordid and illegitimate system by seeing on the horizon, possibly for the very first time, realistic prospects for liberation from a racist system. Maybe, that inspirited courage now proved to be the decisive difference between the white South and the black South. This passion was not new, of course, and we should remind ourselves of its prowess today as our country, at the beginning of the third decade of the twenty-first century, faces a plethora of challenges, many of which suggest that the denial of freedom and opportunity can somehow win out over that passion which counts on the human manifestation of exactly the opposite proposition.

The South receives the tag of "Bible Belt" as a result of the perception that the region condones an avowed fundamentalism and greater literal adherence to biblical scripture. Indeed, white Southerners frequently cited Bible text to justify separation of the races, notwithstanding the fact that the human being is only one species and has become, over the years since the human stood and walked, a thorough amalgamation of those humans who associated with other humans, regardless of skin color.

Historically speaking, the white churches in the South, more often than not, generally spoke the preferred voice of segregation. Reared on the cusp of the Mississippi River Delta in the 1950s and early 1960s, I didn't hear a lot of sermons on race from the pulpit at the First Methodist Church in Monticello. Normally, sermons drew from the scripture readings, especially from the Bible's New Testament, and the ways one is expected to treat her or his neighbor, but with little concentration on who constituted our neighbor. The Little Rock Central High confrontation made many of us blossomed teenagers in Arkansas think more about our neighbors: who were they: also black or only white? I've told the story of how one minister in town at the First Presbyterian Church left soon after he decided to side with the proposition that blacks were also neighbors by agreeing to protect, in clerical garb, the Little Rock Nine as they were to enter Little Rock Central High School through a mob of whites trying to prevent educational integration by African-American students. We didn't hear that sermon in Monticello except by example from the Presbyterian minister, and I'm sure that sermon wasn't preached in a significant number of white churches throughout the "Bible Belt" South.

Soon after leaving for college, I found myself drifting away from the church as I had known it, an all-white institution which I had comfortably attended, an institution where I felt at home over the years of schooling in Monticello. Many, if not most, college students drift like that when left on their own to choose if, when, and where to attend church. Away from the direct and sub-rosa language and practices of Southern racism—on my own, as it were—I thought a lot about the question of "neighbor." Much in the newspapers and on television then propelled the nation to think about the question of "neighbor." I detected that the absence of that definition from my religious background, largely shaped in Monticello, left me more than a little at sea when it became obvious that African-Americans were also my neighbor—our neighbor. The absence of that component part from my past religious affiliation caused me to question the value of religion entirely. One could say that for a period of my life, the absence of a rightful definition of "neighbor" impelled me toward my own individualized form of agnosticism. At that time, I simply failed to recognize that the problem wasn't with the religion of the Judeo-Christian lessons I learned at the First Methodist Church; rather, it was the means by which those lessons were relayed. The institution had failed in its inclusion. Left to the lessons, "neighbor" would never, ever mean mainly white folks in the sanctuary and only other white folks throughout town. "Neighbor" would never, ever exclude African-Americans with whom we lived and breathed every day of our lives in Monticello. And yet, those in town who walked away from church every Sunday as Methodists, Baptists, and Presbyterians were left with that absent resolution.

The black church of the American South was not burdened by the narrow, if not vacant definition of "neighbor." It was not bequeathed that piece of damaged heritage, which weighed down the authenticity of churches serving the white South. Rather, "neighbor" included us all. The black church could be more legitimate in its interpretation of scripture, and that made the black church in the South stronger and certainly more germane.

I cannot divorce the Civil Rights Movement from its spiritual roots. If one listened closely, the speeches Martin Luther King, Jr. gave during those years were not speeches at all, but sermons. This comment alone reflects the influence the black church in the South had on the Movement. The black churches, sometimes even in small towns, seemed to be places fueling attention toward freedomland. Black churches were not only sites for the message; they were also physical fortresses for resistance and organization. Where did the "call to arms" occur for the Montgomery Bus Boycott, and in Selma, where did the victims of Bloody Sunday go for solace and strength? Where did the black activists and organizers convene in Birmingham from the mayhem of police dogs and fire hoses? Black churches.

While I underwent a period of agnosticism or indifference, if not downright periodic reproach, for religion and my own religious affiliation, the indomitable source of strength that the black church gifted to African-Americans in their remarkable struggles to break the shackles of racism also succeeded in wearing away the indifference and ennui I frequently felt toward spiritual matters and religion. This effect from the heavy reliance the black liberation movement placed on the black church empowered my own faith then and continues to support me even now. To have the courage exhibited by African-Americans to confront the palpable hatred and violence, combined with the power of codified legal and administrative structures existing against blacks in the South at that time, persuaded me to look at Judeo-Christian spirituality again. In a real way, the black church in the American South salvaged my Judeo-Christian beliefs.

The Civil Rights Movement of the 1950s and 1960s declared by civil disobedience and litigation that it was time for immense adjustments to our laws and ways, and for these purposes, the black church in the American South cleared the path. For those of us who witnessed complicity in racism by white Southern churches of numerous denominations at the very moment the Civil Rights Movement needed support from those churches, we white Southerners had irrefutable reasons to abandon those institutions. Yet, the black church with its message of courage to power and courage for purpose beyond one's self brought many white Americans back to the abundant message of the Judeo-Christian tradition.

I know so many American whites have great difficulty with expanding their scope of honest inclusion, affection, and love beyond "their own kind." Multiple white Christian churches go a long way to prove my point. I have long felt that churches are where people's hearts reside—that is, they are the places where comfortable social gatherings occur, for communal worship finds us at our most conspicuously vulnerable, and people desire to express themselves at worship services with a community of peers where most feel secure and less exposed or subject to external circumspection. And yet, such isolation and segregation run quite counter to the code of conduct Christian catechism would call for. With much personal experience to justify this conclusion, I surmise that most white Christian churches are only marginally more integrated today (and maybe, even less so) than they were during slavery. When one thinks in these terms with an eye toward both the past and the future, to arrive at this judgment is quite an indictment of countless white Christian churches, but I cannot see it any other way.

Following Freedom Summer and my return south, I occasionally attended my former church, but the areas garnering attention inside the church walls bore little connection to the contests and struggles occurring in the region outside the church walls. I never could quite decide whether there was an intentional strategy by that white church and other white churches to become a world apart, a sort of safe haven from the challenges that the Second Civil War, the Civil Rights Revolution, had thrust upon white Southern congregations. At the same time, I often wondered how the white church could recover from that time. This is not to say that a few Southern white clergy didn't step forward, but they weren't so numerous or so obvious as to alter a prevailing, broader view of, at best, demonstrated passivity by most Southern white churches toward racial subjugation or, at worst, active support for the continuity of racial inequalities.

When I returned to the South and Monticello following Freedom Summer, there was a man with whom I spent time and will call G.P. He was African-American and lived alone, just beyond and along the western boundary of our tree farm, south of Wilmar, the tiny hamlet west of Monticello. On occasion, as I walked over the farm and examined the condition of timber stands and seedling growth, the softwood pines, and the hardwoods that clung to a narrow stream winding its way through the trees, I would stop off to talk with G.P. at either the beginning or the end of my perambulations. I had known him a long time. If he happened to notice anything wrong on the farm, he'd notify Mother; for example, if adjacent landowners painted ownership lines on trees inside our boundaries, which happened now and then, G.P. informed us. He could get paid out of cutting proceeds for his scrutiny. I liked G.P. He must have been in his fifties then, but I didn't know and didn't have a reason to ask. We were friends and called each other by our first names.

During these inspections and occasional cuttings, I found myself stopping off regularly at G.P.'s home, built of large pieces of mostly hardwood and resting on numerous tree stumps that had been painted with a sealant and were lodged, to create a ballast, beneath the flooring of his house. At the beginning of my stopovers to talk with G.P., he discussed what he knew currently about our tree farm—where rotten trees had fallen inhibiting growth of smaller trees, and the like. On my return car trips here and there, I'd buy a bottle or two of liquor to share with G.P. on his porch with its makeshift chairs. He had regular odd jobs that put food on the table, although he also went hunting a lot for rabbits and squirrels, occasionally catching a deer unawares, which, cured and smoked, could feed him for a long spell. He'd walk into the hamlet of Wilmar a few days a week to talk with black friends and watch their television sets. G.P. loosely kept up with important news events; he could read and write to some extent, work with basic math, and was quite self-sufficient in a Thoreauian sort of way.

Even out in the woods, G.P. gathered the possibilities and personal uncertainties that faced blacks at that time. I never pressed the subject on him, but I occasionally asked him what he knew about the Civil Rights Movement and what he thought about it. At first he demurred, but as I dropped by more regularly, and we drank whiskey together more frequently, our conversations gravitated less awkwardly to the topic. From time to time, he raised it himself, having read a used newspaper or watched a television program at a friend's home.

G.P. lived a life surrounded by time, space, and human relations that cried out separation and segregation of a severe kind. It was all he had ever known. G.P. was almost as far removed from black activists in SNCC, CORE, or the SCLC as my life was removed from his. He sympathized with the goals of the Movement, and he readily admitted that opinion, but the tactics for getting there he felt he couldn't discuss. Now and then, G.P. accompanied me on day trips to Mississippi or elsewhere. We occasionally were joined by a young professor of literature from nearby Arkansas A&M College, later to become UAM (University of Arkansas at Monticello). I didn't pretend to know how often G.P. had been away from Wilmar.

Usually, G.P. and I traveled without the professor, and it gave us more of an opportunity to talk about the Movement, particularly what was happening in the region. I soon received a message that he feared the small places would be left out of the Movement or rather the results of the Movement. In other words, what could force the white folks in Wilmar to be fair with him or other blacks like him? Who and how can folks make sure that black children in places like Wilmar received the same opportunities as white children? The cities with their newspaper reporters and television and radio stations tell everyone what's what, but who actually cared about a bump in the road like Wilmar as the reporters and government officials sped from one large spot to another? He obviously had a point. The future ushered in Christian academies and private education institutions for many white children, bypassing associated public education systems and leaving public schools for African-Americans. These academies represented a more sophisticated and devious form of segregation. G.P. also feared that local whites could get meaner and more vengeful in small places like Monticello and Wilmar. G.P. remembered occurrences of white intimidation when blacks were expected to vote for certain candidates, and he worried that those episodes could get worse even if new laws went into effect.

Whenever I attended the University of Arkansas at its main campus in Fayetteville, located in the opposite corner of the state, I wouldn't see G.P. for months, but we always established ties quickly whenever I returned, even for brief visits. Once I had moved to New York City in 1968, the legacy of our friendship dissipated, and even when I returned to teach in the all African-American public school in Monticello following King's assassination, I saw G.P. much less. On occasion, I wondered over the years how G.P. coped in Wilmar after the anti-racism legislation and regulations went into their complete implementation. I wondered whether all the efforts and sacrifices by black activists had actually altered G.P.'s life for the better. Surely, future generations of African-Americans would extract a new and more acceptable life and benefits, but did G.P. notice any appreciable difference? Maybe, in fact, his fears about white vengeance were realized. Were his life and limitations so based in the separation and segregation of the races that his days rolled from one into another with regularity and uniformity and without change? Did Wilmar hold such an abiding inter-personal resonance for him that the Racial Revolution had largely swept by him, practically speaking, without one adjusted moment in his current and final days?

I thought of older African-Americans like G.P. who had difficulty imagining themselves with an advantage from the remarkable progressive prospects that future generations of blacks realized from the days' fertile contentions of the 1960s, and I despond at the loss, the magnitude of human loss, that our white damaged heritage caused innumerable blacks. What would we all be as a civilization if we whites had somehow not fallen heirs to or followed our damaged heritage? I began to appreciate that it was not enough for white folks to identify the damaged heritage of their ancestors; rather, it was critical that they establish a real difference between that past and their own actions—that was what could be done affirmatively in setting a juxtaposition to that past, that damaged heritage. Did the white Southerner envision herself or himself as someone like a character in a Faulkner novel or a person willing to accept a challenge from James Baldwin in his then recently (1963) published *The Fire Next Time*?

In Biblical fashion, the epoch of the Civil Rights Movement could not accommodate white moderation. Extremes were left to fight for, to capture the soul of the South. In fact, it was a treacherous time for white moderate opinion-makers who found fault with tactics on both sides, but who in turn were attacked by both sides—on the one hand, for being unduly compatible with blacks and their expansion of civil rights' measures, and on the other, for being part of the recalcitrant and demonic white past and for resisting progress in racial parity and immediate change. Events and initiatives ran over white Southern moderates like a transport truck barreling over road kill, for they enjoyed no vocal or proactive constituency. Temperate thinking and proposals bore no consequence and, more often than not, died immediately on the vine at conception.

As I followed my own nose through numerous peregrinations with Little Car, I let myself wander over some of the South's, the white South's traits. For instance, the physicality of the South and its racism had walked hand in hand through history. The rest of America had granted to the South the close connection that has existed between these two unmistakable features. This muscularity of the South has been prominently displayed in white Southern literature through characters like Popeye in Faulkner's *Sanctuary* or in James Dickey's poetry and in his popular novel, *Deliverance*.[4,5] The rest of the country often looked askance upon the South for its obsession with physicality, a quality many white Southerners felt comfortable exhibiting for all to see, ranging from racial beatings to football as a violent religion or to beauty pageants as an obverse reflection of the region's devotion to muscularity.

I ascribe the reason for this avowed bedevilment with the physical to the land, the soil of the South. Both Southern blacks and whites have articulated their own special attachments to the land there. One can, of course, say the love of land has been primordial, displayed over an endless array of cultures and places since the beginning of time, but it was mostly a different combination in the South at play. To the white Southern landowner, the land and black labor were joined; they were inseparable, and to work the land was, historically speaking, to work the blacks. Violence itself became part of the economic enterprise for many white planters—not for all, but for far too many. Also associated with this nexus between the land and the economics of physicality for the white Southern agrarian was the procreation by birth of slave assets, often through the white owners' own seed. So, a culture evolved out of Southern agrarian economics tying physicality, if not violent physicality, to the land. Part of the Southern damaged heritage claimed a comfort with physicality that other parts of the country did not experience nor absorb to a corresponding degree.

Violence sanctioned by and incorporated into an economic system takes on an authority and cultural acceptance for leisure, pleasure, and social contract purposes. The apparatus in support of the positive function of violence, as historically viewed by many white Southerners, meant the South would feel more aligned with physicality, even for casual expressions. This historic proclivity toward violence was employed for multiple generations to control blacks. So, why wouldn't violence again be applied during the Civil Rights Movement to attempt to do the same? Subtle and not-so-subtle threats of violence, spoken and unspoken, came at blacks generally and black activists more particularly during the Civil Rights Movement, stressing death and harm if African-Americans didn't stay in their accustomed place with visions of past brutalities permeating even random discussions about race. The Civil Rights Movement acknowledged that white Southern males simply wouldn't give up the use of violent threats, for why wouldn't white Southerners think their use could work again? The tactics needed to be a little different and applied a little differently—more public displays for a broader audience but at least as frightening.

At the same time, how can I explain the attachment by Southern African-Americans to the same land? Did they see the land as a venue for economic freedom? So many blacks desired with a passionate desire to own land there. I have heard blacks describe their attachment to Mississippi River Delta land as their own inheritance, if not economically, certainly culturally and even spiritually, for they had had multiple years and forebears tilling and toiling in the earth of Dixie. Not being black, I cannot readily explain this black devotion to Southern land, or the earnest wish to have land in the South to call their own. I would have thought their own histories on those lands were so bound with violence and the bloody earth that Southern blacks could hardly stand upon the ground for a second longer than necessary in order to leave it. Certainly, many people with the means and desire did. But clearly, I was wrong in my assessment of the attachment that breathed between many Southern blacks, who chose to remain, and Southern land.

A principle existed in the South that secrets should not be released, secrets of previous generations. The same year I left Harvard to go south after Freedom Summer, a new book, *Mississippi: The Closed Society*, by James W. Silver, a white professor at Ole Miss, caused a bit of a stir. While the doctrine of the book developed out of the Mississippi experience, the message would also be appropriate for the white South more generally. What occurred to me then and has continued to occupy my thoughts from time to time is the feature of the closed society that relies on secrecy, for the inference of secrecy dwells as an unavoidable part of the white South's orthodoxy and milieu. Information is controlled. What is communicated consists of only that information acceptable for communication, which supports or enhances the closed society's orthodoxy. Professor Silver put it this way: "Perhaps the greatest tragedy of the closed society is the refusal of its citizens to believe that there is any view other than the orthodox."[6]

The incentive to focus on the Silver book started with my accidental discovery in 2008 of the Elaine Race Massacre. Although this major onslaught against African-Americans happened only one county away from the county of my youth, I previously knew nothing of these murders of black sharecroppers and their family members. The Elaine example merely confirms the secrecy that prevails in a closed society and leads one to wonder how many murderous incidents have occurred, yet to be uncovered.

We do know that a benefit of the Civil Rights Movement that has slowly developed is the unmasking of pogroms, lynchings, and onslaughts previously assigned to oblivion or purgatorial history. Growing up in Monticello, I knew little or nothing of lynchings from the town's history, and there were no educational symposia, no acknowledgments, no tablets or markers unveiled about any of the six known lynchings.

A major piece of the white Southerners' damaged heritage meant the continuation of secrecy of past moments, such as the Elaine Race Massacre and other well-hidden lynchings. The Civil Rights Movement threatened an opening to that history, a divulging of multiple secrets spread over the region. More than one African-American has said that only God could possibly know the number of blacks murdered at the hands of white Southerners without ever being recorded or confirmed.

I wouldn't suggest that the prospect of disclosure of secrets or the threat of the elimination of secrecy, essential for a closed society, primarily drove the white Southerner's opposition to the Civil Rights Movement, but I do believe that part of the protection of the past which occupied the white Southerner did involve a desire for containment of secrets from previous generations, who participated in, instigated, or presided over racial crimes. As I contemplate previous revelations that came my way, I'm still somewhat amazed that my mother decided to convey to me Lonnie's involvement in the Massacre a number of years earlier when I had been only about thirteen. It may be that the integration of Little Rock Central High School in 1957 caused a lot of white parents in Arkansas to tell secrets they would have otherwise been averse to reveal.

❖

Although the South lost the capability to continue the institution of slavery, it did win the right to retain an immoral system for the subjugation of African-Americans. So, for a century following the first Civil War, the South had been victorious in its prolongation of an overt form of immorality. Why wouldn't there be confidence in the region that the white South could do it again in the face of the Civil Rights Movement? Life is far from perfect, and immorality prevails more often than we are prepared to admit, so the white South had reason to believe it could succeed with an extension of its racist system even if still judged to be immoral.

We have learned that morality carries with it a potent force. People do listen to its message and often follow a call to action for an exercise of moral principle against immoral adversity. Moral forces don't always win, but they do have the advantage of the higher ground. Nonetheless, the white South relied on its past to buoy its optimism that the Civil Rights Movement could be stopped, and if not stopped, its impact could be mitigated. After all, the white South played the long game: the African-Americans could win here and there with much fanfare, but when the noise and cheering stopped, it should be possible for the white South to get its way again, if not then, later.

But this time, it became more problematic for white Southerners to ride out the bumps. What tactically proved to be a difference in favor of the Movement when previously white Southerners found they could salvage situations to maintain white domination? One of the reasons deserving of further commentary embodies the combination of transparency and national, if not world attention. Wherever major developments materialized in the Civil Rights Movement, the electronic press was present, a phenomenon the white South despised. There were more than a few incidents where the electronic press faced attacks from peckerwoods and other Southern groups hostile to visibility. White Southerners recognized the power of transparency, which had an immediate, transformative effect; for the country and the world to witness firsthand on a television screen, virtually as they are happening, assaults by a white mob of law enforcement officers against defenseless women, children, and black activists in Selma, Alabama would be infinitely greater in impact than for someone just to read about the attacks in the next morning's newspaper. Moreover, it is infinitely more provocative to watch and hear Martin Luther King, Jr. pleading the case for black sanitation workers in Memphis, Tennessee than for someone to read an excerpt or two from a speech in the next newspaper edition. Although it took a long time for white Southerners to learn the lesson, it was far more problematic for them to be seen as patently cruel when only the lens of the world separated the perpetrators from a limitless audience. The white South abhorred this constantly visual exposure to its tactic of random and institutionalized violence that had worked so well in former times when such transparency was not so available to victims.

Even from the vantage point of a long perspective, we can seriously underestimate racism's influence. We have too often thought of racism primarily as being limited to individual, personal relationships, but when a culture decides that one race deserves to be superior to another, then its legal, professional, and organizational structures are shaped to accommodate that false belief in superiority. It seeps into everything and every moment and consumes preoccupation. At its rapacious worst, racism directs the personality of us as individuals and us as communities, and it saps the intelligence, verve, and potential of the society. Virtually every choice an individual and the associated society will make incorporates racial elements and will, more often than not, predetermine the outcome. Without realizing the effects, race occupies time and talents unconsciously, and the more racist cultures lose the most while the least commit less resources and useless pursuits to the topic, leaving assets, attention, and deliberations for more fertile endeavors. Towns fall to impoverishment from racism's influence, and individuals lose vision and opportunities to its simple and evil persuasions.

I often wondered why blacks, all blacks, didn't just leave the South en masse, particularly in connection with the Great Migration during the 1940s and beyond when mechanization in agriculture left little work and employment for African-Americans on the agrarian lands of the region. Unfortunately, many African-Americans constantly faced a Hobson's choice: to stay in the South with its normal and embedded racism, which was at least familiar, or to subject themselves to the harsh life of the North and West exemplified by such places as Harlem in New York City, the South Side in Chicago, or Watts in Los Angeles. Danger was always present in the towns and cities of the South, but was it as close and contagious as the drugs, prostitution, and criminal action that permeated African-American communities in so many cities of the North and West? Should one believe the characterization of urban black life portrayed in *The Fire Next Time* by James Baldwin or in *The Autobiography of Malcolm X*?[7, 8] The trappings of that life had not been exaggerated, based on the numerous children and grandchildren of African-Americans in Monticello who turned away from the black urban ghettos and told their stories in places like Monticello of the narrow options existing for blacks in urban confines where criminality lurked down the hall, on the steps of the stoop, at school, at work, with friends and enemies alike. So, parents frequently sent children back south to insulate them from those trappings, while other parents who ventured elsewhere braved the tough environments they and their offspring encountered.

Migrating from Arkansas in the 1950s, Sheila Walker settled in with her mother, Sara Black, and several siblings, but Sheila's affirmative life would stand in contrast to that of her two sisters who died from drugs, falling to the dangers in Chicago's African-American urban life. Yet, Sheila proved that a life well-lived could evolve out of those dangers through a will to conquer, combined with a courage to love and to work with others to lift the community at large, a goal instilled by Sheila's mother and a goal for which Sheila still labors daily.

Sheila believes that one of the reasons African-American families often sent children to the South from the North was for educational purposes. In her own case, for example, she did not have an African-American teacher in her Chicago schools until she reached the upper grades. Parents felt that black teachers in the South were preferred over the racism that white teachers frequently displayed overtly toward African-American students in places like Chicago. Indeed, only much later did teachers finally recognize Sheila's intelligence when she was assigned to honors classes at her integrated high school in Chicago.

Either choice—urban environments of the North and West or forthright, severe racism of the South—can numb the soul of child and parent; certainly, I had no right passing judgment either way.

At the time and even afterwards, I heard from African-Americans that the success of the Civil Rights Movement augured well for blacks remaining in the South, for the diaspora of black families then became less necessary. The blacks who voiced this belief relied on the proposition that established African-American higher educational institutions, combined with increased political power from black voting throughout the South, should meaningfully enhance black influence. Retrospectively, considering the solid conservatism of the solid South with the prodigious success of the Republican Party in the region among white Southerners, the anticipated exercise of major, pervasive black power in Dixie may have been a little too optimistic.

When I left Harvard toward the end of the summer of 1964, I went south for a learning experience as part of a broader and more personal understanding of the country's Racial Revolution. By the time I left Arkansas for New York City in early 1968, my views on both race and the liberation of African-Americans had crystallized more fully. I came back to the South after Freedom Summer mainly as a student although I had my inclinations and underlying suppositions. Still, to speak on the subject then would have probably been to posit a series of interrogatories about the situation and the black struggle. By 1968, as I left Arkansas, I had a firm grasp of myself in the context of race and the black liberation movement. In about eighteen months and after the murder of Martin Luther King, Jr., I returned once again to southeast Arkansas, but this time, I put my more congealed and codified views about race and black liberation to work by teaching, before integration of the local public education system, sixth through the twelfth grades at Drew School, the all African-American public school in Monticello.

7

DREW SCHOOL

O n Sunday, April 23, 2017, as soon as Sheila Walker and I completed our two presentations to the local community and wider audience and furnished answers to the plethora of questions posed at the "Reflections and Reconciliation" symposium in Phillips County, an African-American clergyman from Elaine, who had been constructively engaged in bringing insight about the Massacre to local residents, walked up and asked a question that startled me: "Chester, did you teach school in Monticello years ago?"

His question formed an instantaneous flashback of nearly fifty years when I returned to Monticello following the assassination of Martin Luther King, Jr., to teach in the all African-American public school. A world so distant in time: how could this man know about that moment in my life and my African-American students?

He continued: "I couldn't believe it. I was talking with my good friend, who is a clergyman in Jonesboro (Arkansas). I told him about this symposium you and Sheila were holding for local residents on racial reconciliation, and I mentioned your name. He said he knew you, but I told him he couldn't possibly know you since you live in New York City. But he argued that he knew it had to be the same Chester Johnson who taught at Drew School. He was very certain."

"Well, he is right. I did." America had a different slant on race then. So much had been accomplished between Till's vicious murder and King's murder; and while King's death created a pall over the Civil Rights Movement, most believers felt the pall to be temporary; rather, the mantle shall pass, and the push for black equality would continue apace. An hiatus may ensue briefly, but believers in black liberation would do what they could to honor King's memory and keep hope—and progress—alive.

Back then, cynicism and inertia had not yet threatened progress in racial equality. Nixon had been elected president, sure, and the Southern political strategy of Republicans had already begun in earnest with all its racist elements. Still, we thought we could continue to ride a wave of goodwill in the nation. Maybe, as some of us thought at the time, the efforts should be focused at the local level, and there was reason to think King's own credo may have orchestrated the Movement in that direction anyway. So, there I was then, again back in the stringently segregated Mississippi River Delta, but in 1969 I was on a mission to try to make things a little more right—both as social policy but also as an act or form of a kind of personal exorcism from the damaged heritage that was mine to address. It had been a time when folks truly believed we were in a period of worthwhile change and national atonement for past racism. We owed much of it to King. It was the least to be done. So, there I was, honoring King in Monticello, ensconced in Drew School with my students, ranging from the sixth through the twelfth grades; enthralled with the prospects, I still wasn't sure where that moment could lead.

The former student at Drew School, a black clergyman who lived in Jonesboro, was very sick; I talked with him three times by phone, each time briefly—the last time from his hospital bed. I can only hope he realized to the end that I meant to let him know he had always been part of my life—like him, though nearly fifty years had passed, I'd never forgotten my experiences and time there.

For the rest of our trip in April, 2017 to Phillips County, Sheila and her good friend, Barbara Love, who taught social justice education for decades at the University of Massachusetts in Amherst, Massachusetts and who grew up in Dumas, Arkansas, only a short distance from the Elaine Massacre site, listened to my soliloquies continuously, resulting from the astonishment I felt that one of the Drew School students also remembered.

The three of us flew into Memphis and traveled together to the county, driving down the Mississippi side of the Great Muddy until we crossed the bridge to Arkansas into Helena. We spent much of the next several days there in each other's company. Barbara and I shared stories of growing up in segregated southeast Arkansas—her from the African-American perspective and circumstances and mine as a white Southerner. Both Sheila and Barbara wanted to delve into the ways I had been treated by both the black and white communities when I taught at Drew School, and I tried to convey to them the remarkable tensions then present in both racial communities as they moved toward integration of the public schools, scheduled for the following year of 1970–71.

For the white community, I seemed to add just one more, sometimes unnerving, pressure to those it already felt on race, and for many blacks—students, parents, and fellow teachers—I represented a precursor to the following years when African-American students would be integrated with white students. I hoped to buffer the shock for black students as they were to be not actually integrated, but rather absorbed into the white school system.

While studying at the University of Arkansas in Fayetteville, I decided that at some point in the near-term future years, I would wish to teach in the field of secondary education, so I secured requisite course credits to do so. Initially, I projected this training to be manifested through VISTA, the domestic peace corps, but as chance or Providence chose, I ended up employing that part of my university course work—a license to teach—right where I came from: Monticello.

So, did I feel the need to come back to the campestral Mississippi River Delta after the assassination of Martin Luther King, Jr., to teach in an all

African-American school because a white man killed him? Not necessarily, for in a way, King himself probably would have thought such a gesture, on its face, had unnecessary racial overtones. And yet, I do feel that white Southerners should have sought redemption with King, who understood white Southerners needed forgiveness for their damaged heritage, which impelled them to continue that heritage into each and future generations. There was some of that gratitude for his forgiveness to which I felt an obligation as I again traveled south. I wanted to *do* something; King deserved white folks recognizing his legacy in a concrete way—with action—and striving for his legacy could and should mean a turn in history by whites.

King had been a vital part of my maturation process. From the time civil rights rose to be a conscious feature for my then young mind—from Montgomery in 1955 to Little Rock Central in 1957–58 when King attends the high school graduation for Ernest Green to Birmingham to the March on Washington to Selma, my teaching at Drew School seemed like something one does for an old friend, a mentor, someone who taught me a germane and special lesson that shall last a lifetime. The manner in which I viewed civil rights and racial equality could be traced in large part to him, and I owed King for this attitude. I needed to repay him. He also helped restore my Judeo-Christian faith which had largely slipped away; he demonstrated the courage emanating from that faith while I had been surrounded among Southern whites with a denial of human love for African-Americans.

King survived the terror of being driven through Southern backwoods by local law enforcement as he must have disquietly waited to die or be tortured and mutilated the way so many black men had been before him in the South, and yet he did not break or yield under the weight of terror. It was the character he exhibited that allowed me to regain my faith. King illustrated how faith could be put to action to achieve meaningful, progressive change, rooted in Judeo-Christian traditions, elevating African-Americans from their subjugation and, at the same time, releasing whites to be free of their extreme sin of commission. The whites' damaged heritage could be forgiven. Not only I, but all white Southerners owed him for that. And with this in mind, I entered the halls of Drew School for a formative year.

The remarkable thing was that, at the end of my time teaching there, Drew School would no longer exist. All the students and all the facilities would then be folded into the white school system. Even the vestiges of the black institution would immediately evaporate: the gold and blue colors and the moniker of the "Lions." Although the black populace, both general and student, had been substantial in numbers for towns along the Mississippi River Delta and in Monticello, the process for integration meant nothing short of absorption for the African-American students with the institutional white names, colors, and moniker remaining completely intact. The black students now became Billies in Monticello, as generations of white students had been, and also involuntarily assumed the colors of blue and white, as generations of white students had done in the past.

Of course, Monticello held other options for integration of the two schools at its disposal, such as merging white and gold (a color from each school) or starting from scratch with an entirely new moniker and set of colors. But I don't think African-American students anticipated anything other than absorption, which simply reflected another mechanism for subjugation of blacks in the community. But Monticello wasn't the only town to follow an approach of absorption at the time.

It did not take me long to appreciate that among the town's African-Americans, Drew School had become a source of pride, and for good reason. The blacks didn't have the options available to whites for physical improvements to school facilities; rather, for example, a prisoner-of-war camp had been located during World War II on the outskirts of Monticello, just outside the city limits, and at the conclusion of the war, camp buildings became available to the locality. The black community in Monticello then requested and obtained several of the POW buildings to add to the black school's corpus. According to the history which I received from black faculty at Drew, a large number of African-Americans in town organized a disassembling of several structures at the camp, hoisting pieces of buildings onto horse drawn and mule drawn wagons, and carting the segments to the location of Drew School where they were reassembled and adjusted to serve as additional facilities for black students. Thus, the complete disappearance of Drew School as an institution became its own form of negation of black achievement.

Drew School occupied a plot of land only about three blocks from the eastern end of East Shelton close to the house where I lived during my grammar (grade), junior, and high school years before departing for college. The one-level structure of the school where I taught was largely inconspicuous with its dull, off-greenish, gray exterior, which resembled and reflected its former use as a component of the prisoner-of-war camp. Being a short distance from my earlier, childhood address at 308 East Shelton, the school served as one of several reminders of my previous days in that part of town. Largely invisible from the main road, which passed some thirty to forty yards in front of Drew, were also a couple of trailers situated immediately behind the single building and employed to supplement fixed class space.

Unlike the white school, which fielded football, basketball, track, and tennis teams at the time, Drew School had only a basketball team, but each home game constituted a community event for the town's black population. Home basketball games for the white school, as I, when a "Billie," recalled them, were also a community event, but for Monticello blacks, these games were different, for the African-Americans now had far fewer opportunities to cheer their "Lions" to victory, as the town's blacks realized that the 1969–70 year was the very last season African-Americans could come together in celebration for themselves, their children, their school, their Drew School, at a gold and blue, "Lions" game. I found the enthusiasm at cheers notably high in volume, pitch, and intensity at any scores by the Drew team. I occasionally wondered if I emphasized too much the possible effects of the coming absorption of Drew School into the white school and its traditions. Maybe, the fervor I found at these basketball games was normal and comparably repetitive of the passion shown in former times. Had this commitment to Drew teams been so routinized previously that what I observed now was no different? How could I ever know one way or another? It was their world, and I was a sojourner.

I predicted during my tenure at Drew that to chaperone bus trips for "away" basketball games shall persist for me, in later years, as a highlight to remember. As soon as students, players, and cheerleaders boarded the bus for the destination to another African-American school somewhere in southeast Arkansas, electricity struck the receptive interior. Virtually for the entire ride to McGehee, Dumas, Dermott or to some other regional town, unending and well-rehearsed cheers, along with associated systolic pounding of feet against the floorboard of the bus kept excitement astir, and the cadential noise procession, without a break in decibel, rolled right into the gymnasium of the school that we, Drew High Lions, were visiting. Of course, none of these games were reported upon by local area-wide newspapers or other outlets; only the African-Americans were aware of the pending competition between the black public schools on the basketball court, but the unheralded nature of the events seemed to increase the devotion and fun on both sides. I always luxuriated in the home games too, but the away games were replete with sparkling, galvanic anticipation during the ride to a neighboring black community.

Maybe, my students eagerly awaited giving up Drew School to prove themselves, on an equal footing, with whites. Maybe, my students preferred the absorption by the white schools on white terms so that no one could ever second-guess black accomplishments when they occurred as a Monticello "Billie" in blue and white. However, based on many pertinent classroom conversations, the whole constellation of black responses was complex, and for some, they still preferred Drew School; yet, for others, they wished to look at white Monticellonians and not blink. Many years later, former black students decided to celebrate their beloved place of education, which then no longer existed, by holding a demonstrative parade through Monticello in remembrance of Drew School, the "Lions," all in resplendent blue and gold colors. I could only imagine the potency of emotion and multitude of recollections the black participants experienced during the celebration.

Especially for the lower grades I taught, a deep divide surfaced along a certain line, having nothing to do at all with intelligence or subject matter. Quite surprisingly, the divide fell between those who had lived their entire lives within the strictures, racial and otherwise, of Monticello and those who had resided for a time in other parts of the country. Some of my students had lived in St. Louis, Chicago, California, and elsewhere, and these students brought a more critical, worldly, and angry point of view to the classroom. The latter group was generally ready to oppose local, conventional thinking and codes, and they were also quicker to oppose authority figures, including yours truly. They had had less time to be "touched" by vicinal and prototypical protocol and responses.

The home-grown students repeatedly deferred to the emigrants who took more extreme views on issues raised in the classroom. Frequently, these emigrants to Monticello still had parents elsewhere and were shipped to southeast Arkansas to escape the temptations and dangers of urban America or to benefit from educational opportunities not available where too many distractions presented themselves. These emigrants represented educational resources for us all, as they generally weren't afraid of controversy. I had not anticipated the relevance of these students, who complained about white Southern words for people, places, and things, who opposed white schools, who felt they could walk anyplace in town at most any time as a black person, who voiced what their lives had been elsewhere, who occasionally appeared at the front door of my apartment simply to know how I lived, who sometimes even asked me embarrassing questions about my own set of white privileges. Now and then, the emigrants visited the places from where they had come and reported to us their impressions outside the world of Monticello.

Maybe, in those larger places, urban distractions for both student and parent were too much. Maybe, as Sheila Walker has opined, even for integrated schools in the North, racial bias against African-Americans was quite prevalent with fewer black teachers and less attention being paid to the array of black students. Maybe, also, the close-knit family environment for blacks in Monticello cultivated concentration by children on their studies.

A challenge regularly arose for me balancing the contributions between the two groups. While the most controversial, and frequently intentionally so, these emigrant students were frequently the least well-versed in their study preparations. As I now look back, I realize that one English class for eighth graders, consisting mainly of young males, haunted me. Even though this mostly male class was the most boisterous and presumably confident, these students were instead the most vulnerable, for they came to class the least ready with the weakest reading and writing skills. I routinely worried about their future opportunities with limited skills and with not-so-subtle anger.

On one occasion, I had this class work from a mimeographed sheet on spelling and writing names of friends and on completing words and sentences with letters missing. The whole class, twelve to fifteen students, were all at my desk in the center of the room, hanging off the side of my desk or hanging off me when the African-American principal came into the room. I momentarily panicked, thinking he disliked the apparent chaos, but instead he just looked at what they were doing, and before leaving, congratulated me on the engagement of these particular and, to me, special students. In later years, I wondered so often about these children whom I feared might adjust poorly to the broader, adult world outside their families and school.

It was the school year of 1969–70, a decade and a half after the torture and murder of fourteen-year-old Emmett Till. Reportedly, while being attacked by white supremacists, Emmett Till called out for his mother back home in Chicago.[1] And why not? After all, he was only a child, approximately the same age as the eighth-grade young men I taught and I worried over.

It is one thing to be a racist with all that it means to be a racist, but for the life of me, I cannot imagine how a group of men, some bordering on middle age, could take a fourteen year old boy, regardless of color, and do to him what Bryant, Milam, and their white companions did to Emmett Till that summer night in 1955. Timothy Tyson's 2017 book, *The Blood of Emmett Till*, brought that conundrum back with full force. How could anyone have stolen away with one of these eighth graders of approximately the same age and proceed to torture and mutilate him with aplomb? The act itself went beyond anger. Of course, young Till took a dare and may have spoken to Bryant's wife in a certain way, but at fourteen, what did any of his innocent, braggadocio words matter, if he had indeed uttered them? No, it wasn't anger that drove the death squad the night of August 28, 1955; no, it wasn't anger, for anger implies a reasonably rational form of proportionate justification; rather, the brutality toward Emmett Till can only be described as a demonstration of madness, an absence of balance or measure, the absence of a sense of value, the absence of anything remotely edging toward the genuinely human; it was simply an adherence and entrustment to madness.

As I read Tyson's account and returned, in my memory banks, to those eighth graders, I could almost literally see Emmett Till's face reflected in each of those male students' faces. But for the vagaries of time and distance, any one of those eighth graders was across the Great Muddy, the Mississippi River, near Money, Mississippi that summer night in 1955 when Bryant and Milam paid a visit to the home of Emmett's granduncle, Mose Wright, and absconded with the child into the metallic night of horrors. I wish I didn't occasionally dwell on this image and theoretical prospect, but Emmett Till and those eighth graders were bound like brothers in the panoramic visions I have of the land and history along the Mississippi River.

A variety of opinions and attitudes dwelled among my students about the benefits and tactics of the Civil Rights Movement. Some were barely conscious of the recent or even distant accomplishments forged for African-Americans. Then, there were others fully current on the status of the Movement who voiced concerns about the absence of King and who also held definite views about the prophetic legacy of Malcolm X. Admittedly, a scattering of other levels of knowledge and perspective fell among those positions.

Many of my students at Drew were ready and desired to embrace the challenges of the coming integration, the coming absorption, into the white schools. I often took mental bets with myself about how some of my students would fare in 1970–71 and afterwards. There were those for whom I had no worries at all and those I expected to struggle but ultimately graduate, and then there were those who could simply fall away from the process and be destined for menial jobs without even a completed high school education—these were the African-Americans to be used for comparison purposes by white racists arguing that integration simply didn't work, ever. Of course, whites making this argument normally failed to admit the associated point that approximately the same commensurate number of whites fell into the same category.

I wondered about the seniors in my afternoon history class, who missed the chance to execute their skills, both academic and athletic, in a wider venue. They knew how they had performed at Drew School, but what about their performance across town at the white school with its better facilities, broader choices, and opportunities? For years, these seniors may possibly debate with themselves the consequences of being one year older than those who faced the challenges now falling to the juniors, several of whom attended the same history class I taught.

This class of seniors would be the last to graduate from Drew School. They already asked out loud whether it was an honor or a patent reminder of loss, but they couldn't possibly hazard a solid answer to that question for years to come. Indeed, much later, they may be quizzed: what was it like attending an all-black public school with its African-American traditions, practices, and language away from the dominant effects of the prevailing white culture? Did blacks maintain the integrity of their past with more authority and truth inside Drew School than classes of African-Americans did under the fate of an integrated system that put white names, colors, moniker, and other white privileges above the placement of blacks? The year's senior class could not answer questions of that nature, for those students shall not have the knowledge to compare, yet they will have the benefit of transmitting the advantages that accrued to students in an all-black public school with unfortunately the abundance of recognized disadvantages as well: the below standard facilities, teaching materials, and dated information passed on to succeeding African-American students. The year's senior class would be able to impart those latter conclusions, both good and bad, but will those conclusions be enough for black students who had traveled through the deeper waters to the other side?

During the initial phase of my teaching, I think I was appreciably out of touch with my students, or at least it surely seemed that way. I relied on mimeographed lesson plans and texts. But very soon it occurred to me that in order to break down the mythologies of what blacks and whites felt about each other, I needed to do a lot more talking. Formality remained the deadliest of forces. By figuring out more immediate and less restricted ways of listening and talking to each other, we then had a better opportunity to penetrate preconceptions and routine stereotypes, another conduit as a learning experience for them and me. So, talking and listening were what I started to do within the parameters of the topics we studied—English and history.

Thereafter, I often ditched lesson plans. I wanted to know more about my students, so I told them more about me, relating that side to the subjects in which we were engaged. What had my life been like, even in Monticello? Where had I been? What books had I read and why? And how did all of that associate with the topics we studied and who my students were? I needed to be unembarrassedly myself by giving them the ability not only to talk about the subjects we were examining but also to talk to me as a white person who knew Monticello from a white vantage point. After all, the next year, most of my students would be inundated with everything white, and I could attempt to have them ease into that process right then and there in the classroom we shared. So, I began to talk and ask them to talk. Not chaotic talking but relating black and white literature, language, or history to my experience and to their experience with admittedly dissimilar recognition. Periodically, for my stronger classes, I had them write about themselves in the context of these discussions.

In many ways, the students and I were on a quest together. Could we make it? Could our goodwill make it happen? The school had become an agency for change to me—and hopefully for my students as well in their own ways. We were embarking on new paths of relating, of co-inhering, if you will, black and white; that's what I trusted we both wished to attain: a vision and quest in a strange land that in the past did not allow new ways of behaving or relating or embarking between the races, and yet here we were, and we were trying, undoubtedly trying, and in our own manner, succeeding, though we didn't know it or say so.

I heard from white friends that a rumor circulated among a group of whites that I was stirring up black students at Drew School. An attempt at inspiration, yes, but an attempt at "stirring up," hardly. And to what end? I heard the rumor repeated after a school-wide, parent-teacher meeting at Drew where I spoke.

The year had become a time to learn; for me to learn far more about the African-American community and the children of that community, and for those children to learn about whites, Southern white folks, from me, and to learn about me as a sort of passageway to that local white culture. How much would the town actually change once I observed it through the eyes of blacks, disclosed to me through the eyes of African-American children?

A phrase repeatedly floated in and out of my consciousness at various times during that year: I was there in part, in large part, to find those I'd known but not found. The phrase threw me back to the years I lived on East Shelton Street, only a few yards from East Jackson, just behind our family's home—my black friends who disappeared in a cloud of institutionalized racism and my black friends' families whom I barely recalled at all from the time I grew up on East Shelton Street. People I had known but hadn't found. There was a lot of motivation invoked from those earliest of days when I had fallen into the confines of Monticello, a town that increasingly became less innocent than I had wanted it to be, less innocent than the place I previously desired to be my home always, my refuge, but never again to be that anchor of comfort and peace I projected years ago. It could never contain that unrealistic dream again, certainly not after I discerned its place under the sun for driving me to the conclusion I had come here once more, but this time, I had done so to find those I had known but not found.

I visited black homes, and I now encountered limitless conversations with African-Americans of all ages, who remained cautious with me as they felt they should be with any white person, a wariness about whites that had virtually infiltrated the black DNA. Did I uncover from the black viewpoint an underbelly of Monticello translucently new and unadulterated? This was a question that could not be answered simply, for there were the overlays of inter-personal, black-white relationships of long-standing that played a critical part in any conclusions about these black views. At the time, I received the distinct impression from some African-Americans, especially older ones, that they actually accepted the proposition whites should be in charge. On the other hand, a schism manifested between some of the older blacks and younger ones, including many of my students, who believed and articulated that whites had for generations arrogantly relegated to themselves, as a result of tradition and, in my words, damaged heritage, that right to rule over African-Americans, for God had not made any such choice at all, but too many blacks just accepted white dominance without question and without reacting against history, traditions, economics, and politics. I decided that in an ironic twist, even in small towns of the South at the time, the schism, which often pitted in my generation a few white children against their parents, uncles, aunts, grandparents, and other whites, had a mirror image of similar behavior among numerous African-American families.

❖

He was a little younger than my brother and a little older than me. Later, he habitually visited with my mother when my brother and I were away. To him, Monticello could not be more of a home; he knew every white person in town, and every white person knew him. One could even call him a master of language that stayed at the surface; humor was natural like seasons, and he practiced, in every situation, to keep the monologue or dialogue going, whichever suited him at the time. I liked him, even if my interests and attitudes didn't reside closely to his favorites. He wanted Monticello to remain exactly as it had been, for it was a masterpiece, and so he committed himself to the status quo, the everlasting status quo. Monticello had everything he ever wanted or needed, regardless of his income or finances—he'd somehow make ends meet. In fact, he never thought much about money or budgets or a career: he was too busy being himself in the context of his beloved town and all the white townsfolk. He was acquainted with a number of African-Americans, but they were simply separate and apart; he never paid them much attention.

In late summer of 1969 when I arrived back in Monticello, he immediately came to welcome me home, to his hometown. He never once asked me why I had come back. I guess he assumed everyone wanted to return to his hometown; the question didn't need to be asked. He never mentioned anything about the Civil Rights Movement or its meaning for the future of Monticello. Of course, being who he was, African-Americans didn't matter much in his universe, as he followed the town's white code, including the occasional use of verbal pejoratives about blacks whenever he found them useful; from his persona nature with white folks, those words had presumably become part of his orthodox vernacular, although he didn't employ them much around me.

Since I infrequently, after a day of teaching, accompanied him on a drive somewhere, I did not find it unusual when he called one night and requested me to join him late the next afternoon. He offered no reason; he didn't need one. The next day, he explained there was a corral where several horses were being broken (meaning they could be ridden once tamed and trained by a steady and well-rehearsed hand), and he wanted to stop by for a while.

When we arrived at the enclosed corral several miles from Monticello, no horses were being broken. All I saw were several peckerwoods lounging about and sharing a couple of whiskey bottles. The leader of the pack, who also owned the corral and adjoining few acres, immediately started to harass me: why was I teaching at the n_____ school? Why did I want to improve the education for n_____s? What kind of a white person was I, anyway? He also declared he didn't like my hair, which wasn't very long, but for some reason offended him. He wanted to teach me a lesson. So, he came at me with bottle in hand and other peckerwoods at his flanks. Instantly, I knew my problem wasn't just the leader but consisted of the group as a whole.

As I retreated backward, our family "friend" for years just stood away, for he had successfully delivered me, and that's what he had been expected to do—to deliver me to be taught a lesson not to ever violate the local and regional codes: whites and blacks don't mix, and whites don't take deliberate steps, meaningful actions, to improve the lot or education of blacks. I had violated both, and I needed to be brought to task. An example should be advanced for the white community; no one violates the racial canons without paying dearly. The peckerwoods realized they were authorized to advance that point on behalf of other whites in town with similar ideas and inclinations.

Once they started to grab, a wall of a man, some seven years older than me, out of nowhere, like a holy specter, stepped in. To this day, I don't know where he had been or for how long or whether he had been there for the intimidation or not, but he simply stepped in front of the leader of the surge and stopped him; by intercepting the leader, he thwarted the others as well. This wall of a white man, a local football hero, who, only a few years previously, played center for one of the professional teams in the National Football League, could not be physically daunted by anyone in Monticello. I had watched him play football on television for years with some parochial and native pride, and I certainly didn't count him as a close friend, but here he was, positioned right in front of me, separating me from the phalanx and proclaiming clearly and unequivocally, "This is not going to happen," a phrase I remember without effort decades later with a decisive ring of deliverance, a ring of unrelenting and redemptive certitude. My deliverer proposed I leave the corral, and as I exited,

I discovered another white friend who just pulled up in a sedan, whom I asked to take me home.

At the time, I was naturally thrilled with the coincidences of the former football player rescuing me and another friend—a true friend—conveying me home. However, it then seemed all contrived and too pat. But as I surmised, several people in town heard of the planned attack and its timing, and these two friendly whites took an initiative to interfere, even if they were slightly late to the party. The person who delivered me to the peckerwoods always talked too much for his own good. Thank God for gossip and rumor in a small town.

After relaying this narrative, I've heard it said that I communicate the encounter with little emotion and little anger. If this be true, it's a function of the combination of two reactions on my part. First, the peckerwoods didn't shock or surprise me; they had a mission. I was simply in the wrong place at the wrong time, but I wasn't hurt, after all. Second, much more important was the intriguing response by the local football hero: what caused him to come to my defense? We weren't particularly good friends, and yet when confronted with the prospect of the attack, he rescued me. He, a homegrown, white son of Monticello. What caused him, in good conscience, to make the statement he did through his actions, a statement that would eventually be known by others in town? By far, that's the more crucial question, if not message.

The duration and termination of innocence are whimsical, unpredictable, and enigmatic. I commented earlier on the forces that, at times in years past, drove me to adore the town of Monticello; I was ensorcelled by the acceptance that fell my way there as part of my adolescence, the fast adoption of me by the white community as though I were a member with entitled family status. At points in my young life, I didn't dare dream of living out a life anyplace else. But later, as black liberation flowered into personal and doubtless persuasion, I sensed something else brewing in the cauldrons of the town's racism, the malignancy reflected in a variety of manifestations. What did Monticello have to say about the unfolding of six local lynchings, spread over several decades during the post–Civil War Era of 1868–1921? What was I to think as a teenager when the owner of a popular restaurant in town ran an African-American man, in obvious distress, asking for help, out into the street calling after him vicious and inexcusable names? What was I to think when the white community determined to impose, at the integration of the local public education system, by absorption, upon black students, the existing moniker, colors, school name, and more of the white school, rather than seek a fairer treatment and accommodation to cause the African-American students to feel more at home?

How could my captivation with the town from an earlier phase stay the same when a life-long friend gratuitously and intentionally set me up for an attack by a group of provincial peckerwoods whose sole mission was to teach me a lesson for being at Drew School, for showing concern and care for young African-Americans? The peckerwoods collectively could offer the assault against me to the white community as a token of the perpetrators' commitment to the principles, practices, and absolutism of white supremacy? Only a few months later the same former family friend attempted to execute a strategy to harm me again for my affinity and association with the town's black population.

The almost unqualified innocence with which I previously endowed Monticello had since departed with the causes for this perceived loss of innocence resting on matters of race. With the lack of a planned, true integration welcome to my students for the next school year of 1970–71, with the inability of the town to confront its past racist acts of lynchings, and with the rest that surfaced when one scratched the town's underbelly, an ambit of innocence became impossible and implausible. But it is not an easy process to redefine, to reinterpret the innocent into something else. Also, how far does one let the image slide into other territory and remain reasonable? One must be wary of the influence of disappointment, which can accelerate the slide into a new notion beyond its proper place. After all, since we often manufacture attributes of the innocent, we can commit the same error when we look at the same object from a dissimilar prism, the obverse prism. Although I have been at this exercise for many years, I have yet to fully resolve and create a suitable balance in the conflicting forces impacting my complete view of Monticello.

From the former perceived innocence and related exaltation of the place, the town's underbelly found its way into a more limpid line of vision, and I then admitted to myself that if I still had a compulsion toward Monticello, it was a compulsion to discharge change for the local African-American community of which I now realized I was a part.

❖

The opportunity to work for change in race relations at a more public, governmental level occurred soon thereafter in the middle of the school year, when the long-standing mayor of Monticello decided to step down from the position and pursue other available choices for employment. The position of mayor of the town enjoyed an ability to impact policies and programs at all strata of life in the community, both black and white. I had discussions with many African-Americans about what the black populace should do to give African-Americans a greater say toward equal status in Monticello where black voters constituted a meaningful portion of the electorate. If blacks were to vote solidly behind a candidate, then a smaller number of whites should be required to sway an election. While African-Americans in town did not represent a majority, the black population approximated a substantial minority, and those votes could be put to an advantage in a mayor's race. Who should the candidate be? It was thought I enjoyed a better chance of pulling more white votes so that, combined with a large number of African-American voters, a win loomed possible leading to a more progressive approach in race relations to benefit the black populace; in turn, various young, visible white adults also concluded time for change had descended upon Monticello and therefore supported me. A coalition was formed, a rather serious coalition, so at the age of twenty-five, I could possibly be elected mayor.

At the outset, I realized the problem wasn't with young African-Americans or, to a large extent, with certain, young white voters except for young whites so racist they would vote against me on the grounds of where I taught. The question became: how would middle age and older African-Americans decide to vote? The best I could do was to make myself available to every voter in Monticello, young or old, to improve my chances across the board; I therefore committed myself to canvas every house in town. I chose to knock on every front door of every home in Monticello. However, my African-American friends said blacks didn't easily open the door to a white man at night, for history always warned them danger from a white man lingered, at nighttime, on the other side of the front door.

Therefore, young black men about my age whom everyone recognized in the black community volunteered to chaperone me from house to house in the African-American parts of town. Over the course of the campaign, assistance from young black men proved to be logistically a boon for getting me into black homes to talk about the benefits of a new vision in Monticello, consistent with the expectations and goals of the broader racial equality movement nationally.

During every hour of every day not devoted to teaching or developing plans for classes or getting a little rest, I was talking to potential voters, mostly in their homes, black and white homes. People listened courteously and asked questions, but sometimes whites stated their reservations and concerns about my racial views. From a number of white households emanated the question: "Why are you teaching at Drew School?" The wife of a white employee for the City lectured and upbraided me for stirring up young blacks to have a different attitude toward racial norms and behavior.

Over a few weeks, nervousness occurred among older white politicos and probably a plutocrat or two who opposed my being mayor as our campaign showed strength and decent prospects. The first line of response from that group was the easiest to attempt—that is, to exclude me from the race on eligibility grounds. So, a question surfaced: should an employee of the school district be allowed to run for public office in Monticello? The question was debated by the school board without a determinative conclusion and was then referred to an outside counsel, who opined that no legal reason existed eliminating me as a candidate for the position of mayor. When that tactic failed, another, more serious question was posed: did I comply with state law residency requirements in order to run for mayor? I applied to the State of Arkansas to issue the judgment, and it ascertained that though I had just previously lived in New York City, I still maintained locally my permanent residency when I voted absentee in a recent local election. Thus, the two technical, potential obstacles were resolved in my favor.

The face of opposition challenging my ability to run on the basis of residency had been none other than the former family friend. Not as another mayoral candidate but as an agent for those whites who opposed my election, he had previously contributed to the failed peckerwood assault at the corral. The same former friend who set in motion the earlier attack to teach me a lesson about adhering to the rules and modus operandi as a white person in Monticello. Nothing should change, and nothing would change if the peckerwoods, enforcers of Southern white supremacy, and those who authorized them had their way. It wasn't the former friend's desire to be a peckerwood, for he only associated with them when necessary. Rather, he desired to be linked to those in law enforcement, business, politics, and the like who enjoyed the caste and who asked him to help them keep the status quo without disruption. To him, Monticello may need to abide by a few new racially liberating laws, but there were to be far fewer changes than white folks feared; and Monticello didn't need any more accommodation for the blacks, and it didn't need for blacks to have immediate access to the mayor's office. For the good of Monticello, that's all.

Although the former friend didn't succeed in removing me from the ballot, I've often wondered whether he would have ever taken that responsibility upon himself if Mother had been around, who was decidedly the member of the three-part Johnson family closest to him. But alas, she determined to spend much of the year I taught at Drew School in Arizona with John Maxie, my older brother, a vascular surgeon, and his family— away from the strum und drang my instruction at the African-American school apparently caused among some of her friends. I suppose Mother judged it just wasn't worth dealing with a series of awkward moments. Since she desired not to be any part of my involvement at Drew School, I refrained from telling her during her elongated visit to Arizona about my bid to be the next mayor, and surprisingly, no one called or wrote her about the election until after the ballots were counted. She loved me; I knew that without a doubt. She was a very good mother, demonstrating great patience with few reservations, most of the time, for letting me be me, but she had no idea what drove me to Drew School, and as far as she was concerned, it could only be bad news. Better to be away from it all without having to answer the inevitable and fateful question: "Why is Chester teaching at Drew School?"

Freed from the technical encumbrances that challenged my run for mayor, I could now better embrace plans for getting elected: having friends call friends and neighbors, having more than one mailing to households in town, continuing my visits to every house in Monticello, preparing for the City Hall debate. And I couldn't let my teaching slip for a moment; the children must not pay for my energies being applied elsewhere.

Little did I know then that a loud beat of major competition sounded in various parts of town. The former county judge for Drew County had been persuaded or had decided on his own to come out of retirement and run for the mayoral position himself. At that time, county judges exercised more authority and control than any other public official in Arkansas counties, with tentacles threading throughout most every executive and judicial function. Later, a new state constitution withdrew many of the powers from the state's county judges, but when this new candidate for mayor had been county judge, he enjoyed all those extensive and privileged powers. Indeed, as Governor of Arkansas, Bill Clinton indicated that he based his political strength in the state on the influence of county judges.[2] On top of it all, this new entrant was still popular with a large segment of the citizens of Monticello, which was and is, after all, the county seat for Drew County.

I wasn't conceding, of course. There is an ole saw that politicians generate more enemies while in office than friends, and who knew—with all the variables on race, current and pending, now facing the town, the mayoral outcome could be quite unpredictable, so I forged ahead with my plans. My march to every house in town carried a message with it: how much better would I know Monticello at the end. An urgency of necessity drove the desire every day that I proceed with the walk.

Years later, I wrote, as part of a group of poems entitled "Meditations on Civil Rights Activists," a composition on Ida B. Wells, the African-American anti-lynching advocate and historian. One of the final lines in that persona poem consists of these words: "We are what we have to see."[3] Upon reflection, I believe this line portrayed my vision and attitude as I stopped at every home and talked with as many occupants present, including children. At the end of this pilgrimage, one conclusion stood out more than the rest: I had not previously imagined or realized the poverty which gripped so many persons, black and white, in this small town. Most everyone invited me into their homes with my taking advantage to survey the interiors of each abode. The homes along the town's major arteries retained a certain ease and comfort, having well-maintained physicality and pleasant personalities. However, once away from those houses, poverty exuded everywhere, especially throughout the internal parts: completely worn out and broken furniture; tattered blankets spread over holes in chairs and sofas; three or four children sometimes sleeping in a bedroom; beds or make-shift cots in the living room; a television set that barely functioned. Even though I grew up on "the other side of the tracks," I hadn't observed this degree of indigence up and down East Shelton, but for maybe one or two cases. As a child, I didn't dwell on poverty.

In the areas of Monticello where African-Americans lived in their isolated, segregated, and compartmentalized fractions of town, it was much the same as many white homes I visited, for poverty struck those Monticellonian whites nearly as hard as it struck African-Americans. Was every small town in southeast Arkansas the same where hidden, expansively hidden poverty suffused through many of the secondary arteries, those off the primary streets, which occupied the attention of most people?

Maybe, this discovery had its more formidable point: poor whites and African-Americans held so much in common, and yet it was out of this more impoverished white community that the peckerwoods evolved, those whites who were the most anxious and ready to inflict physical harm on blacks. Why? I never fully bought into the argument that the ferocity of racism among impoverished whites had more to do with the fact that no class below poor whites abided on the economic scale other than African-Americans, which engendered competition between the two, felt acutely by the whites. This argument alone seemed too easy, a too conventional explanation. Something more sinister was also at play. I concluded over time that lower caste whites, beholden to higher caste whites in small towns, targeted blacks to leverage attitudes of the more elevated persons to keep African-Americans in their place, to keep the status quo firm and unamendable.

The visits began to have a purpose all their own—in some respects, well away from the election for mayor. For instance, as I mentioned earlier, African-American men escorted me at night through their parts of town; on one such night, two of us appealed our way down a dirt street I'd not previously explored. At the very end of the street, a house, more worn than others, was steadied on two-foot cement blocks. A child's voice from within probed the dark, "Who is it?" My partner for the night's visits identified himself and said, "I want ya'll to talk to someone." The door opened into a tired room of two double beds, the room's only furniture. A white man, about sixty, maybe less, gasped for air in the older bed; he paid us little attention. The young girl, who led us inside, was one of my students and stood close, pointing to the white man, bedridden, who suffered near us. In a matter-of-fact monotone, she declared, "Some call him 'Bill'; others call him 'The Mixer.'" Suddenly, I focused on the lighter tinge of her complexion.

A small town is a universe. At least, that's my view, for one can elicit conclusions and applications that reach well beyond the tailored and limited scope that many people place on the provincial code of conduct and moral structure of a small town. Monticello was such a place, and I gathered general insights into human nature from its ways. Having been swept into the lyrical and dynamic character and artistic potency of the story just recounted, I composed "The Mixer," which has been mentioned earlier and which was published in 2017 in my *Now And Then: Selected Longer Poems*;[4] the piece rested heavily on the miscegenational family whose children were seeded by a white man who resided in the African-American section of the profoundly segregated society of a town like Monticello. There would be more prose and poems to resonate out of the transverse of black and white America and out of the transverse of black and white Monticello.

Not to belabor the race for mayor, I continued to charge ahead, metaphorically speaking, but the embedded qualities and long-serving public experience of the former county judge, combined with the suspicions about my racial views by many white Southerners in Monticello, proved too weighty to overcome. I had a respectable showing, but the drawbacks cast the election to him.

I gained pleasure from the engagement and education afforded my students by the election, for we often talked about issues and developments that arose, allowing them to think through and articulate concerns, suggestions, and attitudes, which turned the race into a learning experience for them. Importantly, they ingested the lesson that a system of government and politics can be challenged, and while one doesn't always win, the process and will to make the effort, even in the face of defeat, proved valuable. Without prompting, a number of students got involved, asking to deliver circulars and discussing the election with family members, many of whom were eligible to vote. On election day, several older students availed themselves of family cars to take African-American voters back and forth to the polls, an initiative the principal of Drew School didn't appreciate, fearing that the students' participation implied that the school took a position on the election, a conjecture he wanted to avoid at all costs for very good reasons.

Upon reflection, I wondered why the peckerwoods in town, who had been foiled in their physical assault by a local football hero, did not take advantage of my vulnerability at night as I walked alone through various enclaves of Monticello. I can only surmise either they judged or they were persuaded to judge that an attack on me potentially created a meaningful backlash or unwanted public and press attention. Otherwise, my nightly visits and strolls from house to house offered a target that would have been hard for peckerwoods to resist if left to their own devices and proclivities.

Soon, spring came. The earth breathes and sighs fully and luxuriously in the vernal Mississippi River Delta. It is planting season, and the rich, darkened black and gray soil is turned to receive cotton, soybean, and other plants, setting the stage each year for the grand finale at fall's harvest, the closing of the region's high mass. Shaking off cold's slow trudge, the air tingles from excitement with huge pieces of agricultural equipment crawling over Delta highways and obstructing traffic on the way to unlimited spaces of flatland re-engineered and moved about each spring in anticipation of the autumnal rows of lush and sumptuous cotton, beans, and other crops. For those of us who have witnessed repeatedly this dramatic production that concludes in the fall, it is virtually impossible not to be seduced as the weather leaves hibernal months, and the mornings warm, and the ground starts to exude its familiar and alluring, redolent smells of procreation, a sort of analogue to the procession of human seeding and impregnation. One can then understand how folks, black and white, are drawn to be part of life along the Mississippi River Delta notwithstanding all the rest that beggars romantic attachment.

Over the course of the school year, I had often stood by the windows in the classroom where I glimpsed cars traveling east and conforming to the patterns of Highway 35. Only Dermott, one smaller municipality, perched along Highway 35 closer to the Great Muddy—the Mississippi River, that recognized spine of the country, celebrated in song and poetry and so integral to the Union victory during the Civil War. Here we were, each of us, so resultant of the arbitrary nature of that prodigious river with its alluvial caprice depositing prime soil residue upon its banks. Everyone in my classroom, at any one time, had somehow been piloted by the presence of the Great Muddy: descendants of slaves who tilled the land; and I, descendant of slave-owners who wished to build an empire for themselves and who came across the Mississippi River to limit competition for coveted land. We, both black and white, were of the very same root; the Great Muddy didn't attend to any artificiality of division between black and white, for we were one in our reliance on this national spine that bequeathed the agricultural gold of cotton along its shores, and we had all been drawn to it—some ancestors by will or greed, other ancestors by whip and the price of slave labor. Like the alluvial soil, we had been deposited here by the collective vagaries and power of the Colossus rolling its massive amounts of water and more at the very end of a road, on the other side of Dermott, bearing east a few miles out of Monticello.

As days continued to warm into hot in southeast Arkansas, I would now and then relieve the students from a steamy classroom by holding sessions outside in the shade of an oak or elm tree that hung inside the school's boundaries, and as we started to approach the end of the school year, I allowed, on Friday afternoons, weather permitting, my eighth grade English class, those mostly young males, to hold short baseball games on the open, dirt fields behind the school.

On the whole, my students and I knew where we would be come fall. Of course, my seniors were different—some headed to college, while most headed to find a job somewhere, anywhere they could hold on to a decent and steady job, one good job, possibly for the rest of their lives. However, more of my students were now destined for the white Monticello school system that gestured with little welcome for African-Americans. A few would, no doubt, confront the situation with bellicosity, but most wished for constructive change and remained curious about their white classmates and the novel days ahead. How would they be treated? How would the facilities compare with those at Drew? How much racism would manifest from white students and teachers? These realistic questions saturated the remaining days of our school year.

By spring leading into summer, I had decided to return to New York City, the direction north toward home. I'd miss my students very much—all of them; not just the well-behaved and smart, but also those who gave me grief, who found ways to get in my face and challenge me, not as a teacher, but as a human, the ones who would never truly settle down, those who will be set against more obstacles than they know, simply of their own making. I would love to fathom a year ahead to learn how all coped and weathered the storms, but such witness wouldn't be possible, for I was leaving Monticello.

Counting the time I spent intermittently in town after Freedom Summer, combined with my tenure at Drew School, Monticello had had enough of Chester Johnson, and I guess I had had enough of Monticello. Indeed, I decided during the 1969–70 school year that for all practical purposes, I had foresworn being a white Southerner, burdened with its persona from a damaged heritage. In so many ways, I settled into opposition to the persona of a white Southerner—for all that it meant or for all that it meant to me. For the seven years that succeeded my teaching at Drew, I did not return to Monticello; during that period, my mother came to New York City for any visits, or we would sometimes meet at a third location. Since then, I've returned to Monticello from time to time, mainly in connection with visits to my mother when alive and for her funeral, a reading I gave from a new book of my verse, and an award I received from the local college. I've also attended a couple of high school reunions, which I enjoyed, but Monticello can never be home again. Although I frequently challenged and argued in solitude a point here or there on racism in that town, I always acknowledged, regardless of place in time where I may be, I could not have lived with myself if I followed a path that didn't lead north toward home.

8

IN MEMORIAM

n October, 2010, I was in Fayetteville, Arkansas, located in the extreme
northwest corner of the state and home for the University of Arkansas,
to receive the University's Distinguished Alumnus Award. As part of this
campus visit, which lasted several days, the Pryor Center for Arkansas Oral
and Visual History, an entity of the University, interviewed me through
Scott Lunsford, associate director of the Center, for upwards of ten hours.
At some point during this interview, we began to explore the issue of race
and its impact on my life, and as the discussion progressed, I veered toward
the Elaine Race Massacre that had already begun to occupy a good deal
of my intellectual attention, as well as my time, including a considerable
amount dedicated to research on the particulars of the conflagration and
its legally significant aftermath.

When I asked Scott whether he had ever heard of the Elaine Race Massacre or maybe the same historic assault but described as the Arkansas Race
Riot, he replied he wasn't aware of it and didn't believe anyone at the Center

knew anything about it either. So, I proceeded to discuss the causes, the roles of the local white posses and white federal troops, the approximate magnitude of African-American deaths that resulted from the onslaughts, and the associated ramifications, including the precedent-setting case, *Moore v. Dempsey*, which evolved out of the local and state litigation from the Massacre and which would impact measurably and nationally the ability of African-Americans to achieve equal rights and equal protection.

Learning about the Elaine Race Massacre transfixed Scott, who expressed a strong desire to learn more: books, articles, videos, whatever he could acquire and devour on the subject, for Scott was now into this moment of Arkansas and national history. Less than two years later in August, 2012, he and I would together visit Phillips County and explore the Massacre's killing fields, the town of Elaine, and the nearby county seat of Helena.

After the Fayetteville interview, Scott's next stop on the Elaine Race Massacre trail resided in Phillips County where he scheduled an interview with David P. Solomon's father, also named David, who was a patriarch for eastern Arkansas. At that interview held in Helena, both Davids were present and added much color and commentary to my former introduction to Scott about the Massacre. During his conversation with the two Davids, Scott recounted my comments from the earlier interview, at which point the younger David responded that he knew me. After all, we had been classmates at Harvard College, although we hadn't known each other very well then.

Soon thereafter, David P. Solomon and I met coincidentally at a party in Manhattan (New York City) and began to discuss the Elaine Race Massacre. Both being residents of New York City, we then started to meet regularly for lunch, principally to discuss the particulars of the Massacre, and shared our family connections to the event. David explained how one member of the broader Solomon family was refused participation in the local white posse because he had two young children, and how another Solomon imprinted a role on the conflagration by signing a telegram in January, 1920 to Governor Henry J. Allen of Kansas asking for the extradition to Arkansas of Robert L. Hill and then in late 1923 by signing a petition of clemency for the Moore Six.[1,2] I described Lonnie's background and how he came to participate in the Massacre while in the employment of MoPac, which, through individual employees, exhibited a significant role in the event and afterwards. I also explained that I lived my earliest years with my maternal grandparents, Hattie and Lonnie, during which time my grandfather became my principal caregiver. We discussed the importance that the Massacre and its consequences had locally and nationally, including the remarkable impacts of *Moore v. Dempsey*.

We agreed on the need for a memorial and deliberated over the reasonable options for location, including the grounds of the State Capitol or near the Phillips County Courthouse where so much torture and judicial malice and skullduggery took place. Early on, David asserted his preference for the Memorial to be placed in Phillips County near the Courthouse; the politics of getting the state to agree to a memorial on the campus of the Capitol would be virtually insurmountable, and though the role of the state had arguably been decisive (i.e., calling in the federal troops to suppress a "phantom" black insurrection and the state's noteworthy involvement in the litigation phase), the Massacre was local, and the need for racial reconciliation had been distinctly felt in Phillips County, which the Memorial would help to address.

At our lunches, David reflected from time to time on his mother's progressive views about civil rights and her desire for racial equality and unbiased treatment of blacks by whites. He indicated that throughout her life as a mother, she tried to instill those qualities and attitudes in her three sons. While his father's beliefs had been no different, they were less vocally expressed, resulting mainly from the confidential nature of his father's legal practice serving both blacks and whites as a prominent attorney. Toward the end of the father's career, he received a citation from a regional legal organization in the state commending his services for "improving the condition of the poor in Eastern Arkansas." I found it quite special that the Solomon family, which assisted in the establishment of Helena's synagogue, enjoyed abiding and far-reaching roots in and commitment to the local community, spanning several generations. In fact, I concluded early that it was this family's lengthy and vigorous association with Phillips County, consisting of governmental, economic, legal, and social prominence, combined with the vicinal relevance and criticality of the Massacre, that drove

David P. Solomon to take on the initiative—with valuable facilitation and input from his law dean brother, Rayman—to support, organize for, and fund the Memorial, which he wished would be remembered as a family legacy to the county.

From the outset, he made it abundantly clear that his father would be an integral part of the family's decision to proceed or not to proceed with the Memorial. In September, 2014, during a symposium on the Elaine Race Massacre held at St. Paul's Chapel in downtown Manhattan, he announced publicly, with both of his brothers in attendance, the commitment of the Solomon family to the Memorial. Thus, the father had commended the management of the Elaine Massacre Memorial to the next generation.

According to numerous members of the local community, little of useful import about the Elaine Race Massacre had been voiced among white citizens in Phillips County for the better part of a hundred years. It was often a topic deliberately eschewed, even in casual conversations. For some whites to feel more comfortable about this part of the county's history, the gravitas of the event had been consciously downplayed—from a massacre to a skirmish and from at least over a hundred dead African-Americans to twenty-five and less. For several generations, the county never came to terms with an appropriate way of dealing with the conflagration. To hide the Massacre had been a suitable method for many, those who wished the historical recall just to disappear altogether. And yet, ultimately the size and broad relevance of the Elaine Race Massacre would not be denied, as one credible and comprehensive treatise after another—Cortner's *A Mob Intent On Death*, Stockley's *Blood in Their Eyes: The Elaine Race Massacres of 1919*, Woodruff's *American Congo*, Whitaker's *On the Laps of Gods*, and Francis's *Civil Rights And The Making Of The Modern American State*—disembodied the logic and reality of misrepresentation and silence about the onslaughts and the judicial outcomes.

It is understandable why a white community would not wish to confront the dark, probably the darkest, episode from its past. Undeniably, history is a mirror—a merciless, accurate, in its detail, mirror—and the truthful acknowledgment that a racial massacre happened and happened according to the best available facts sets in motion a series of terrifying prospects that challenge both previous and current behavior. Indeed, admitting that a race massacre transpired—in the degree that it occurred—means to assign responsibility, reasons, lessons, and incentives, which, in the face of a damaged heritage, bring a white legatee face-to-face with the limitless, most heinous aspects of his or her racism. Further, the employment of terrorism to achieve racist goals, as manifested in Phillips County during the fall of 1919, illustrates the extremes to which racists will go to achieve their ends for economic and filiopietistic reasons.

Others, who have written about the Elaine Race Massacre, and still others, black and white, residing for years in Phillips County as witnesses to behavior there, have explained that most African-Americans in the county were also reluctant to talk at length about the Massacre and its aftermath. Perhaps, since I am white, I can better understand the basis for whites to shun a concentration on the Massacre to keep reality and a direct allusion to their damaged heritage as far away as possible, but I initially found the historical hesitancy of African-Americans to explicate the event somewhat baffling until I acknowledged for myself the local world that blacks still confronted in places like Phillips County, Arkansas. For instance, if I walk alone the streets of Helena in the very early morning hours before daybreak with the realization of the Massacre descending like a consumptive spell and then imagine I too am black, I think I can appreciate the demonology striding alongside each one of my steps. For indeed, how far away are those whites who came to raid African-Americans at Hoop Spur the morning of October 1, 1919? How can blacks stop today's prototypes of those whites who would not be satisfied until they vanquished blacks that first dreadful morning of the conflagration? Is that appetite barely below the surface, ready to surge again in another shape or medium? Will raising the former moment of a hundred years ago release momentum for a possible repetition? Will an honest revisiting of the Massacre invoke, adjure the beast once more?

In 2017, a video documentary about the Massacre appeared on a Little Rock television channel, and I'm told that someone—today's analogue to a member of the white posses of October 1, 1919—posted a response to the documentary, saying that the main problem with the Elaine Race Massacre was that it had only happened in Phillips County; rather, that post was reported to have suggested that the Massacre should have been conducted statewide. With this kind of proposal being offered a hundred years later, it is no wonder that many local African-Americans have shown over time concern about raising an event that conceivably can elicit another call to arms against blacks.

What does it mean when one local African-American says about the Phillips County community that "we sweep the Elaine Race Massacre under a rug, but then we keep stumbling over the rug"? I will hazard a speculation that this maxim refers to those situations where one temporizes a discussion through obfuscation, dismissal, or denial of a facet of the Massacre to run then headlong right into recognition of a major, associated incident, such as the murder of the four Miller brothers, the slough killings, or the sizeable attack north of Elaine by the federal troops. In this way, no one knows how to react, for there is no context by which to view the disclosure or ascription leading either to the obfuscation, dismissal, or denial (under the rug) or to an authentic moment (the infamous stumble). Without a reconciled and agreed upon context, there is no common view of the appropriate and definitive facts concerning the Elaine Race Massacre: what were the causes, who did what, how did the ramifications express themselves afterwards?

In concrete terms, what did it mean to sweep the Massacre "under a rug"? It may simply mean that the conflagration to some never happened or, if it did, then its importance can be disallowed or dismissed. Either way, those who perished or were physically or emotionally scarred can have little value to those who endorse or perpetrate the sweeping. They who do the sweeping have decided to stand above the event, the Elaine Race Massacre, and take on responsibility for arguing against its consequences or magnitude, and then, by becoming a nonobjective arbiter, they may even savor disinformation about and disrespect for the victims.

Similarly, what does it normally mean that "we keep stumbling over the rug"? Instances occur there that cannot be explained or described without an allusion to or confirmation of the Massacre's pertinence to the community and to specific, individual members of the local community, while the illusionists or deniers (or quasi-deniers in support of a much lesser crime) stand firm according to their own rationale with the expectation that the public will abide with an obeisance to untruths that can continue to be an essential part of a vicinal rendition.

What are the consequences for a community that does not reconcile divergent and often unreliable assumptions and facts that surround such a weighty event as the Elaine Race Massacre? For one thing, a community without full appreciation of both its past and the increments or steps that led to the present can remain poised in fixed incertitude. Of course, communities can go through a long process of development and the setting of goals and achieving them without a decision to reconcile a momentous part of their history, but I submit that the "soul" of such a community suffers as a result, with fewer common tracts existing on which the public may rely, and moreover, peculiarities have a tendency to arise often without explicable provocation—that is, cliques have better reasons to grow and expand, and artificial divisions between citizens have a greater likelihood of happening. A common center, the "soul," if you will, has more difficulty forming, stabilizing, and surviving.

It is hard to identify and address the very express characteristics of a community that does not reconcile racial effects created by an event, such as the Elaine Race Massacre, for the dynamics of a town are so multi-faceted and complex, and yet it is worth the effort to attempt to discern those features cascading on a locality with citizens who may choose to disregard the impacts of manifold race murders of blacks by whites. Subtle innuendo, ordinary disagreements or dissents, turns of dialogue, especially in the normal discourse between blacks and whites, can mean more than may otherwise be apparent, balanced precariously on the edge of a conversation.

So, how does a memorial to the 1919 racial attacks bear on these matters? The Elaine Massacre Memorial is now prominently set in front of the Phillips County Courthouse, which, a hundred years ago, had a jail attached, and it was at the Courthouse complex where black sharecroppers and certain members of their families faced torture immediately following the Massacre so that the white version of the Massacre, developed by the County's Committee of Seven, would be the dominant interpretation of the event, resonating in the abbreviated and quickened trials of the African-American sharecroppers. But the trials held in that Courthouse were so egregiously unfair that for six of the convicted blacks—the so-called

Moore Six—the U.S. Supreme Court threw out the convictions in the landmark and celebrated case of *Moore v. Dempsey*. Thus, the historic and racial pertinence of the Elaine Massacre Memorial applies not only to the locality and region, but also to the nation as a whole.

The people who collectively participated in the numerous conversations and considerations about the design, size, and message of the Elaine Massacre Memorial, unveiled on September 29, 2019, anticipated that it would not only honor those who died, known and unknown, in the conflagration, but also function as a reminder of the Massacre to many who would now have the chance to gaze upon the structure. Of course, there were those who would feel neutral toward the Memorial, and then there were those who knew very little about the Massacre, and for them, the Memorial should open an entirely new area for exploration and discovery.

Nonetheless, as a result of the Elaine Massacre Memorial, a catalyst existed for another set of folks, especially from Phillips County. The Memorial would implicitly represent an historical record of the Massacre with the African-American deaths totaling more than a hundred and possibly even meaningfully more. Gazing upon the Memorial, many people shall now confront the moment of the Massacre intellectually and emotionally, viscerally—at the heart of the event. Will it then be memory heard again, a memory they wanted to believe and did? And that's how they may have described the event to others all those years, but they may or may not have fully believed it even then, but talked about the Massacre the way they were told. Now, each time the Memorial is observed, they may begin to conclude something else that's not memory at all, but another, different view to percolate in order to hold something new, specially crafted from ideas and data that correct and lead, not to satisfy expectations or defend what they would otherwise believe or want to believe. No, ideas and data that set a course right back to the fall of 1919 and Hoop Spur, confused days and nights and white posses, and enough murdered black folks to last the county for its lifetime. And then, the military arrives, and the deaths of black folks that weren't ever counted because only a few whites said they believed it, and if only a few believed it could happen, then maybe it never did. But now, they know differently, or they are learning to know differently. Not only does the Memorial put pressure on the local community to come to terms with the essential truths surrounding the Elaine Race Massacre through a broader engagement and education, but it also does so by serving as a constant physical presence and reminder.

The haunt of untruths about the Massacre should be mitigated by the Memorial. One advantage of the Memorial is to emphasize, even by inference, if not by outright declaration, the evident, true accounts of the Massacre, a benefit that should not be understated or overlooked. Where there is no verified information or hard data to the contrary, all rumors, recited folklore, excuses, alibis, intentional prevarications, and all other tales about an event have equal currency and validity, as there is nothing usable in solid contradiction for confuting such statements, for all could be equally true, except for obviously flagrant untruths.

In contrast, for purposes of obviating untrue stories and representations concerning the Massacre, educational initiatives about the conflict have run parallel with the design and construction of the Memorial. Through this educational process for the local community, sponsored by the Elaine Massacre Memorial Foundation Committee and the Delta Cultural Center, a consensus has already begun to emerge that argues against the less factually-based history. Moreover, I expect that attention to the Memorial will evoke accounts from several sides that can be employed to supplement that which is already known and recorded. For example, much speculation surrounds various possibilities about the disposal of the African-American bodies that would have accumulated following the killings, especially by the federal troops. I have heard at least the following ideas about disposal of the black bodies: large scale dumping of corpses into the Mississippi River, which runs close to several of the killing fields; loading of bodies in MoPac railroad cars that were then moved into areas of Desha County, Arkansas, immediately south of Phillips County—stories have been told that African-American workers were paid a $1 a body for all those placed in MoPac cattle cars; creating burial grounds at various spots through the southern part of Phillips County; or the African-American dead may be contained in black cemeteries outside Phillips County in neighboring counties. Probably a combination of these explanations draws us closer to the truth about the disposal of the African-American bodies amassed from the murders. With guidance and professional input for such investigations and educational pursuits, more pertinent information and discerning insights can be gathered to "fill out" the complete, but as yet undiscovered, features that are calling out to be integral pieces of the Massacre's story.

Another factor that must not be overlooked from the vantage point of the influence the Elaine Massacre Memorial can have on the populace of Phillips County consists of the drama that will be brought to the remembrance. Though a writer and poet myself, I freely admit to the limitation of words, for they can be spun into the air and naturally dispersed unless repeated and given special awareness, while the visual arts of architecture and sculpture are often more dramatically persuasive through their unbroken presence for the public day after day. Architecture and sculpture create perspective, and perspective creates expectation—thus, a dramatic impact will reside with the Elaine Massacre Memorial; for drama tempts us into redefinition and adjustment, a kind of blunt instrumentation that alters visions to which there had previously been constant and repetitious reference. A new promise is released, a promise that this time, a people will allow commentary based on facts supporting a complete and unadulterated interpretation of the Elaine Race Massacre as it actually occurred without tendentious interjections and stilted rhetoric meant to deflect and prove something which has actually little to do with the event.

Yet, I cannot accept the proposition that change is inevitable or that a memorial, even with the substance, good will, and veracity the Elaine Massacre Memorial imparts, will always increase the chances change for the better will find a way. Still, where there is growing suspicion about stories that could not have occurred based on the knowable components at play, the use of a memorial hastens the dissolution of fabricated history. In addition, by standing in direct contrast to those who divert by saying, "Forget the past, let's move on," the Memorial recognizes the unfilled need for the local community to come to terms with the Massacre.

The hundred years of silence and deflection since the Massacre illustrate a local inability to articulate the existence and impacts of "white motivation," those underlying elements of greed and mythologized tradition that have driven so often white attitudes toward black and white relationships. Of course, when these elements lead to multiple killings of African-Americans, the inability for whites to acknowledge the role of "white motivation" in these murders is compounded and extended over time, which may also explain, to no small degree, why whites have so often diminished the importance and magnitude of lynchings and other racial onslaughts.

It's not my belief that we humans are born with racism as a natural result of who we innately are; rather, it is a trait we absorb as a condition of what we learn and have to unlearn if we are to rid ourselves of this evil. So, one of the key white motivations, filiopietism, has been incorporated into the way many whites are nurtured and hewed through genera-tions, and there is normally little option for the multitude of young, white lives born into a world that condones and fosters this practice; for many American whites, especially in the South, this learned experience feels like a bequeathed part of being.

Filiopietism, that excessive veneration of the past and tradition, may not be fully apparent to all, but I know it when I experience the way it contributes to white adherence to heritage. Let me set the stage. The Battle of Gettysburg constituted the deepest incursion in the Civil War by Confederate forces into the North for a major military engagement, and Pickett's Charge constituted the most decisive battle at Gettysburg. Wil-liam Faulkner wrote in this novel, *Intruder In The Dust*, about the impact of Pickett's Charge on the future subservience to the mythological power of this event:

> For every Southern boy [*Faulkner is referring to every white Southern boy*] fourteen years old . . . there is the instant when it's still not yet two o'clock on that July afternoon in 1863, the brigades are in position behind the rail fence, the guns are laid and ready in the woods and the furled flags are already loos-ened to break out and Pickett himself . . . waiting for Long-street to give the word and it's all in the balance.[3]

To suggest that every fourteen-year-old, white Southern boy over an entire region of this country feels this extraordinary urge to participate in a failed military charge at the Battle of Gettysburg would qualify as filiopietism—a remarkable commitment of emotional sympathy or empathy to forebears. But maybe that's just me. Faulkner, who, in my mind, unquestionably adopted filiopietism for his art, realized he could tap into that white sensibility for the meaning of Pickett's Charge to white Southern males—Pickett's Charge where Southern forces were decimated by Union soldiers. Was it the defeat that was so attractive to fourteen-year-old Southern white lads? The lost cause? Was it the defense of a regional way of life, including the subjugation of black Americans, that made the Confederate soldiers heroes to subsequent generations? That which we glorify, we emulate. Faulkner's clairvoyance to perceive the effect of Pickett's Charge as a critical moment in a white Southern boy's mythological makeup actually confirms the power that filiopietism has on so many white Southerners. But is the romanticized version for Pickett's Charge, offered up by Faulkner, simply a dangerous and generous helping of severely misplaced reverence? Is this example a piece of the racist fabric by which white Southern racism has been shaped and through which life has been lived, relying on filiopietism as an integral component of the racist profile and composition?

While few American writers are his equal as a purveyor of filiopietism—with the impact of historical mythologies brought forward in time, William Faulkner could still acknowledge the terrors and evil that veneration of the past can perpetrate on the present, illustrated by these words, also annunciated elsewhere in *Intruder In The Dust*: "no man can cause more grief than that one clinging blindly to the vices of his ancestors."[4]

Furthermore, if we, as a country and culture, truly wish to rid ourselves of racism, tradition and legacy have to take less part in our lives, so that we create a society that bears increasingly less similarity in its practices and less veneration to the past. After all, adherence to former times mirrors a history when subjugation of blacks was widespread as a central and acceptable component of white, American life. In this respect, racial issues will disappear more quickly and more completely when we, blacks and whites together, readily move away from any such impactful traditions.

Greed, at the same time, doesn't fall into the same process of learned behavior as filiopietism; greed is not foreign and not a learned response like manners or language. Moreover, the motivation of greed does not belong to the American or Southern brand of whites alone; it is more embedded into human nature: black, white, Asian, European, man, woman, child.

Greed has often been compared to the breaths of air we involuntarily enjoy; it still resonates within us even if society tells us that it is unseemly to demonstrate its existence freely. An appetite, some control this august penchant better than others.

The truth about white motivation may be discernible among African-Americans, as they have watched it unfold over such a long time, but it is very difficult for whites to proclaim these features publicly that translate into recognizable and compelling elements of white racism against blacks.

The first few steps of acknowledgment for the Massacre's causes and consequences lead to a set of admissions that establish a precise shape of white motivations. In this case, it was generally known that the then white farming system had institutionalized an elaborate scheme for economically depriving African-Americans of their fair share. And, of course, the inherited impulses of whites kept intact the traditional beliefs and practices of a damaged heritage that were transferred from one generation to the next. These two aspects produced the balanced legs of white prejudice: the economic and filiopietistic incentives and excuses for the treatment of blacks in a subordinate, unequal manner, in varying degrees, even up to this day.

It is not easy for a community to address an ensanguined past. In Phillips County's case, the length of time taken to look at the Massacre in a more direct, rational, and less fictitious fashion illustrates that conspicuous reluctance. So, what happened that created a firm determination to construct a memorial for a point in the county's history that many folks have shown a strong desire to forget or deflect? For one thing, a family's courage released energy that prevailed to lift up support for the Memorial. David P. Solomon, the oldest of three brothers, voiced hope and a wish that the Solomon family could do something to reconcile wounds from the Massacre that had not yet fully healed within the county. He became convinced that for Phillips County to move usefully beyond its more distant past, something needed to be done about the Elaine Race Massacre—something dramatic and physically compelling for gaining the attention of even those opposed to talking more, much more about an event that many locally believed was better off forgotten. For the older David, the centenarian patriarch, a large enough spark spread to the oldest tree in the forest so that he also became consumed by the passion the son exhibited and conveyed;

so, the father accepted this persuasion of bringing new recognition to the Massacre through a memorial to chase away those persistent demons of the county's past.

Among those locally who lent a consequential hand to help launch the Elaine Massacre Memorial were the Millers and the Cunninghams, whose participation advanced an initiative for the community to accept and endorse the Memorial. Brian Miller, federal judge for the Eastern District of Arkansas, and his brother, Kyle, who runs the Arkansas state agency, the Delta Cultural Center, responsible for promoting the historical and cultural highlights in eastern Arkansas along the Mississippi River Delta, lost several family members during the Elaine Race Massacre, including D. A. E. Johnston, a prominent Helena dentist who was probably the most successful black businessman in town at the time, and Leroy Johnston, a genuine hero from World War I, who survived the war but couldn't survive the racial violence of the Massacre. In addition, there were the Cunninghams, Cathy and Ernest, husband and wife, long-time public servants. To illustrate Cathy's dedication to the public interest, she has been inducted into the selective Arkansas Women's Hall of Fame, and Ernest served as state representative for years, being elected Speaker of the Arkansas House of Representatives; he and Cathy have led numerous restorative, educational, and redevelopment programs and projects within Phillips County.

These four individuals, among others, were local, steadfast cohorts, black and white, who helped galvanize support for the Solomon commitment and plans—visible, high-level, enthusiastic allies of the Memorial. Without these advocates, the Elaine Massacre Memorial would have experienced appreciably greater difficulty achieving public favor.

As co-chair of the Elaine Massacre Memorial Committee, consisting of both blacks and whites, I was struck by the lack of institutional and personal opposition to the Memorial. The group that, in public, demonstrated about the Memorial did not disagree with the necessity of its existence or its purpose, but rather preferred that the location be in the town of Elaine, not Helena. Even though the name for the Massacre had been ascribed to Elaine, the use of the name, Elaine, had been only a matter of convenience, for very few killings apparently happened within the town. Since the most recognizable settlement closest to the killing fields was Elaine, the appellation endured. However, a more precise designation would have been the South Phillips County Race Massacre, for deaths from the onslaughts against African-Americans spread throughout various parts of the southern half of the county. Over time, the Elaine ascription prevailed with no compelling reason to rename the incident or, more accurately, set of incidents—at a certain point, any change in the name of the Massacre would have only confused people.

Over the decades following the Massacre, the community of Elaine increasingly became a town that virtually didn't exist; few, if any, economically viable businesses remained. The opposition to the proposed location attempted to foster an idea that the Memorial could somehow serve as an anchor for redevelopment and that people would travel to Elaine to experience the Memorial. However, many of us involved questioned whether tourists and visitors would choose to travel the thirty minutes or so from the county seat, as opposed to the Memorial being located a few blocks north of one end of the Helena bridge, which is only one of three bridges along the Mississippi River for general traffic traveling to and from Arkansas over the Great Muddy. The site in Helena, in close proximity to the bridge and nearby the Phillips County Courthouse, represented an eminently more accessible place for the Memorial than a location some distance away, reachable by automobile on State Highway 44, a two-lane, largely deserted road.

Why was there effectively so little resistance to the Memorial? One can identify several reasons: residual respect for the views of the patriarch, the older David Solomon, who granted so much time and support to the local community; endorsement of the Memorial by significant, local leaders; preoccupation with the troubling and harsh local economic and associated social problems that sapped personal and group energy for opposition; or possibly, the hope that economic activity and development could be spurred in the county by the Memorial. However, I'd like to think that this lack of resistance illustrated a preponderant viewpoint in Phillips County that it was time for the community to recognize more completely, collectively, and formally the Elaine Race Massacre, putting false aspects of false histories behind with both races anxious to accept the event full-faced, symbolized through the Memorial.

For the writing of this chapter, I traveled to Phillips County and conducted face-to-face interviews on attitudes and expectations about the Memorial with a number of local residents. Toward this end, I talked both with enthusiasts for the project and with those who opposed it. Of course, as part of these interviews, attitudes toward racial matters could hardly be divorced from attitudes toward the Memorial. In this respect, I surprisingly discovered that those who opposed the existence of the Elaine Massacre Memorial did so, in part, for fear that the presence of the monument might stir up passions and resentment among African-Americans about past treatment of blacks by whites. For those persons voicing a potential retribution scenario, a concern existed that blacks, inspirited by a memorial with an implicit purpose to acknowledge onslaughts perpetrated by whites in a former era, may possibly take violent actions against whites. The fact that blacks in the county outnumbered whites by a considerable margin was meant to underscore the logic for this fear. Cited alongside the fear of a possible long-delayed reprisal by blacks against whites resided another fear, one that suggested African-Americans could demand reparations for past injustices committed against blacks during and immediately following the Massacre. Reacting to these worries, certain African-Americans, supportive of the Memorial, recited a countervailing argument that most blacks in the county were simply too occupied with day-to-day problems, including the scarcity of jobs, to be so absorbed by the Memorial in a way leading to these forms of revenge for something that happened a century earlier.

Frequently, fear of blacks by whites, which can often convert itself into attacks against blacks, may just be the work and presence of residual shame. For instance, let's say that I unscrupulously abscond with something of essential value to someone, black or white, such as one's freedom, a most precious basic of life, would I fear that the person against whom I've committed the offense shall try to exact recompense for the painful and decisive loss? So, this fear may just be an especially felt concern that those harmed will return someday to assert revenge.

At the same time, I was informed in several of the interviews with black and white residents of Phillips County familiar with the Memorial that most recent discussions about the potential impacts of the monument occurred among whites. Entire black sharecropper families left the county after the Massacre, while other African-Americans had family members depart sometime later with no desire ever to return to the area. Moreover, I was advised that the economic plight, resulting in depression-like consequences, caused by adjustments in agricultural practices along the Mississippi River Delta and experienced over many decades, hit the African-American community especially hard; though whites bore economic deterioration as well, this decline meant blacks in the county, being particularly vulnerable, needed to focus more attention on making ends meet and dealing with associated, adverse social effects.

In the context of these interviews, I was sufficiently reminded that generational reconciliation is just one more issue to address within the world of race relations. For example, as I arranged these interviews, I received communication from a young, white adult who knew that I had scheduled an interview with one of his parents to talk about the prospective Memorial; residing outside the State of Arkansas, he wished to have separate communications with me to discuss his attitude about the subject, indicating that his opinions on certain facets of race relations and the Memorial departed from those I would probably hear from the parent. Thus, in turn, I held separate interviews with both individuals, and indeed, as the young adult accurately predicted, the sentiments I elicited from each were measurably dissimilar.

During the face-to-face interviews I conducted within Phillips County and others by phone once I returned to New York City, I was told by several people that the racial divide between blacks and whites in the county remained palpable and deeper than apparently both sides wished. One cannot blame the Massacre of a hundred years ago solely for the conceded division, though it certainly didn't aid the situation, and as an outsider, I wouldn't hazard an outright explanation, but I did have the opportunity to grasp the limited comfort zone between the two races. One white person proposed that a generational gap prevailed with a good part of the division between the races laying at the feet of those whites who refused to "unlearn" their damaged heritage that they had previously been taught, including the currency of fictional mythologies about African-Americans. Still, this person also accepted the complexity of the local situation, including the less predictable aspects of certain white behavior toward African-Americans. For example, this Phillips County resident described the ambivalent and paradoxical qualities of some whites toward blacks this way: "There are whites in the community who may privately use the 'N' word for blacks in one breath, and then turn right around and write a check for a black student to attend a better school."

Elsewhere in this book is a discussion about the presentations Sheila and I gave on racial reconciliation before members of the local community. However, there is one vignette that occurred during our racial reconciliation session which should be examined in this context. At one point during the question and answer interchange, an African-American man asked me: "Did you know your grandfather was a murderer?" Subsequently, I learned this totally appropriate, but grim question was actually not meant for me at all; rather, the intent had been for the question to carom off me and squarely hit a particular white member of the audience, a descendant of one of the white planters involved in the Massacre. Indeed, one cannot know precisely the current impact of the long history between blacks and whites in Phillips County, such as the previous ownership by white planters of large numbers of slaves during the nineteenth century, white planters whose descendants were still a meaningful presence. Was the question posed to me targeted with the Massacre alone in mind or for an even greater span of history? I certainly didn't know, and I'm not sure the questioner knew either.

Repeatedly, black and white voices complained to me at the time of these interview sessions that the influence of the Elaine Race Massacre surely continued to be present. The complaints centered on a common recognition that the Massacre with its inhuman and unrelenting milieu continued to pervade life in Phillips County as a pall that simply would not dissipate. I even heard the same jeremiad from folks who didn't live there, suggesting that a persistent motivation to escape the palpable aversion also rested on visitors whenever they journeyed to the county. People who argued vehemently that this phenomenon was indeed real could not be persuaded otherwise; at the same time, they were convinced that the Elaine Massacre Memorial, a physical, but also symbolic monument to honor the Massacre victims and family members and to declare racism as a primary root cause of the historic violence could ameliorate this suffusive heaviness by giving hope that the events of 1919 were now a mutually accepted reality of the past, which shall not unduly invade the reality of the present and future any longer. I was informed that even more emphatically, the Memorial represented the manifestation of a collective desire for the community at large to be redeemed in a spiritual sense. Of course, some had not become so optimistic about the potential, regenerative role of the Memorial, but proponents submitted that the existence of the Memorial and its intimations, as forms of an inspired redemption, would no longer permit an impassive and deathly chronicle and its related shroud to be the controlling personality for this black and white community.

Attention to this memorial comes at an unusually susceptible time for our country. Two African-Americans whom I interviewed for this chapter expressed a strong belief that, in some respects, racial attitudes by certain whites in the United States at present bear a striking similarity to those expressed in 1919. While no bloody race war is at present waged in America, which characterized conditions in many cities and states following World War I, a regrettably notable number of the country's white population now seem to exhibit racial views not unlike those that led to conflicts between African-Americans and whites at the time of the Elaine Race Massacre. The blacks who articulated this comparison between the two periods felt that President Donald J. Trump and a significant part of his constituency take racial positions, exhibited by word and example, that show uncompromising admiration and preference for people, things, and places "white" and for white privilege and an often illustrated disfavor, if not outright disdain and eschewal, for people, things, and places "black" and "brown." The use of disparaging utterances, vernacular idiom with ad hominem purposes, often coarse symbolism, false equivalencies ("very fine people, on both sides," so uttered President Trump, depicting the violent clashes in Charlottesville, Virginia that occurred during August, 2017), and the regular finding of fault with persons of color transparently communicate these biases by the President and a meaningful segment of his core followers, and it was to these racist displays that some black interviewees were undoubtedly responding.

One could try to argue that the greater fault lines existing currently in the country's body politic are political, not racial. For example, at the time of the recent, deadly conflict in Charlottesville, whites were represented on both sides of the conflict. One faction touted its promotion for national whiteness and its aversion to black and brown peoples, together with persons of the Jewish faith and ethnicity, while the other side embraced a more tolerant attitude for a pluralistic composition in our national profile. In this respect, the African-Americans I interviewed who voiced concern about the absence of change in racial opinions over the last hundred years, demonstrated by a certain part of the American white populace, indicated they had reason to fear that incipient violence lies just below the surface of white consciousness.

In furtherance of this conclusion, a relative, whom my wife and I visited for a short while only a few years ago, who unhesitatingly voiced racist comments and who lived only about fifty miles away from Phillips County, maintained a rifle in every room of his house with the exception of bathrooms. He also cherished a locked shed that contained an amount of guns and ammunition we considered shocking. When asked to explain the reason for the abundant arsenal, he replied, without any amplification, that it was there to protect him and his family *"when they came."* He never described who *"they"* were, feeling he didn't need to go that far in clarifying the term. With such a family member being representative of a portion of American whites, I have concluded that the African-American interviewees who opined that we weren't too far removed from 1919 had a credible, though disturbing point.

According to the Equal Justice Initiative, Arkansas, over the period, 1877–1950, ranked fourth in the absolute number of lynchings that occurred in the South, behind Mississippi, Georgia, and Louisiana, in that order. However, on a per capita basis (per 100,000 African-American residents), Arkansas ranked at the very top of the list among Southern states over the period, 1880–1940.[5] Taking a little time to peer back over my own Arkansas past, I wonder what would have happened if a serious proposal were set forth in Monticello to create a permanent marker, sculpture, or other remembrance to the town's legacy of lynchings. What would have been the reaction there? Since I have only been an infrequent visitor to Monticello from time to time, following my tenure when I taught at the African-American Drew School, I could hardly claim to know the town's probable response to a proposal with that goal in mind. Nevertheless, I'm hopeful that over the coming years, white folks in southeast Arkansas generally, including Monticello specifically, will see the wisdom of acknowledging, through perpetual, physical declarations, their own inherited racial violence and brutal racial murders, which were part of the histories of those communities. I further hope that any such physical declarations will also unconditionally state or infer that acts of racial terrorism and assaults will not happen again in those localities where they had previously occurred.

Not surprisingly, it is fair to say that few, if any, communities in southeast Arkansas have families like the Solomons of Phillips County who are able, willing, and courageous enough to envision and execute an entire project to result in the erection of an important memorial to a racially murderous past and who could also foresee the beneficial impacts for blacks and whites alike to be derived from the Memorial. The Solomon family led a reckoning to come to Phillips County, a kind of dispelling of illusory protection that has emanated from a misbelief by some citizens in a mythological equivalency of falsehood to truth. The family had perceived the outgrowths and limitations that insufficient explanations generated over time, and the local community was no better off, but actually much worse as a result. Others in other places should draw solace and strength from the Solomon standard.

By not acknowledging that racial violence and brutal racial murders formerly happened within or near the geographic boundaries of a locality and by not publicly declaring that such illegal and feral behavior will not occur again, communities are remaining ominously silent about the prospects for such paroxysms and killings being repeated. I worry that by not committing to a "Never Forget" community pledge and by not sending the message through a physical marker or other comparable expression, communities are effectively telling local African-Americans in a threatening and not-so-subtle way to stay in their place.

9

A RECONCILIATION
IN PHILLIPS COUNTY

S oon after the 2013 serialization of my long article on the Elaine Race Massacre appeared through the literary journal, *Green Mountains Review,* I heard circuitously from an Arkansas friend who asked, "Why can't Chester leave Elaine alone?" Implicit in that question was the dismissal of the reality that we, without even a conscious effort or conscious admission, reflect the tentacles of our past, whether they be declarative or tenuous. We simply can't help it; that is what we do. We are creatures aligned or askew with our past, meaning that in the case of Elaine, for example, unless we were to restructure the past to evince its reality, we are destined to live out a false past that also makes us false as a people, black and white. Many other places—countries, towns, and cities—have chosen to confront their pasts, and Phillips County, Arkansas has now, through its Memorial, moved affirmatively to do the same. Dissembling about crucial moments in our past forces us to dissemble about the present, and to try to forget about the past means we attempt to accept the present the way it is without consideration as to how or why we currently do the numerous, so often completely inexplicable, things we do.

So, what else do whites need to know in circumstances such as these? Why shouldn't I leave Elaine alone? Because whites need to understand what we have been capable of doing to other human beings of a different color. This information and admission are important pieces for self-definition. Moreover, how can whites ask those whom they have wronged to join in reconciliation without a mutual devotion to a belief in the authentic history emerging out of, let's say, those cotton fields or the Hoop Spur Church, north of Elaine, in 1919? For there can be no change without firm acknowledgment in light of those acts, as deeper still in intensity appears the puissant and prospective acts of altered behavior and engagement with the genuinely human. And if we are to extract the genuinely human in each other, we must recognize and forecast our own capacity for this co-inherence (i.e., they in us, we in them). In terms of the moral code for the historically oppressing white, one must treat the African-American free of any racial presumption or condition with the same respect, care, friendship, and love as one would invoke for another of one's own race. In the exercise of these expressions, the related desire for expiation and atonement, redemption and renewal (attitudinal and behavioral) requires doubtless will and pursuit; without them, other efforts prove inadequate.

The question posed by my Arkansas friend could have also been answered by Milan Kundera: "The struggle of humanity against power is always the struggle of memory against forgetting."[1] This is no small matter, for truth brought forward affects the way we act and react today and tomorrow; based on revised and truthful history, we adjust our current behavior—in Phillips County's case, between blacks and whites. With the Elaine Race Massacre in our backward glance, was I more inclined to lift the carefully fabricated veil of Elaine because my grandfather joined the savage sallies against the African-American sharecroppers? No doubt, but history resides with us regardless of whether we own a genealogy, close or distant, to an act of brutal racism or not, and the absence of such genealogy does not allow us to escape the possible, terrible history of the place where we may find ourselves.

Earlier, I discussed the consequences of the words spoken by an African-American citizen of Phillips County, who voiced the necessity for local reconciliation between the races this way: "We sweep the Elaine Race Massacre under the rug, but then we keep stumbling over the rug." This stumbling contains those surprising, unusual ways blacks and whites, as humans, behave toward each other derived from the history yet to be confronted and addressed, as moments from the past, without warning, burst forward to disturb, confuse, but also to remind unequivocally and virtually without mercy. I chose to illustrate this point by reciting the epigram from an African-American, for I believe those who have been victimized or oppressed inhabit higher ground for reconciliation efforts. But without forgiveness exercised by those who sustained the aggression and aftermath of the conflagration and who continue to carry long-term effects of associated oppression, there is little chance for reconciliation. The oppressing parties are not able to forgive themselves; they have no resources for such an act. Thus, the role of the historically oppressed is a most crucial one in the reconciliation relationship. That is also the nature of the non-violent strategy for social change: the oppressed frees the oppressor from acts of oppression and the residual effects of inhuman treatment and inhuman objectification. I can certainly attest to the unique contribution Sheila fulfilled in pursuit of our own reconciliation. Through her forgiveness of Lonnie and his tendentious, racist opinions and conduct and role in the Elaine Race Massacre itself, she conveyed to me the assurance that I was then allowed to proceed with her to friendship through a closer dialogue, shared views, and personal stories—a shared purpose. On this foundation, a willingness and aspiration could spread and unfold between us to reach agreement on the unassailable facts about Elaine, including the preceding and post history of the Massacre that so directly framed the manner in which blacks and whites have treated each other locally.

As a white man whose "damaged heritage" of subjugation of blacks and whose roots of racism have extended through several generations in the American South, mainly Arkansas, but also inclusive of Alabama, Louisiana, Tennessee, Texas, and Virginia, it is indeed awkward and probably a bit presumptuous for me even to refer to a proposed moral conduct for the historically and racially oppressed African-American. In contrast to the jeremiads expressed against the moral turpitude of oppressing whites, less has been said about moral conduct that should or shouldn't apply to the racially oppressed, though many will remember the confusing words of St. Paul about slavery whose sentiments have largely been discredited as inappropriate for the racism of whites against blacks in America. I will say that Sheila's forgiveness of Lonnie and her demonstrated goodwill and friendship toward me are exemplary models for addressing the issue— and are also largely consistent with the teachings of Martin Luther King, Jr.

Much discussion among those of us involved in the creation of the Elaine Massacre Memorial routinely centered on the desire to raise racial reconciliation as a priority for the Phillips County community, including local citizens, black and white, with antecedents on both sides of the attacks. In turn, I communicated with a local clergyman whose church membership contained descendants of the white planters who had been engaged in the events of 1919. In early 2017, the priest and the head of a local organization, the Delta Cultural Center (DCC), determined that the DCC should arrange to have Sheila and me tell our story of reconciliation over the Massacre to the Phillips County community. The intent was to evoke attendance locally; however, an announcement of our program also appeared on the events calendar website for the State of Arkansas, so the audience actually consisted of both county residents and Arkansans outside the local community. Furthermore, the Little Rock Central High School Museum chartered a bus, thereby providing access to those in central Arkansas interested in hearing Sheila and me speak about racial reconciliation. On Sunday, April 23, 2017, before an audience approximately 65 percent African-American and 35 percent white, we told our story using the Elaine Race Massacre as the plat over which our journey traveled.

Although I had previously heard portions of Sheila's recitation, I remained riveted at each telling, as more questions elevated to my consciousness at nearly every pause she took—this life-long, remarkable odyssey from her birth in Hot Springs, Arkansas to Chicago to New York City to Syracuse and now to Delaware. At seven years of age, Sheila learned about racism in Chicago from the death at fourteen in August, 1955 of another young Chicagoan, Emmett Till, lynched in Money, Mississippi, a death that many termed the start of the modern Civil Rights Movement for its galvanizing of the African-American coalition that had previously been more decentralized. Sheila's mother, Sara Black, peered into the open casket at the shockingly torn, mutilated, distorted Emmett Till whose mother, Mamie Till-Bradley, affirmatively and publicly declared she wanted the casket to be opened for her son's Chicago funeral to show the world what Mississippi segregationists had done to her son. Sara Black came home from the funeral clearly shaken, an effect that Sheila remembers to this day, an effect that propelled Sheila to the issue of racism, for she then, even at her young age, understood that something, like the murder of Emmett Till, could happen to someone who looked, based on skin color, like her.

From her mother's reaction to the Till funeral, Sheila also told the Arkansas audience about her life in segregated Chicago with only white teachers until Sheila reached the eighth grade. She described her family's relocation to the City's South Side where she took advantage of a program at the University of Chicago for underprivileged children that gave her access to learning experiences which otherwise would have been denied, and yet racism in Chicago persisted for Sheila through innumerable aspects and tinctures of her daily life. Active early in the Student Non-violent Coordinating Committee, she picketed, boycotted, sat-in, and demonstrated and would have shared in the Freedom Rider efforts to integrate federal interstate transportation except for the fact Sheila was simply too young at the time. This activism drew on inspiration from her mother, who participated in local opposition to housing discrimination and in tenant organization actions to correct landlord malfeasance in Chicago.

Sheila continued to inform the Arkansas audience about stories of the Elaine Race Massacre that circulated now and then through her life, caught in disturbing conversations she overheard about Albert Giles who went to jail and who had been sentenced to execution in the electric chair for reasons associated with a place called Elaine. Moreover, after Sheila's marriage in 1973 at the age of twenty-five, she and her husband, Ivor, took a trip from the Bronx, New York, where they were then living, back to Hot Springs, Arkansas to visit her grandmother, Annie. While in Hot Springs, Sheila heard Annie begin to explain one piece of the ordeal that dealt with the September 30, 1919 meeting, which Sheila's grandmother attended with Sheila's great grandmother and two granduncles in the Hoop Spur Church for the local chapter of the Progressive Farmers and Household Union. Annie continued to paint verbally for Sheila the picture of the church interior when shots were fired into the meeting with black sharecroppers and family members hitting the floor or escaping through windows and running into nearby woods and cotton fields. At that point, Annie could not continue the telling as her body and voice quivered, and her verbal systems shut down from the trauma of recollection. Certainly, something tragic had happened then or later during the Elaine Race Massacre, which persisted over several more days. Sheila never did receive the complete story from Annie beyond that point, and when she later asked her mother, Sara, about the inability of her grandmother to proceed, the answer came back with a short, summary explanation, "Oh, she must be speaking about Elaine," to which Sheila would ask, "Elaine, like the name?" "Yeah, Elaine."

Two decades later, Sheila acquires a computer, which gave her the ability to conduct more thorough research on the Massacre. Initially, she studies various old accounts from both the African-American newspaper, the *Chicago Defender*, and the *New York Times*, among others, back to 1919 when the Massacre exploded. As she read the first day reports and then the second and third day pieces about the conflict, a relative's name rises, Milligan Giles, whom Sheila's mother would explain was the person Sheila knew as Uncle Jim. These early news records, reflecting the white attitude that a conspiracy existed among the African-American sharecroppers to kill white planters in Phillips County, Sheila found to be embarrassing, something to be left alone, at least for a while.

Sheila continued with her comments to the DCC audience, telling them that periodically thereafter, she returned to searches into Elaine, and in 2001 uncovered a very recent book on the subject, Stockley's *Blood in Their Eyes: The Elaine Race Massacres of 1919*, which she then acquires and stunningly affects her. Upon reading the book, Sheila unearths pertinent facts and information, such as the discourse on her great-uncle, Albert Giles, one of the Arkansas Twelve,[2] meaning he had been a member of twelve sharecroppers who, immediately following the Massacre, were convicted of the murder of white men who perished during the Massacre; the Twelve were expected to be summarily executed within a few short weeks after their trials. Sheila explained that through the brilliant and tenacious legal work of the African-American, Little Rock attorney, Scipio Africanus Jones, the Arkansas Twelve were freed a little over five years following their rapid and unfair convictions.

Members of the Giles branch of Sheila's maternal family had been mentioned by Stockley in his book, and she also realized, for the first time, that the Elaine Race Massacre represented not only an important moment in the twentieth century for her own heritage, but also a seminal link in the chain of history for black Americans. Sheila surmised at that point the Massacre embodied a subject to which she would devote much intellectual attention and considerable time in future years to understand better the familial pieces and to discover the broader relevance of the event for the state of Arkansas and the nation as a whole.

Sheila relates that several years later in 2008, another book on Elaine is published, Whitaker's *On the Laps of Gods*, which draws its title from a letter written to Scipio Jones by Walter White, who at the time was an official with the National Association for the Advancement of Colored People but who would later lead the organization for a quarter of a century. In his letter to Jones, composed shortly after the legal arguments had been presented to the U.S. Supreme Court in *Moore v. Dempsey*, White writes, "The cases lie on the laps of the Gods."[3] Whitaker, starting on the first page of his book, features, in the telling of the story, three of Sheila's forebears who lived through the Elaine Race Massacre: Sallie, Albert, and Milligan Giles, the latter two having been seriously shot the first morning during the white posse attacks.

That Sunday afternoon in April, 2017, Sheila poignantly describes her absorption with the Whitaker book. From her immersion in *On the Laps of Gods*, she revisited the lives of immediate family members, the difficult lives of siblings and others. What if her antecedents, as sharecroppers in Hoop Spur, north of Elaine, had been able to take advantage of the extraordinarily high cotton prices at the time? What if the family could have used part of that extra money and purchased a small farm and made something more of their lives for themselves and future generations? How this difference could have altered the worlds for progeny who instead lived out lives often destructively. Sheila relayed to the crowd that both her younger and eldest sisters died, having been addicted to drugs.

Years after the Elaine Race Massacre, Sheila's family became part of the Great Migration of African-Americans from the South to the North with large numbers of those immigrants making their way to Chicago, where Sheila was raised poor, very poor—she and family members living in poverty. Sheila and her husband, Ivor, had done better, but it was also a struggle. Sheila pondered, as she became increasingly familiar with the Massacre, the various ways life could have possibly been better for so many with a little more income from the 1919 cotton harvest. Whitaker in his book brought Sheila closer to those ancestors and to that earlier time for her family. As a result, Sheila decided to locate Whitaker and recount for him her connections and reactions to his book, to which he expressed an animated answer, telling Sheila that she was the first African-American descendant he knew, other than a federal judge, who lost several anteced-ents, directly connected to the Elaine Massacre. Whitaker also indicated to Sheila that he had been in touch with me and inquired of her whether she would be interested in meeting someone with a family member who had been a participant in the conflagration.

At this point, Sheila conveys her recollections of our first phone call, our long first phone call. She tells the audience that "I haven't laid eyes on this man. I'm listening to a white male with a Southern accent, but there's a connection. We connected sight unseen." She relays that we agreed to meet soon thereafter in Boston where her son lived, and that I took a train up from New York City. She tells the story of staring anxiously out a window the morning of my arrival, looking and waiting for me to come walking up the street. Sheila continued:

"When we met in the foyer, I could do nothing but embrace Chester, and when we sat down on the sofa, I don't know how, or when, or why it happened, but either I reached out or Chester reached out, but the next thing I know we're holding hands. . . . You know when people are real. I've been in law enforcement. I can look and kinda make a judgment about when someone is being honest and totally open with me. And that's what I got from Chester, a mere stranger, but no, not a stranger. Because something brought us together and when I look back and reflect on that, I look at the intervention, the divine intervention that has played a role for putting Chester and me together. . . . But I know upon that first meeting with Chester that I had an ally. I didn't know where it was going to lead me. . . . Chester was like 'split' as far as his feelings for his grandfather, reconciling what his grandfather participated in, what his grandfather had done. . . . It isn't for me to hold on to something terrible that happened. Knowing the history of this country, knowing what happened in the Jim Crow era, knowing what happened during slavery, knowing what happened to my people in this country—as black people, we're very forgiving. Chester was a human being like me. This was something that happened to both of our families, and something brought us together. I call it God. I call it divine intervention. . . . As I have been on this path and this journey, things just fell into place as far as our connection is concerned."

Challenging the audience directly, Sheila stated, "We must collectively push forward to heal our minds of this tragic event and learn to connect with each other. This is a community that needs to learn connection, white and black, Hispanic, to learn how to join collectively to heal. . . . white people, talk to your own white people about not only Elaine, but just about the general field of racism in America. We need as black people, we need white people to help end it, and as white people, we need black people to help end it. . . . We're all human, we're all humans, we're all born to be good."

Sheila would then go on to touch on several other topics, such as various conversations we've had and the distinctions between the Ware Six and the Moore Six of the Elaine Twelve, and then it was my turn to talk to the local community and the expanded number of Arkansans who came from outside of Phillips County—to the mostly African-American assemblage. Sheila had done a remarkable job relaying the story of the conjunction we established with each other as legatees of our respective heritages received from the Elaine Race Massacre. I had anticipated Sheila's capable explication covering sensitively that crucial area for the audience, so I would be free to focus on certain untrue perceptions about the Massacre that enjoy devotees in the county and that work to prohibit racial reconciliation. Here are a few of my associated comments:

"Sheila Walker, my partner in this journey, clarified the underlying relevance of the Elaine Race Massacre to our reconciliation, for Elaine is part of our own individual histories. We have therefore been reminded that our past is never far away, which should impel us to relate to it for our sanity and for our own humanity. The concept, occasionally articulated in the context of the Elaine Race Massacre, that we should just forget it and move on confounds anyone with even a modicum of sensibility. Either Sheila or I or any of us must address the association with and the impact of that past for such an important event as the Massacre, or we are left to fight with it every day and throughout the night, as Jacob in the Old Testament fought with the imposing and unrelenting stranger until dawn. Sheila and I recognize the mandatory nature of this necessary struggle with history, and I'm absolutely certain that many of you here today acknowledge it as well.

"From Sheila and me, you hear that we believe emphatically reconciliation to be the outgrowth of a common acceptance of certain crucial facts about Elaine. You hear we wish to achieve a shared understanding about determinative aspects surrounding the event itself in order for us to talk with honesty, perception, and empathy about the roles that our respective forebears played in this moment of American racial history.

- Five white men were killed during the onslaughts, while there is a reasonable possibility that two of the five may have actually died from friendly fire;
- It is simply unclear how many African-American deaths can be attributed to those groups of white vigilantes who came to participate in the Massacre from Tennessee, Mississippi, and surrounding Arkansas communities; and
- It is certain that the volatile and combustible environment existing at that time in Phillips County, such as the fear of black sharecropper

unionization among white planters and other racial and economic roots of contention that arose following World War I, stoked the simmering flames of conflict here.

"What we don't know—and this topic has led to misunderstandings for decades—is the number of African-Americans killed in the Elaine Race Massacre. There is one narrative that surfaced soon after the event, which argues that fifteen to twenty blacks died that first day from the white posses operating in an area just north of Elaine. This narrative states that those African-American deaths are the only ones inflicted on blacks during the entire conflict. Under the scenario, federal troops came to restore order, and that's all the military did.

"However, the pertinent and decisive information about African-American deaths during the Massacre does not end there. Based on military records and further supported through investigations and interviews with the federal troops by the Federal Bureau of Investigation, at least fifty to eighty blacks were killed at the hands of the military alone. According to a report submitted to the U.S. Department of Justice by the FBI within days of the conclusion of the Massacre, at least twenty African-Americans died for refusing to halt when so ordered for resisting arrest. In addition, the FBI report concludes that other African-American deaths by the military came from an advance through woods where 150 black sharecroppers were hiding, as federal troops, being under shoot-to-kill orders, cleared the area with machine guns. Of course, there were more ad hoc killings of blacks away from the federal troops and away from those deaths inflicted the first morning by the white posses; such other ad hoc deaths included Dr. D.A.E. Johnston, the black dentist, and his three brothers and the killings of African-Americans by the white marauding vigilante groups. Thus, the total of African-Americans who perished would reasonably be in excess of a hundred.

"For my 2013 article on the Massacre, I quoted from a note I received from Robert Whitaker, who stated specifically for my piece his estimated figure for African-Americans who died, 'It is the documentation for the killing by the military, which I write about in *On the Laps of Gods*, that is the best evidence, in my opinion, that the total number killed was above

100.'[4] At the same time, a security agent for the Missouri Pacific Railroad, who had been especially involved during the Massacre and the torturing of the sharecroppers and the trials following, asserted in an affidavit that hundreds of African-Americans had been killed by white posses.[5]

"I hope that as a result of our going through this data, we can put to rest the untrue narrative that the only blacks who died during the Elaine Race Massacre were those killed on that first day by the white posses before the federal troops arrived.

"The first step toward reconciliation resides in acceptance of a common set of vital truths relevant to an occurrence, such as the Elaine confla-gration. Moreover, in this instance, of course, a most immediate and compelling truth would focus on race and those facts bearing on racial elements within the event. Though economic factors were surely present, the Massacre happened as a racial onslaught against blacks by white vigi-lantes, white posses, white federal troops, a white Governor, and the white Woodrow Wilson Administration. These are prima facie facts. I don't think we need to debate the conclusion."

Elaborating on pivotal steps toward reconciliation between blacks and whites, I offered another aspect for the audience to apprehend and accept:

> "By pursuing reconciliation, one is not simply receiving, in good faith, the most accurate and well-recognized facts for a particular moment in history; one is equally accepting the proposition that each generation must embrace, on its own, what is genuinely human, not bound by those who come before.
>
> "It has also become a powerful declaration that Sheila and I chose reconciliation over the alternative, fated by silence and fated by untruths. Yet, race is not the only area that cries out for reconciliation. While it is not so obvious, generational reconciliation also has its special place."

Because of my early upbringing by maternal grandparents, especially Lonnie, I felt a strong compulsion, at least during the initial phase of my intense focus and research on the Massacre, to pursue an expression of generational reconciliation, if for no other reason than my love for Lonnie and my appreciation for the life he and Hattie arranged for me during my very early years after my father died and my mother abided the best she could. This generational consequence would have to be reconciled alongside Lonnie's part in Elaine. As I relayed to the audience,

"At the beginning of my journey to and through the Massacre, I thought I could find that moment, that location where I would understand how Lonnie could be such a loving grandfather, the most present person in my early life, and then participate in the Elaine Race Massacre. Maybe, that moment or location could be found in those rows and along the public dirt roads I walked among the killing fields north of Elaine. But I admit I never found that moment or location. I utterly failed at my attempts to effect the sought after generational reconciliation. I was likely destined to fail, for the generational dissonance between Lonnie and me was not driven so much by a difference in age as by our respective difference in racial views.

"Rather, Lonnie has become a split figure, a bifurcated figure. Both sides explain him, I guess: loving grandfather and contributor to attacks against African-Americans. But I can't take the two sides as representative of a blended person. He simply became both to me. Still, however, as I wrote my serialized article on the Massacre, I indulged myself by deflecting his actual involvement in the conflagration, not unlike other white descendants from racial onslaughts might have done.

"A partial denial of Lonnie's part surfaced when I wrote the article as I applied the conditional word, 'likely,' to his participation, though all of the information tied him directly to the racial attacks. In other words, 'likely,' which softened the vision I allowed myself of Lonnie at Elaine, became my own form of subtle denial."

I also took refuge in a quote by Sheila Walker for an article about our reconciliation when she proffered the idea that 'I didn't know Chester's grandfather, of course, but I'm more forgiving of Lonnie than even

Chester. People aren't bad. Circumstances make people do bad things.' It is a lesson one may learn on Elaine, as I took from Sheila's observation that racial reconciliation can also include acceptance of the view that circumstances make people do bad things. Yet, the truth remained that my grandfather now consisted of two separate persons, and I therefore no longer desired or expected to make my peace with generational reconciliation.

I have often wondered who else may have chosen to align themselves for a similar historical episode on a decision tract like the one to which Sheila and I have adhered. Who also discovered the redoubtable reasons to search for reconciliation amid evidence that a racial lynching or lynchings of blacks by whites had transpired? For I have also wondered about the continual distress such a fraught, historical moment can relay to the descendants of the oppressed and oppressors in the absence of a well-intentioned reconciliation to render the inter-generational scars and legacies less palpable and less resonant.

According to anecdotes that several of us had heard on trips to Phillips County, conversations recently intensified locally about the Massacre, though some citizens, committed to the discredited white narrative, nevertheless persisted in voicing those beliefs. Apparently, however, there had been a noticeable diminution of local support for the white narrative with its simulacrum of a smaller number of African-American deaths and its reliance on a black insurrection as the causation for the Elaine Race Massacre. Rather, new areas for exploration had ensued, such as the method by which African-American bodies may have been removed from the killing fields. Of course, silence about the event still permeated much of the community, though I heard that new stories and reprised lore were percolating. So, there were signs of an awakening. Whether the reconciliation remarks by Sheila and me, the prospective memorial, or other vicinal causes had any relevance for this awakening and related conversations was hardly consequential, but the shape of those discussions had been altered, and a bit of fresh air on old myths cleared away some of the dust.

Nevertheless, what do we really understand about reconciliation? We do perceive how people are more humanely treated when reconciliation has been achieved, when reconciliation strips away a previous context and replaces it with a more direct, candid, conducive, sympathetic, responsive, and realistic one, one that matters more personally, one that has set aside the evils and rages of damaged heritage and filiopietism, one that has more fully taken on co-inherence, empathy, agape love, and the adoption of the genuinely human. To receive another's situation captures the will of one's own purpose, thus finding one's self in the place of another. Further, for someone connected to the oppressing (historically speaking) side, this act of pursuing reconciliation with another of a separate race, combined with an acceptance of forgiveness from those oppressed can remove the dominance of a seemingly immutable past transmuted to the present. For someone associated with the oppressed, to be co-inherently bound to a representative of past oppression is to transfer freedom to that person, and the act of imparting freedom can serve as an illumination and passage to a consciously elevated relationship.

In commentary from his influential book, *Black Theology and Black Power*, Professor James H. Cone, a progenitor of black liberation theology, declares that in true racial reconciliation, "the wall of hostility is broken down between blacks and whites, making color irrelevant to man's essential nature."[6] This conclusion is fundamental and completely accurate. Dr. Cone and I came to know each other only a few years before his death in 2018. He grew up in Bearden, a small town located in south Arkansas, west of Monticello and farther into the interior of the state. His childhood life of severe segregation and racism there impacted Cone enormously. Soon after publication of my long article on the Elaine Race Massacre, he showed considerable interest in the event, so that, in turn, he and I shared, during the summer of 2013, a number of lunches together, just the two of us, discussing the Massacre, but also our erstwhile lives in that part of Arkansas, our personal histories, race matters, and theology. I admire his writings and viewpoints very much.

I propose we bring Dr. Cone's words for reconciliation into a more fully human setting, into a setting in which we can relate to genuinely human possibility—simply put, to ourselves. For instance, dealing with the special nature of race, we too often assign too much of our individual commitments to institutions, to the all-powerful father and mother of an institution, forsaking prospects we know we otherwise can bring entirely to bear between individual blacks and whites. While there is no doubt that much greater white activism, at all levels, is needed today in responding to racist episodes and comments, racial reconciliation is bi-racial, aligned with personally intense involvement and commitment. Unfortunately, many white-dominated institutions, attempting to improve the situation through white-dominated, racially sensitive seminars and the like, actually contribute to white reluctance to participate more actively in racial reconciliation by diverting energies and attestations away from more personal, bi-racial engagement.

Both Sheila and I have considerable reservations that institutions can be the most effective facilitators leading to black-white reconciliation—until those institutions actually break open and free individuals of good will, black and white, to find each other in personal missions that result, on their own, in authentic and public expressions for the genuinely human. Reconciliation between Sheila and me did not and does not rely on facilitation by one or another institution to fuse our inter-personal bond. Rather, we depend instinctively on each other for the contact, words, sentiments, favored dialogue, and humanity to circumvent obstacles embedded in so many past ways and habits.

If an act of reconciliation reaches success, it does so by forming a one-to-one understanding and does not presume to be accessible through an abetting institutional structure. Many may even consider one-to-one reconciliation too optimistic; still, I encourage each person to take the step toward this prospect, for the result can be extraordinary.

Institutions depend on their own order and protocol, normally reflective of complex political, economic, and organizational composition and the organization's own best interests, all of which can be impediments to the pathway leading to inter-personal reconciliation. There is co-inherence, the genuinely human, empathy, forgiveness, agape love—powerful tools available for our remarkable use and behavior—qualities only humans, in the image of God, can elevate beyond understanding. For after all, we are left to ourselves, simply as we should be, to give and receive reconciliation, to love each other, if you will; the chance is indeed ours, as one and another, black and white, to reach well beyond those cruel assumptions our racial history declaims and to be more than the past had ever promised we could be.

AFTERWORD

The obstacles that undermine and stymie African-American equality in this country today differ from those facing African-Americans during the Civil Rights Movement, which sought legislative and administrative redress from barriers that by institutional fiat had achieved separation of the races. For example, the absence of voting rights for many blacks in the South at that time had the unqualified imprimatur of state and local government enforcement, which, with minimal subterfuge and without hesitation, reflected the desires and Jim Crow agendas of hardcore racists.

The landscape over which racism applies today is normally less elemental (though not always) than earlier times but still can turn insidious. Except for the most virulent racists, few will dare say publicly that America should deny equal education opportunities to persons of color, but separately private, recurrently religious, educational academies have popped up over the years and operate regularly populated by white children, leaving many public schools for non-white students. In addition, state legislatures often create gerrymandering of districts so that non-white communities are routinely underrepresented through the election process with courts frequently serving as partners for state legislatures in efforts to limit strength and participation in governance by non-white citizens. Today, racist agendas are carried forward not by "white citizen councils," but by many mainstream names and organizations, which are nonetheless similarly meant to thwart civil rights.

A mantra during the African-American Civil Rights Movement, harkening back to the cadence of Psalm 13, was "How long?" The mantra today could be "How far?", meaning "how far" back will we return to a former time? At this point, the country should be more concerned about our retreat than our being placated about how far we, as a nation, have come in achieving racial equality. Let's consider the recent steps and devolution carrying us, as a people, back in time: the striking down by the U.S. Supreme Court of important sections of the 1965 Voting Rights Act; the use of voter ID laws as the new poll tax that kept minorities from voting for generations; and various, other examples of increased implementation of public policies decidedly racist in nature, such as the Flint, Michigan water supply fiasco and the nation's restrictive approach to immigration for persons of color.

Of course, there has been progress in many respects for African-American civil rights from the 1950s and 1960s to the present, but the will to achieve racial equality, in all its multiple possibilities and forms, has effectuated much less than the country proudly heralds, and the very progress actually attained seems to militate against further strides by African-Americans to reach true equality. Judged by this state of affairs, one must question the extent to which the genuinely human has a chance to guide this nation, as a whole, toward greater racial reconciliation.

While much was accomplished as a result of the African-American Civil Rights Movement by converting many white hearts toward a more open, freer, and fairer society, we whites are still far from where we should be. In terms of white participation in dealing with equal justice and equal rights for African-Americans, three white groups and gradations of these groups dominate the white perspective in the United States today; they also illustrate the absence of a general consensus for vigorous commitment among whites to equal justice and equal rights for African-Americans. First, there are the out-and-out racists; we recognize them, and they, for the most part, recognize themselves. Second, there are those who think racial issues impact their lives and other peoples' lives on the margin; they go about their jobs and leisure routinely accepting normal traditions and patterns that have encompassed and will continue to encompass them—with racial matters a sort of subliminal reality. Then, there is the third group of American whites that has known all along the country is far from resolving its racial issues, and members of this group take steps, constructive steps, every day, big and small, institutionally and personally, to foster the genuinely human between blacks and whites and move us toward a comity of resolution. This group comprehends that while it is virtually never stated in these terms, racism is directly and routinely attached to most of the critical issues of our time. This third group acknowledges there is no end in sight to the terrible struggle between our racist history and traditions and the beautiful pluralism that is also part of America, of being American.

For those of us who look back to the 1950s and 1960s Civil Rights Movement with a reflection of saddened hope and unrealized expectations for what many of us thought could have been the beginning of authentic racial equality on a broad scale, we maintain a view that whites in this country should have thoroughly embraced the message of Martin Luther King, Jr., as the methodology for racial change. He offered white racist Americans personal renewal, a cleansing of historical and diabolical sins, and reconciliation through public action and white acknowledgment of previous sins and prior subjugation of American blacks from centuries of grotesque laws and traditions. In spite of this gift, less than a desirable number of whites took advantage of the prospects for cleansing renewal and redemption that King's inspired reasoning generously granted.

Some devotees to black liberation theology suggest that American whites are born with a greater depth of Original Sin, and the roots for that belief are borne by the inherited consequences of subjugation by whites of blacks over many generations. I happen to believe there may be more than a whit of truth to this conclusion by the passing of evil and injurious behavior from one white generation to succeeding ones, as damaged heritage is not transferred without associated and accumulated effects, whether they are recognized as such by the legatees or not.

Since segregation and the subjugation of African-Americans have existed in this country from the early 1600s, many white Americans perfunctorily convince themselves to accept the proposition that the plight of blacks had somehow become a permanent, institutionalized way of life. This conclusion among some white Americans defies the spirit and realistic response to structural human violation, regardless of the passage of time that an unfair and injurious system has been in place. In turn, derivative of this history, there is little doubt that part of the rage white racists feel toward African-Americans infers the unjust and brutal lives that white Americans have thrust on their black brothers and sisters. Some may call this response guilt, but I think it goes beyond guilt into that measure of shame which is greater than guilt and eats even more deeply into the fabric of the white human soul. I discern that reaction when I observe the ferocity with which many white racists espouse their views or choose to demean or confront blacks. Although guilt devalues and enervates, shame is more dangerous and creates spite as it also inspires irrational and hungry vengeance.

So, then, how do American whites individually begin the work toward racial reconciliation? We must have the willingness and courage to implement a change that sheds both the inhumanity of our damaged heritage and the inhuman shield of tradition, history, fabrication, and filiopietistic devotion to the past. This decision additionally means that sometimes we shall walk away from those who cared for and adored us, including those who may be our parents, grandparents, siblings, or friends. Occasionally, we shall even withdraw, if necessary, from the full acceptance of our own grown children, for whenever we continuously adhere to historical patterns, images, stereotypes, or other, multiple forms of damaged heritage and filiopietism that dishonestly exhort the past and enflame the present, we forego a chance to gain access to the realm of the genuinely human, a first step toward racial reconciliation.

ELAINE MASSACRE MEMORIAL

Dedication: September 29, 2019

ON DEDICATING
THE ELAINE MASSACRE MEMORIAL

Read by the author: September 29, 2019

They will end; all of them will end:
Words to flare a conflagration.

They will end; all of them will end:
The plots setting hue against hue.
Yes, they will end.

But time and the river shall
Never end; for they begin
To begin, again and over again,
As time and the river wash
Through the land, and over
Its dreams, schemes,
And lauded and unlauded past.

We've told our stories here
While others listened,
Thinking mainly of their own:
Of those who died killing,
Or of those who found
No finding of an escape
From onslaught upon onslaught.

Now, we gaze on the Memorial,
Which tells of days
That went unclaimed,
Which tells things a hundred years
Of the Elaine Race Massacre
Did not care to hear: that
All history is a struggle
Between what we must end
And what we must begin;

As time and the river ever
Flow between now and then
And delay for neither those
We honor here nor those
Who have or will come here.

Of time and the river,
Beckoning no escape,
Leaves no choice:
So, we shall no longer wait
For more light that we may
Better see light, nor wait
For other dreams that we
May better inspire dreams.

A poem by J. Chester Johnson

ACKNOWLEDGMENTS

A special thanks goes to both Grif Stockley and Robert Whitaker, who, through their respective, necessary, and revelatory books (Stockley's *Blood in Their Eyes: The Elaine Race Massacres of 1919* and *Ruled By Race* and Whitaker's *On the Laps of Gods*) furnished the nation intelligent and well-documented reasons to give the Elaine Race Massacre of 1919 and the consequences of its aftermath greater awareness as seminal occurrences in American history. I must also express my particular gratitude to Robert Whitaker, who accompanied me as I searched out the evolving truth of the Massacre to its absolutely bitter and unadulterated end, when I ultimately came to the realization that my beloved, maternal grandfather, Alonzo W. Birch—or, as I knew him, "Lonnie"—had a role in the Massacre, working for the Missouri Pacific Railroad.

I am deeply grateful to the staff of *Green Mountains Review*, especially to its Editor-in-Chief, Elizabeth A. I. Powell, for the diligence and care paid to my 2013 article, "Evanescence: The Elaine Race Massacre." The special attention *GMR* rendered to the piece raised the visibility and importance of the Massacre for many readers, resulting in a broader interest for this historic conflagration and its influential, legal repercussions. The account of the Elaine Race Massacre and its aftermath, as portrayed in Chapter 1 ("A Changing of America") of *Damaged Heritage*, reflects information contained in my *GMR* article.

A series of images, pertinent to the accurate and realistic telling of the Massacre's story, are included herein. I want to express my thanks to the Butler Center for Arkansas Studies, Central Arkansas Library System, particularly Brian Robertson, and to the Arkansas State Archives, particularly Elizabeth Freeman, for their assistance and cooperation in making the images available.

I wish to extend my appreciation to Trinity Church Wall Street, New York City, for its assistance in acknowledging and distributing the various messages—germane and decisive for the nation's racial history—that are part of the Elaine Race Massacre. Trinity is the venerable and historic Episcopal church that has been in lower Manhattan at Wall Street and Broadway in New York City for over three hundred years and whose cemetery contains numerous American luminaries, such as Alexander Hamilton, Robert Fulton, and Albert Gallatin. In September, 2014, Trinity sponsored a packed-house symposium at its separate St. Paul's Chapel on the Massacre. After the symposium at St. Paul's Chapel in which I participated as a speaker, I was requested by Trinity's Task Force Against Racism to be the Martin Luther King, Jr., birthday guest preacher at Trinity Church Wall Street for 2015, following many distinguished MLK birthday speakers at Trinity, such as Jesse Jackson, Marian Wright Edelman, and Andrew Young. I gave four separate presentations over the 2015 weekend, exploring further the Elaine Race Massacre. It would be impossible for me to thank individually all those persons who were instrumental in support of these Trinity gatherings; however, my sincere gratitude goes to the institution at large and to each of those persons responsible for the successful planning, organization, and execution of these various events.

For the better part of a decade, the Solomons, a prominent and well-known family in Phillips County, Arkansas, site of the Elaine Race Massacre, have led an effort with devoted, if not heroic, and especially public-spirited leadership, headed by David P. Solomon, for the construction of the Elaine Massacre Memorial, located in front of the Phillips County Courthouse. Previously, there had been no permanent memorial to the Massacre. By 2018, construction on the Memorial had begun and related agreements were in place; in addition, a bi-racial Elaine Massacre Memorial Committee had been created. The formal dedication of the Memorial occurred on September 29, 2019, one day before the Massacre's centennial. Pictures of the Elaine Massacre Memorial appear in this book, and I'm thankful to David Gruol for the use of these images in *Damaged Heritage*. The courage exhibited in all matters concerning the Massacre and the Memorial by my good friend, David P. Solomon, and by the entire Solomon family, has bolstered and energized me in more ways than they can imagine.

Soon after the establishment of the Elaine Massacre Memorial Committee, a decision was made by the local Delta Cultural Center and the Committee to sponsor an education program for the purpose of informing citizens of the county and beyond about the Massacre and its historically significant legacy. Toward this end, Sheila L. Walker, having several forebears as victims of the 1919 white onslaughts, and I, whose grandfather participated in the Massacre, were the initial presenters in this multi-disciplined education program that included periodic lectures in Phillips County, Arkansas in advance of the dedication of the Memorial. Sheila and I spoke in April, 2017 on racial reconciliation using the Massacre as the backdrop for our remarks. I wish to thank Dr. Kyle Miller, Director of the Delta Cultural Center, for this unusual opportunity given to Sheila and me.

As a result of our respective antecedents being on opposite sides of the Massacre, Sheila and I have been engaged for several years now in a pilgrimage of reconciliation, and I cannot imagine a more considerate and supportive partner with whom to be on this journey. Of course, this pilgrimage would have been incomplete without the remarkable participation and contribution of her husband, Ivor, and other immediate members of Sheila's family: Apryl, Aubrey, Franziska, and Marcus. Much in this book is devoted to the story of our attitude, determination, and efforts toward the mutual achievement of reconciliation, beginning with the big-hearted and genuine act of forgiveness, tendered both privately and publicly, by Sheila of my grandfather, Lonnie, for his role in the 1919 conflagration. From this signal act of forgiveness, the story unfolds in these pages exemplifying a deep and honest friendship Sheila and I hope can be a blueprint for others, as blacks and whites in this country move, we pray, to a comity of affirmative resolution.

For dedicating her book, *Scipio Africanus Jones*, seven hundred copies of which have been distributed to Arkansas schools, to the reconciliation to which Sheila and I have been committed, and for composing and placing a statement to us, entitled "Authentic Reconciliation," in Turning Point Park in Elaine, Arkansas, I wish to thank Patricia Kienzle. For their support, knowledge, friendship, and assistance along the way in my quest to find the answers for then and now to the Elaine Race Massacre that have led to my writing of *Damaged Heritage: The Elaine Race Massacre and A Story of Reconciliation*, I wish to thank Ray and Royce Brown; Hannah, Jamie, and Mary Callaway; Cathy and Ernest Cunningham; Herbert and Mary Donovan; John and Kay DuVal; Cornelius Eady and Sarah Micklem; Ruth Antoinette Foy; Kathy and Lowell Grisham; Roslyn Hall; Barbara Love; Scott Lunsford; Davis McCombs and Carolyn Guinzio; Catherine Meeks; Brian Miller; James and Elgenia Ross; Warren and Martha Stephenson; Virgil Trotter and Lindsey Allen; Rosanna Warren; and Jeannie Whayne. I also wish to thank our daughter, Juliet, for her love and for her continuous and unmitigated choice to be part of a more expansive and affirmative black-white community in our country.

There are heroes in Phillips County, Arkansas—women and men, black and white—who have added meaningfully and measurably to an adjustment in attitude toward the Massacre that has helped nurture support for the creation of the Memorial. I would like to give acknowledgment and thanks to those many resolute and fair-minded souls, who know who they are.

I wish to thank my agent, Peter Rubie, for his vision of this book's importance and for his contributions in bringing *Damaged Heritage* to reality. I also wish to thank my editor at Pegasus Books, Jessica Case, for her talent, steadfast assistance, and constant thoughtfulness.

Certainly, I could not close without acknowledging the essential and bountiful help and encouragement I receive from my loving and generous wife, Freda. I surprise her all day long with questions of varying degrees of importance, and even with these habitual interruptions, she then, in turn, routinely and with good cheer, agrees to read drafts I write, offering skilled insights and much valued suggestions and wisdom. As one longtime and discerning friend reminds me, "You married well." Indeed, I did.

ENDNOTES

INTRODUCTION

1   Alisdair MacIntyre, *After Virtue: A Study In Moral Theory, Third Edition* (Notre Dame, IN: University of Notre Dame Press, 1981) p. 221.

2   Roger Frie, *Not In My Family* (New York: Oxford University Press, 2017) p. 67.

3   *New York Times* Editorial Observer: Brent Staples: "The Death of the Black Utopia," November 29, 2019 p. A26.

1: A CHANGING OF AMERICA

1   Robert Whitaker, *On the Laps of Gods* (New York: Crown Publishing Group, a division of Random House, Inc., 2008) pp. 46–47.

2   Nan Elizabeth Woodruff, *American Congo: The African American Freedom Struggle in the Delta* (Chapel Hill: University of North Carolina Press, 2012) pp. 80–81.

3   Whitaker, p. 1.

4   Whitaker, p. 98.

5   Whitaker, p. 91.

6   Whitaker, pp. 91–92.

7   Grif Stockley, *Blood in Their Eyes: The Elaine Race Massacres of 1919* (Fayetteville: The University of Arkansas Press, 2001) p. xxiii.

8   Stockley, *Blood in Their Eyes*, p. 36.

9   Whitaker, p. 132.

10 Email exchange between J. Chester Johnson and Robert Whitaker, December 19, 2012.

11 Grif Stockley, "Elaine Massacre," *The Encyclopedia of Arkansas History & Culture*, encyclopediaofarkansas.net/encyclopedia/entry-detail .aspx?entryID=1102; Stockley, *Blood in Their Eyes*, p. 80.

12 Whitaker, p. 130.

13 Whitaker, p. 133.

14 Whitaker, pp. 141–142.

15 Whitaker, p. 142.

16 Stockley, p. xxvi.

17 Stockley, p. 129.

18 Stockley, p. xxvii.

19 Whitaker, p. 181.

20 Stockley, p. xxviii.

21 Stockley, p. xxviii.

22 Stockley, p. 169.

23 Whitaker, p. 229.

24 Stockley, p. xxix.

25 Whitaker, p. 238.

26 Whitaker, pp. 239–241.

27 Stockley, p. xxx.

28 Woodruff, p. 99.

29 Stockley, p. xxx.

30 Whitaker, p. 268.

31 Whitaker, p. 277.

32 *Moore v. Dempsey*, 261 U.S. 86 (1923), supreme.justia.com/cases/federal /us/261/86/.

33 Megan Ming Francis, *Civil Rights and the Making of the Modern American State* (New York, NY: Cambridge University Press, 2014), pp. 127–128.

34 Richard C. Cortner, *A Mob Intent on Death: The NAACP and the Arkansas Riot Cases* (Middletown, CT: Wesleyan University Press, 1988) p. 189.

35 Stockley, p. xxxi.

36 Stockley, p. xxxi.

37 Whitaker, p. 300.

38 Whitaker, p. 301.

39 Stockley, p. xxxii.

40 Stockley, p. xxxii.

41 United States Census Bureau, censusviewer.com/city/AR/Elaine.

42 Ibid, US Decennial Census: 1950, 2000, 2010.

43 Yevgeny Yevtushenko, *Yevtushenko: Selected Poems*, translated by Robin Milner-Gulland and Peter Levi, S.J. (Penguin Books, Ltd, 1962) p. 82.

2: THE GENUINELY HUMAN

1 William Faulkner, *Requiem for A Nun* (New York, N Y: Random House, 1951) p. 73.

2   E-mail to J. Chester Johnson from Sheila L. Walker, October 1, 2019.

3   Melinda Thomsen, "Stop Being Normal: A Review of *Now and Then: Selected Longer Poems* by J. Chester Johnson" (*BigCityLit*, Fall 2019/Winter 2020).

4   Woodruff, p. 2.

5   Whitaker, p. 148.

6   E-mail to J. Chester Johnson from Rosanna Warren, September 6, 2014.

7   Soren Kierkegaard, *Fear and Trembling* (Cambridge, United Kingdom: Cambridge University Press, 2006) p. 107.

8   *I'll Take My Stand: The South and the Agrarian Tradition* (Baton Rouge, LA: Louisiana State University Press, Louisiana Paperback Edition, 1977, 2006) pp. 260–261.

9   Robert Penn Warren, *The Legacy of the Civil War* (Lincoln, NE: University of Nebraska Press, 1998) p. 58.

10 *I'll Take My Stand*, p. xxxi.

11 E-mail to J. Chester Johnson from Rosanna Warren, dated May 6, 2019.

12 Ida B. Wells, *The Autobiography of Ida B. Wells* (Chicago: The University of Chicago Press, 1970) p. xvii.

13 Larry Siedentop, *Inventing the Individual, The Origins of Western Liberalism* (Cambridge, MA: The Belknap Press of Harvard University Press, 2014) pp. 10–12.

4: MARCH 15, 2014

1   J. Chester Johnson, *Auden, the Psalms, and Me* (New York, NY: Church Publishing, 2017) p. 146.

2   Charles Williams, *The Descent of the Dove* (Vancouver, Canada: Regent College Publishing, 2002), p. 138.

3   Charles Williams, *The Image of the City* (Berkeley, California: Apocryphile Press, 2007), pp. 104–105.

4   Williams, *The Descent of the Dove*, p. 46.

5   Williams, *The Descent of the Dove*, p. 236.

6   Woodruff, p. 99.

5: MONTICELLO, ARKANSAS

1   Gene Dattel, *Cotton And Race in the Making of America: The Human Costs of Economic Power* (Lanham, Maryland: Ivan R. Dee, Publisher, 2011) pp. 30–31.

2   Donald Holley, "A Look Behind the Masks: The 1920s Ku Klux Klan in Monticello, Arkansas" (*The Arkansas Historical Quarterly*, Volume 60, No. 2, Summer, 2001) p. 136.

3 United States Census Bureau, censusviewer.com/city/AR/Monticello.

4 Carolyn Gray LeMaster, *A Corner of the Tapestry, A History of the Jewish Experience in Arkansas, 1820s–1990s* (Fayetteville: The University of Arkansas Press, 1994) p. 278.

5 LeMaster, p. 39.

6 Grif Stockley, *Ruled By Race* (Fayetteville: The University of Arkansas Press, 2009) p. 281.

7 Justiceunbound.org/carousel/brown-v-board-the-little-rock-nine-and -presbyterian-public-witness/.

8 www.encyclopediaofarkansas.net/encyclopedia/entry-detail.aspx?entry ID=8376.

9 Ida B. Wells, *On Lynching* (Amherst, NY: Humanity Books, 2002) p. 201.

10 www.encyclopediaofarkansas.net/encyclopedia/entry-detail.aspx?entry ID=346.

11 www.encyclopediaofarkansas.net/encyclopedia/entry-detail.aspx?entry ID=8346.

12 www.encyclopediaofarkansas.net/encyclopedia/entry-detail.aspx?entry ID=8376.

13 Douglas A. Blackmon, *Slavery By Another Name* (New York: Anchor Books, 2009).

14 Stockley, *Ruled By Race*, pp. 266–267.

15 Stockley, *Ruled By Race*, p. 266.

16 "Mississippi: Is This America," Eyes on the Prize III, (1962–1964).

17 www.encyclopediaofarkansas.net/encyclopedia/entry-detail.aspx ?entryID=6921.

18 Arkansascivilrightsheritage.org/freedom-riders-and-the-desegregation -of-public-facilities/.

6: AFTER FREEDOM SUMMER

1 Willie Morris, *North Toward Home* (New York: Vintage Books, 2000).

2 www.encyclopediaofarkansas.net/encyclopedia/entry-detail.aspx?entry ID=4773.

3 Timothy B. Tyson, *The Blood Of Emmett Till* (New York: Simon & Schuster, 2017) pp. 205–206.

4 William Faulkner, *Sanctuary* (New York: Jonathan Cape and Harrison Smith, 1931).

5 James Dickey, *Deliverance* (Boston: Houghton Mifflin, 1970).

6 James W. Silver, *Mississippi: The Closed Society* (New York: Harcourt, Brace & World, Inc., 1964) pp. 154–155.

7   James Baldwin, *The Fire Next Time* (New York: Vintage Books, 1993).
8   Alex Haley and Malcolm X, *The Autobiography Of Malcolm X* (New York: Ballantine Books, 2015).

7: DREW SCHOOL
1   Timothy B. Tyson, p. 205.
2   encyclopediaofarkansas.net/entries/office-of-county-judge-5720/.
3   J. Chester Johnson, *Now And Then: Selected Longer Poems* (Haworth, NJ: St. Johann Press, 2016) p. 158.
4   Johnson, p. 3.

8: IN MEMORIAM
1   Cortner, *A Mob Intent on Death: The NAACP and the Arkansas Riot Cases*, p. 61.
2   Stockley, *Blood in Their Eyes*, pp. 224–225.
3   William Faulkner, *Intruder in the Dust*, Second Vintage International Edition (New York, N.Y.: Vintage Books, 2011) p. 190.
4   Faulkner, *Intruder in the Dust*, p. 47.
5   Equal Justice Initiative, *Lynching in America: Confronting The Legacy of Racial Terror*, Second Edition (Montgomery, AL: Equal Justice Initiative, 2015) pp. 40–41.

9: A RECONCILIATION IN PHILLIPS COUNTY
1   Milan Kundera, *The Book of Laughter and Forgetting* (New York: Penguin, 1981) p. 22.
2   Stockley, *Blood in Their Eyes*, p. xxvii.
3   Whitaker, p. 285.
4   Email exchange between J. Chester Johnson and Robert Whitaker, December 19, 2012.
5   Whitaker, p. 260.
6   James H. Cone, *Black Theology and Black Power* (Maryknoll, NY: Orbis Books, 2012) p. 147.

J. Chester Johnson is a well-known poet, essayist, and translator, who grew up one county removed from the Elaine Race Massacre site in southeast Arkansas along the Mississippi River Delta. He has written extensively on race and civil rights, composing the Litany for the national Day of Repentance (October 4, 2008) when the Episcopal Church formally apologized for its role in transatlantic slavery and related evils. At the height of the Civil Rights Movement and following the assassination of Martin Luther King, Jr., Johnson returned to the town of his youth to teach in the all African-American public school before integration of the local education system. Several of his writings are part of the *J. Chester Johnson Collection* in the Civil Rights Archives at Queens College, the alma mater of Andrew Goodman, one of three martyrs murdered by white supremacists in Mississippi during Freedom Summer. His three most recent books are *St. Paul's Chapel & Selected Shorter Poems* (2010), *Now And Then: Selected Longer Poems* (2017), and *Auden, the Psalms, and Me* (2017), the story of the retranslation of the psalms in the *Book of Common Prayer* for which W. H. Auden (1968–1971) and Johnson (1971–1979) were the poets on the drafting committee; published in 1979, this version became a standard. Johnson, who served as Deputy Assistant Secretary of the U.S. Treasury Department in the Carter Administration, owned and ran, for several decades, an independent consulting firm for large domestic governments and non-profit organizations on capital finance and debt management. His poem about the iconic St. Paul's Chapel, relief center for the recovery workers at Ground Zero, has been the Chapel's memento card since soon after the 9/11 terrorists' attacks (1.5 million cards distributed); *American Book Review* said of the poem: "Johnson's 'St. Paul's Chapel' is one of the most widely distributed, lauded, and translated poems of the current century." One of fifteen writers selected to be showcased for the inaugural Harvard Alumni Authors' Book Fair, he was educated at Harvard College and the University of Arkansas (Distinguished Alumnus Award, 2010).